A Longman C

William Shakespeare's

HAMLET,
Prince of Denmark

Second Edition

Edited by
Constance Jordan
Claremont Graduate University

PEARSON
Longman

New York   San Francisco   Boston
London   Toronto   Sydney   Tokyo   Singapore   Madrid
Mexico City   Munich   Paris   Cape Town   Hong Kong   Montreal

Vice President and Editor-in-Chief: Joseph P. Terry
Development Editor: Barbara Santoro
Executive Marketing Manager: Ann Stypuloski
Production Coordinator: Shafiena Ghani
Project Coordination, Text Design, and Electronic Page Makeup: Dianne Hall
Cover Designer/Manager: John Callahan
Cover Illustration: *Hamlet and Horatio in the Cemetery* by Eugene Delacroix:
   The Bridgeman Art Library
Senior Manufacturing Buyer: Alfred C. Dorsey
Printer and Binder: R. R. Donnelly & Sons Company / Harrisonburg
Cover Printer: Coral Graphics Services, Inc.

Library of Congress Cataloging-in-Publication Data
CIP Data is on file at the Library of Congress.

Please visit our website at http://www.ablongman.com

ISBN 0-321-31729-7

1 2 3 4 5 6 7 8 9 10—DOH—07 06 05 04

For Ethan, Simon, Devin, and Josie Marie

Contents

List of Illustrations

About Longman Cultural Editions

Reading always seems to vibrate with the transformation of the day—now, yesterday, and centuries ago, when the presses first put printed language into wide circulation. Correspondingly, literary culture has always been a matter of change: of new practices confronting established traditions; of texts transforming under the pressure of new techniques of reading and new perspectives of understanding; of canons shifting and expanding; of informing traditions getting reviewed and renewed, recast and reformed by emerging cultural interests and concerns; of culture, too, as a variable "text"—a reading. Inspired by the innovative *Longman Anthology of British Literature,* Longman Cultural Editions respond creatively to the changes, past and recent, by presenting key texts in contexts that illuminate the lively intersections of literature, tradition, and culture. A principal work is made more interesting by materials that place it in relation to its past, present, and future, enabling us to see how it may be reworking traditional debates and practices, how it appears amid the conversations and controversies of its own historical moment, how it gains new significances in subsequent eras of reading and reaction. Readers new to the work will discover attractive paths for exploration, while those more experienced will encounter fresh perspectives and provocative juxtapositions.

Longman Cultural Editions serve not only several kinds of readers but also (appropriately) their several contexts, from various courses of study to independent adventure. Handsomely produced and affordably priced, our volumes offer appealing companions to *The Longman Anthology of British Literature,* in some cases enriching and expanding units originally developed for the *Anthology*, and in other cases presenting this wealth for the first time. The logic and composition of the contexts vary across the series. The constants are the complete text of an important literary work, reliably edited, headed by an inviting introduction, and supplemented by helpful annotation; a table of dates to track its composition, publication, and public reception in relation to biographical, cultural, and historical events; and a guide for further inquiry and study. With these common measures and uncommon assets, Longman Cultural Editions encourage your literary pleasures with resources for lively reflection and adventurous inquiry.

Susan J. Wolfson
General Editor
Professor of English
Princeton University

About the Second Edition

This edition of *Hamlet* uses the text established by David Bevington for *The Complete Works of Shakespeare* (Longman, 5th Edition); the notes to the play are also his. Bevington bases his text on the Second Quarto of 1604–1605 (Q2), with substitutions chiefly from the Folio (F) and some from the First Quarto (Q1) to achieve better readings. (A list of variants appears right after the printed text of the play.) The result, for the most part a conflation of Q2 and F, gives us the entire play that Shakespeare wrote. We need to keep in mind, however, that because this conflated *Hamlet* is too long for any single production, most versions of the play in performance will show some careful cutting. For further discussion, see Paul Bertram and Bernice W. Kliman (eds.), *The Three-Text Hamlet: Parallel Texts of the First and Second Quartos and First Folio* (1991); Kathleen O. Irace (ed.), *The First Quarto of Hamlet* (1998); and Stanley Wells and Gary Taylor, "Hamlet," in *William Shakespeare: A Textual Companion* (1987), pp. 396–420.

For this new Longman Cultural Edition, I have added some texts to the "Contexts" section to show more of the cultural and ideological settings in which Shakespeare wrote and contemporary audiences saw the play. Early modern Englishmen and women remained seriously divided over matters of religion, law, and social behavior during Shakespeare's lifetime. Some interpreted irrational events by invoking spiritual agents; others rejected claims for supernatural activity in the world as fraudulent. Unusual human behaviors, whether suggesting transient emotional stress or persistent mental disturbance, were considered symptomatic of "melancholia," a generalized disease of the spirit. Religious practices were no less controversial: Catholics regarded the doctrine of purgatory as true to the teachings of the apostolic church, while Protestants believed it had no basis in Scripture. Debate, which transcended social ranks, could lead to lethal outcomes; but for those who faced martyrdom, the hope of salvation surpassed any benefit mortal life could provide. In a more worldly key, tragedies of revenge, a very popular genre in the theaters of Shakespeare's day, were staged in the midst of a culture of respect for the law, especially its guarantee that everyone accused of a crime had a right to a fair trial. Another subject of law, suicide, was just as prone to contradiction. While suicide was a legal crime, and the church regarded it as a mortal sin (a form of murder), there were other views so sympathetic to its psychology as almost to justify it under certain circumstances. All these questions register in the last unit in the "Contexts" section, on the varied interpretations of *Hamlet* on the page and on the stage. All texts in these units have been modernized. When quoting passages from Scripture, I have followed the text of the English translation of the Geneva Bible (1595).

I am grateful to the co-editors of *The Longman Anthology of British Literature* for their help in publishing this edition, especially to Susan Wolfson, who oversaw its production from start to finish. I am also grateful to Anne Ehrenworth, who edited this manuscript, and to Barbara Santoro, who oversaw this edition. I wish further to thank my students and colleagues at Claremont Graduate University, particularly my research assistant Ambereen Dadabhoy, who went through Bevington's text and notes, supplying me with much useful information; my colleagues Professors Marc Redfield and Molly Ierulli, who helped me find texts to illustrate past performances of the play; and to Carol Bliss, who guided me through databases for illustrations of the play.

Constance Jordan
Claremont Graduate University

Introduction

Of all Shakespeare's tragedies, *Hamlet* is the best known. The figure of its hero, lonely, pensive, and shrouded in black, is recognized as a character quite independent of the play itself. He circulates within the limits of our cultures; he finds as many representations as readers and audiences. His face, whether Olivier's or Branagh's, Barrymore's or Gibson's, or that of one of the many other actors who have played the part, seems altogether familiar, a part of our world. And yet, what do we really know of Shakespeare's most enigmatic character?

Unlike Macbeth, the man of action to whom he is most often contrasted, Hamlet has appeared to epitomize the thoughtful hero. The great German playwright Goethe saw him as all-encompassing consciousness; the English poet Coleridge agreed. Their contemporary, the critic William Hazlitt, judged the play to be so dreamlike that he thought it should not be performed at all. And yet, *Hamlet* is action-packed, full of plots and quarrels, schemes and murders, plays and duels. The hero himself takes action, not once but a number of times—killing Polonius (although inadvertently); sending Rosencrantz and Guildenstern to their deaths (although they are guilty of no particular crime); tormenting Ophelia (although she appears to be ignorant of his motives). And he finally takes the revenge he has pledged himself to perform.

It's worth recognizing how many kinds of interpretations have yielded new visions of *Hamlet* and its hero over time. The hero of the Romantic poets now shares a place with others who speak to our present cultural concerns: Feminist criticism has shown us a Hamlet contending with Gertrude and Ophelia, contending, too, with questions about his own manliness; psychoanalytic criticism has exposed his unconscious drives, his unacknowledged desires; postmodern critical theory has shown how far he is a creature of language; and materialist criticism has revealed the social determinants of his career. Recent historicist criticism has helped us see the play and its hero in the complicated and, in a sense, conflicted cultural moment in which Shakespeare wrote and acted—a moment shaped by the troubles and triumphs of its fleeting present and its enduring memories. If some of these concerns may evoke little modern sympathy, they were fascinations for Shakespeare's contemporaries. Other issues, especially those having to do with questions of belief (or doubt), knowledge (or ignorance), loyalty (or treachery), and fortitude (or frailty) can still speak volumes to us.

From the beginning of the play, Shakespeare places his hero in a situation of almost unbearable constraints. Called to avenge his father's murder, Prince Hamlet must defy the social and political order if he is to accept the charge; he must rise above the law and be the judge and plaintiff in his own (and his father's) cause. The conventions of revenge tragedy, followed by Shakespeare himself in *Titus Andronicus*, represented revenge for honor's sake as a plausible if horrific act. Understood in terms of late Elizabethan England society, however, revenge was tantamount to treason. These are the terms that Shakespeare imports into his play; he makes Hamlet alone responsive to them. Neither Laertes nor Fortinbras, both vengeful characters, finds himself exactly in Hamlet's situation. Laertes desires a revenge that, although unlawful, is aided and abetted by the present king, a man who is supposedly the incarnation of the law. Fortinbras, the Norwegian prince whose father lost Denmark to the old king Hamlet, recovers this property not by taking action but by biding his time. The moment of his success is quite unforeseen—the vantage he acts upon at the end of the play is the "now" of an unanticipated present.

The social and political strictures that force Hamlet's careful questions of himself and his filial duty are compounded by other uncertainties. His father's ghost tells Hamlet that he comes from purgatory. Could a loyal Elizabethan subject believe in such a place? Protestant doctrine had dispensed with the idea of a nether world of purgation as a vital feature of Christian faith, calling it nothing more than a clerical fiction. Are we seeing a deluded Hamlet? And if purgatory does not seem strange to us, nor Hamlet's unquestioning acceptance of it unjustified by doctrine, what of the fact that it is his father's ghost that incites revenge? Catholic teaching maintained that souls in purgatory asked for graceful prayers, not earthly satisfactions. And finally, what was a ghost? Some who wrote about spiritual experiences said ghosts were merely figments of a supersensitive imagination. Others thought it possible that the real and material world was bound up with an invisible sphere of spirituality, but they usually remained unclear about how that spirituality manifested itself. Yet Shakespeare represents the ghost of the old king (an embodied character in the cast) as working his way through purgation, atoning for his sins. Shakespeare chose to dramatize such contested issues, conceiving a hero compelled to recognize and confront their complexities.

We should notice how quietly the play ends. Before the violence that brings the action to a conclusion, Hamlet's words to Horatio speak of a providence working in and through the natural world. He declares that he will defy "augury," the forecasting, planning, and anticipation of events: "If it be now, 'tis not to come; if it be not to come, it will be now; if it be not now; yet it will come, the readiness is all" (5.2.205–207). With these words, Hamlet gestures toward an essentially Calvinist eschatology. He implies that the terms of a particular death and the sense of ending it anticipates lie beyond human apprehension. All that matters is individual "readiness." True, there is something very bleak about the way Hamlet and his antagonists meet their death. Comforts for the dying which adhered to old Catholic rituals are represented as pernicious: the "unction" on Laertes' sword is a poison parody of the spiritual healing ointment of extreme unction; the wine in Claudius's "cup" is no eucharist but yet more poison—corrupted by the effects of a deadly "union" that separates the company forever.

These quotation-marked words draw vital historical meaning from current political and religious contexts. *Hamlet* is still embedded in these contexts, even as it speaks to subsequent ages. In addition to the rich and useful criticism that has informed its readings and performances, we can recognize a fundamental attitude of mind that embraces a creative skepticism, sustained at last by a comprehensive grasp of a providential design. Hamlet's testimony—arguably fatalistic were it not for its echo of Scripture (Matthew 10.29)—addresses the question that opens the play, "Who's there?" and reflects at length upon the noncommittal response it gets, "Nay, answer me." *Hamlet* tells us that we are ignorant of more than we know or can know, that what we do in the confidence of being right risks unintended, even ironic consequences. To question, to reflect, to think: these are the activities of a conscious mind. The Romantic poet John Keats saw them as Shakespeare's achievement of a "Negative Capability"—a capacity for being "in uncertainties, Mysteries, and doubts" (as he wrote in a letter of December 1817), and perhaps, too, a capacity for tempered inaction. The end of *Hamlet* is marked by a quietism made courageous by a belief in providence. Shakespeare's "romances" will show us a providence whose more generous dispensations justify desire and guarantee hope for a brave new world.

Table of Dates

1588–97   England wages war with Spain.

1592   Shakespeare is mentioned as an actor and writer in a pamphlet by Robert Greene.

Thomas Kyd publishes his revenge play, *The Spanish Tragedy*, anonymously.

Christopher Marlowe's revenge play *The Jew of Malta* is performed.

1594   Shakespeare becomes a Charter Member of The Chamberlain's Men.

Shakespeare's revenge play *Titus Andronicus* is performed; Christopher Marlowe publishes *Dr. Faustus*, his last play.

1597   Francis Bacon publishes the first edition of *The Essays*.

1598   A play called *Hamlet*, now lost, is produced.

1599   The Chamberlain's Men occupy the Globe Theater.

1602   *Hamlet* is entered into the register of the Stationers' Company.

1603   Queen Elizabeth dies.

The "bad" quarto of *Hamlet* is published (Q1).

The "good" quarto of *Hamlet* is published (Q2).

1616   Shakespeare dies.

1623   Publication of the first collected edition of Shakespeare's plays in Folio.

HAMLET,
Prince of Denmark

[by William Shakespeare]

HAMLET,
Prince of Denmark

Dramatis Personae

GHOST *of Hamlet, the former King of Denmark*
CLAUDIUS, *King of Denmark, the former King's brother*
GERTRUDE, *Queen of Denmark, widow of the former King and now wife of Claudius*
HAMLET, *Prince of Denmark, son of the late King and of Gertrude*

POLONIUS, *councillor to the King*
LAERTES, *his son*
OPHELIA, *his daughter*
REYNALDO, *his servant*

HORATIO, *Hamlet's friend and fellow student*

VOLTIMAND,
CORNELIUS,
ROSENCRANTZ,
GUILDENSTERN, } *members of the Danish court*
OSRIC,
A GENTLEMAN,
A LORD,

BERNARDO,
FRANCISCO, } *officers and soldiers on watch*
MARCELLUS,

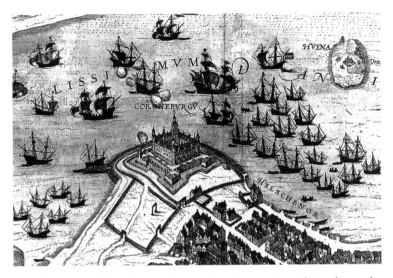

Freti Danici, *Elsinore Castle*. This eighteenth-century etching shows the superbly defensive situation of Kronenborg Castle (the site of the sixteenth-century Elsinore Castle) on a promontory at the very edge of the Baltic Sea. The castle's four corners are protected by v-shaped platforms, each fortified with several cannons, and the entire structure is surrounded by a moat. (By permission of the Folger Shakespeare Library.)

FORTINBRAS, *Prince of Norway*
CAPTAIN *in his army*

Three or Four PLAYERS, *taking the roles of* PROLOGUE, PLAYER
    KING, PLAYER QUEEN, *and* LUCIANUS
Two MESSENGERS
FIRST SAILOR
Two CLOWNS, *a gravedigger and his companion*
PRIEST
FIRST AMBASSADOR *from England*

*Lords, Soldiers, Attendants, Guards, other Players, Followers of
    Laertes, other Sailors, another Ambassador or Ambassadors
    from England*

SCENE: *Denmark*

ACT 1

SCENE 1

Location: Elsinore castle. A guard platform.

Enter Bernardo and Francisco, two sentinels, [meeting]

BERNARDO   Who's there?

FRANCISCO   Nay, answer me.° Stand and unfold° yourself.°

BERNARDO   Long live the King!

FRANCISCO   Bernardo?

BERNARDO   He.   5

FRANCISCO   You come most carefully upon your hour.

BERNARDO   'Tis now struck twelve. Get thee to bed, Francisco.

FRANCISCO   For this relief much thanks. 'Tis bitter cold,
And I am sick at heart.

BERNARDO   Have you had quiet guard?

FRANCISCO   Not a mouse stirring.   10

BERNARDO   Well, good night.
If you do meet Horatio and Marcellus,
The rivals° of my watch, bid them make haste.

Enter Horatio and Marcellus

FRANCISCO
I think I hear them.—Stand, ho! Who is there?

HORATIO   Friends to this ground.°

MARCELLUS   And liegemen to the Dane.°   15

FRANCISCO   Give you good night.

MARCELLUS   Oh, farewell, honest soldier.
Who hath relieved you?

FRANCISCO   Bernardo hath my place.
Give° you good night.

Exit Francisco

MARCELLUS   Holla! Bernardo!

BERNARDO   Say, what, is Horatio there?

HORATIO   A piece of him.

BERNARDO   Welcome, Horatio. Welcome, good Marcellus.   20

---

2 me (Francisco emphasizes that *he* is the sentry currently on watch) | **unfold yourself** reveal your identity   **13 rivals** partners   **15 ground** country, land | **liegemen to the Dane** men sworn to serve the Danish king   **18 Give** May God give

HORATIO   What, has this thing appeared again tonight?
BERNARDO   I have seen nothing.
MARCELLUS   Horatio says 'tis but our fantasy,°
And will not let belief take hold of him
Touching this dreaded sight twice seen of us.   25
Therefore I have entreated him along°
With us to watch° the minutes of this night,
That if again this apparition come
He may approve° our eyes and speak to it.
HORATIO   Tush, tush, 'twill not appear.
BERNARDO   Sit down awhile   30
And let us once again assail your ears,
That are so fortified against our story,
What we have two nights seen.
HORATIO   Well, sit we down,
And let us hear Bernardo speak of this.
BERNARDO   Last night of all,°   35
When yond same star that's westward from the pole°
Had made his° course t'illume° that part of heaven
Where now it burns, Marcellus and myself,
The bell then beating one—

                              Enter Ghost

MARCELLUS   Peace, break thee off! Look where it comes again!   40
BERNARDO   In the same figure like the King that's dead.
MARCELLUS   Thou art a scholar.° Speak to it, Horatio.
BERNARDO   Looks 'a° not like the King? Mark it, Horatio.
HORATIO   Most like. It harrows me with fear and wonder.
BERNARDO   It would be spoke to.°
MARCELLUS   Speak to it, Horatio.   45
HORATIO   What art thou that usurp'st° this time of night,
Together with that fair and warlike form
In which the majesty of buried Denmark°
Did sometimes° march? By heaven, I charge thee, speak!

23 **fantasy** imagination   26 **along** to come along   27 **watch** keep watch during
29 **approve** corroborate   35 **Last . . . all** this *very* last night (emphatic)   36 **pole** pole-
star, north star   37 **his** its | **t'illume** to illuminate   42 **scholar** one learned enough to
know how to question a ghost properly   43 **'a** he   45 **It . . . to** (it was commonly
believed that a ghost could not speak until spoken to)   46 **usurp'st** wrongfully takes
over   48 **buried Denmark** the buried King of Denmark   49 **sometimes** formerly

MARCELLUS It is offended.

BERNARDO   See, it stalks away.   50

HORATIO Stay! Speak, speak! I charge thee, speak!

Exit Ghost

MARCELLUS 'Tis gone and will not answer.

BERNARDO How now, Horatio? You tremble and look pale.
Is not this something more than fantasy?
What think you on't?°   55

HORATIO Before my God, I might not this believe
Without the sensible° and true avouch°
Of mine own eyes.

MARCELLUS   Is it not like the King?

HORATIO As thou art to thyself.
Such was the very armor he had on   60
When he the ambitious Norway° combated.
So frowned he once when, in an angry parle,°
He smote the sledded° Polacks° on the ice.
'Tis strange.

MARCELLUS Thus twice before, and jump° at this dead hour,   65
With martial stalk° hath he gone by our watch.

HORATIO In what particular thought to work° I know not,
But in the gross and scope° of mine opinion
This bodes some strange eruption to our state.

MARCELLUS Good now,° sit down, and tell me, he that knows,   70
Why this same strict and most observant watch
So nightly toils° the subject° of the land,
And why such daily cast° of brazen cannon
And foreign mart° for implements of war,
Why such impress° of shipwrights, whose sore task   75
Does not divide the Sunday from the week.
What might be toward,° that this sweaty haste
Doth make the night joint-laborer with the day?

---

55 **on't** of it 57 **sensible** confirmed by the senses | **avouch** warrant, evidence
61 **Norway** King of Norway 62 **parle** parley 63 **sledded** traveling on sleds |
Polacks Poles 65 **jump** exactly 66 **stalk** stride 67 **to work** to collect my
thoughts and try to understand this 68 **gross and scope** general drift 70 **Good
now** (an expression denoting entreaty or expostulation) 72 **toils** causes to toil |
subject subjects 73 **cast** casting 74 **mart** shopping 75 **impress** impressment,
conscription 77 **toward** in preparation

Who is't that can inform me?

HORATIO   That can I;

At least, the whisper goes so. Our last king,   80
Whose image even but now appeared to us,
Was, as you know, by Fortinbras of Norway,
Thereto pricked on° by a most emulate° pride,°
Dared to the combat; in which our valiant Hamlet—
For so this side of our known world° esteemed him—   85
Did slay this Fortinbras; who by a sealed° compact
Well ratified by law and heraldry°
Did forfeit, with his life, all those his lands
Which he stood seized° of, to the conqueror;
Against the° which a moiety competent°   90
Was gagèd° by our king, which had returned°
To the inheritance° of Fortinbras
Had he been vanquisher, as, by the same cov'nant°
And carriage of the article designed,°
His fell to Hamlet. Now, sir, young Fortinbras,   95
Of unimprovèd mettle° hot and full,
Hath in the skirts° of Norway here and there
Sharked up a list of lawless resolutes
For food and diet to some enterprise
That hath a stomach in't,° which is no other—   100
As it doth well appear unto our state—
But to recover of us, by strong hand
And terms compulsatory, those foresaid lands
So by his father lost. And this, I take it,
Is the main motive of our preparations,   105
The source of this our watch, and the chief head°
Of this posthaste° and rummage in the land.

---

83 **Thereto . . . pride** (refers to old Fortinbras, not the Danish King) | **pricked on** incited | **emulate** emulous, ambitious   85 **this . . . world** all Europe, the Western world   86 **sealed** certified, confirmed   87 **heraldry** chivalry   89 **seized** possessed 90 **Against the** in return for | **moiety competent** corresponding portion   91 **gagèd** engaged, pledged | **had returned** would have passed   92 **inheritance** possession 93 **cov'nant** the *sealed compact* of line 86   94 **carriage . . . designed** purport of the article referred to   96 **unimprovèd mettle** untried, undisciplined spirits   97 **skirts** outlying regions, outskirts   98–100 **Sharked . . . in't** rounded up (as a shark scoops up fish) a troop of lawless desperadoes to feed and supply an enterprise of considerable daring   106 **head** source   107 **posthaste and rummage** frenetic activity and bustle

BERNARDO   I think it be no other but e'en so.
    Well may it sort° that this portentous figure
    Comes armèd through our watch so like the King   110
    That was and is the question° of these wars.
HORATIO   A mote° it is to trouble the mind's eye.
    In the most high and palmy° state of Rome,
    A little ere the mightiest Julius° fell,
    The graves stood tenantless, and the sheeted° dead   115
    Did squeak and gibber in the Roman streets;
    As° stars with trains° of fire and dews of blood,
    Disasters° in the sun; and the moist star°
    Upon whose influence Neptune's empire stands°
    Was sick almost to doomsday with eclipse.°   120
    And even the like precurse° of feared events,
    As harbingers° preceding still° the fates
    And prologue to the omen° coming on,
    Have heaven and earth together demonstrated
    Unto our climatures° and countrymen.   125

                                  Enter Ghost

    But soft,° behold! Lo, where it comes again!
    I'll cross° it, though it blast° me. (*It spreads his° arms*) Stay,
       illusion!
    If thou hast any sound or use of voice,
    Speak to me!
    If there be any good thing to be done   130
    That may to thee do ease and grace to me,
    Speak to me!
    If thou art privy to° thy country's fate,
    Which, happily,° foreknowing may avoid,

---

109 **Well . . . sort** that would explain why 111 **question** focus of contention
112 **mote** speck of dust 113 **palmy** flourishing 114 **Julius** Julius Caesar
115 **sheeted** shrouded 117 **As** (this abrupt transition suggests that matter is
possibly omitted between lines 116 and 117) | **trains** trails 118 **Disasters**
unfavorable signs or aspects | **moist star** moon, governing tides 119 **Neptune's**
. . . stands the sea depends 120 **Was . . . eclipse** was eclipsed nearly to the cosmic
darkness predicted for the second coming of Christ and the ending of the world (see
Matthew 24.29 and Revelation 6.12) 121 **precurse** heralding, foreshadowing
122 **harbingers** forerunners | **still** always 123 **omen** calamitous event
125 **climatures** climes, regions 126 **soft** enough, break off 127 **cross** stand in its
path, confront | **blast** wither, strike with a curse 127 **s.d.** *his* its 133 **privy to** in on
the secret of 134 **happily** haply, perchance

Oh, speak!   135
Or if thou hast uphoarded in thy life
Extorted treasure in the womb of earth,
For which, they say, you spirits oft walk in death,
Speak of it! (*The cock crows*) Stay and speak!—Stop it,
     Marcellus.
MARCELLUS Shall I strike at it with my partisan?°   140
HORATIO Do, if it will not stand.   [*They strike at it.*]
BERNARDO   'Tis here!
HORATIO   'Tis here!°
                                                          [*Exit Ghost*]
MARCELLUS 'Tis gone.
     We do it wrong, being so majestical,
     To offer it the show of violence,
     For it is as the air invulnerable,   145
     And our vain blows malicious mockery.
BERNARDO It was about to speak when the cock crew.
HORATIO And then it started like a guilty thing
     Upon a fearful summons. I have heard
     The cock, that is the trumpet° to the morn,   150
     Doth with his lofty and shrill-sounding throat
     Awake the god of day, and at his warning,
     Whether in sea or fire, in earth or air,
     Th'extravagant and erring° spirit hies°
     To his confine; and of the truth herein   155
     This present object made probation.°
MARCELLUS It faded on the crowing of the cock.
     Some say that ever 'gainst° that season comes
     Wherein our Savior's birth is celebrated,
     This bird of dawning singeth all night long,   160
     And then, they say, no spirit dare stir abroad;
     The nights are wholesome, then no planets strike,°
     No fairy takes,° nor witch hath power to charm,°

---

140 **partisan** long-handled spear 141–42 **'Tis here! / 'Tis here!** (perhaps they attempt to strike at the ghost, but are baffled by its seeming ability to be here and there and nowhere) 150 **trumpet** trumpeter 154 **extravagant and erring** wandering beyond bounds (the words have similar meaning) | **hies** hastens 156 **probation** proof 158 **'gainst** just before 162 **strike** destroy by evil influence 163 **takes** bewitches | **charm** cast a spell, control by enchantment

So hallowed and so gracious° is that time.

HORATIO   So have I heard and do in part believe it.   165
But, look, the morn in russet° mantle clad
Walks o'er the dew of yon high eastward hill.
Break we our watch up, and by my advice
Let us impart what we have seen tonight
Unto young Hamlet; for upon my life,   170
This spirit, dumb to us, will speak to him.
Do you consent we shall acquaint him with it,
As needful in our loves, fitting our duty?

MARCELLUS   Let's do't, I pray, and I this morning know
Where we shall find him most conveniently.   175

                                    Exeunt

                        ❖

                      ACT 1
                     SCENE 2

               Location: The castle

*Flourish. Enter Claudius, King of Denmark, Gertrude the
Queen, [the] Council, as° Polonius and his son Laertes,
Hamlet, cum aliis° [including Voltimand and Cornelius]*

KING   Though yet of Hamlet our° dear brother's death
The memory be green, and that it us befitted
To bear our hearts in grief and our whole kingdom
To be contracted in one brow of woe,
Yet so far hath discretion fought with nature   5
That we with wisest sorrow think on him
Together with remembrance of ourselves.
Therefore our sometime° sister, now our queen,
Th'imperial jointress° to this warlike state,
Have we, as 'twere with a defeated joy—   10
With an auspicious and a dropping eye,°

164 **gracious** full of grace   166 **russet** reddish brown

0.2 **s.d.** *as* such as, including   0.3 **s.d.** *cum aliis* with others   1 **our** my (the royal "we"; also in the following lines)   8 **sometime** former   9 **jointress** woman possessing property with her husband   11 **With . . . eye** with one eye smiling and the other weeping

With mirth in funeral and with dirge in marriage,
In equal scale weighing delight and dole—°
Taken to wife. Nor have we herein barred
Your better wisdoms, which have freely gone   15
With this affair along. For all, our thanks.
Now follows that you know° young Fortinbras,
Holding a weak supposal° of our worth,
Or thinking by our late dear brother's death
Our state to be disjoint and out of frame,°   20
Co-leaguèd with this dream of his advantage,°
He hath not failed to pester us with message
Importing° the surrender of those lands
Lost by his father, with all bonds of law,°
To our most valiant brother. So much for him.   25
Now for ourself and for this time of meeting.
Thus much the business is: we have here writ
To Norway, uncle of young Fortinbras—
Who, impotent° and bed-rid, scarcely hears
Of this his nephew's purpose—to suppress   30
His° further gait° herein, in that the levies,
The lists, and full proportions are all made
Out of his subject;° and we here dispatch
You, good Cornelius, and you, Voltimand,
For bearers of this greeting to old Norway,   35
Giving to you no further personal power
To business with the King more than the scope
Of these dilated° articles allow.   [*He gives a paper*]
Farewell, and let your haste commend your duty.°
CORNELIUS, VOLTIMAND
  In that, and all things, will we show our duty.   40
KING We doubt it nothing.° Heartily farewell.
                    [*Exeunt Voltimand and Cornelius*]

13 dole grief   **17 Now . . . know** next, you need to be informed that   **18 weak
supposal** low estimate   **20 disjoint . . . frame** in a state of total disorder   **21 Co-
leaguèd . . . advantage** joined to his illusory sense of having the advantage over us
and to his vision of future success   **23 Importing** having for its substance   **24 with
. . . law** (see 1.1.87, "well ratified by law and heraldry.")   **29 impotent** helpless
31 His Fortinbras's | **gait** proceeding   **31–33 in that . . . subject** since the levying
of troops and supplies is drawn entirely from the King of Norway's own subjects
38 dilated set out at length   **39 let . . . duty** let your swift obeying of orders, rather
than mere words, express your dutifulness   **41 nothing** not at all

And now, Laertes, what's the news with you?
You told us of some suit; what is't, Laertes?
You cannot speak of reason to the Dane°
And lose your voice.° What wouldst thou beg, Laertes,   45
That shall not be my offer, not thy asking?
The head is not more native° to the heart,
The hand more instrumental° to the mouth,
Than is the throne of Denmark to thy father.
What wouldst thou have, Laertes?

LAERTES   My dread lord,   50
Your leave and favor° to return to France,
From whence though willingly I came to Denmark
To show my duty in your coronation,
Yet now I must confess, that duty done,
My thoughts and wishes bend again toward France   55
And bow them to your gracious leave and pardon.°

KING   Have you your father's leave? What says Polonius?

POLONIUS   H'ath,° my lord, wrung from me my slow leave
By laborsome petition, and at last
Upon his will I sealed° my hard° consent.   60
I do beseech you, give him leave to go.

KING   Take thy fair hour,° Laertes. Time be thine,
And thy best graces spend it at thy will.°
But now, my cousin° Hamlet, and my son—

HAMLET   A little more than kin, and less than kind.°   65

KING   How is it that the clouds still hang on you?

HAMLET   Not so, my lord. I am too much in the sun.°

QUEEN   Good Hamlet, cast thy nighted color° off,
And let thine eye look like a friend on Denmark.°

---

44 the Dane the Danish king   **45 lose your voice** waste your speech   **47 native** closely connected, related   **48 instrumental** serviceable   **51 leave and favor** kind permission   **56 bow . . . pardon** entreatingly make a deep bow, asking your permission to depart   **58 H'ath** he has   **60 sealed** (as if sealing a legal document) | **hard** reluctant   **62 Take thy fair hour** enjoy your time of youth   **63 And . . . will** and may your time be spent in exercising your best qualities   **64 cousin** any kin not of the immediate family   **65 A little . . . kind** too close a blood relation, and yet we are less than kinsmen in that our relationship lacks affection and is indeed unnatural (Hamlet plays on *kind* as [1] kindly and [2] belonging to nature, suggesting that Claudius is not the same kind of being as the rest of humanity; the line is often delivered as an aside, though it need not be)   **67 the sun** the sunshine of the King's royal favor (with pun on *son*)   **68 nighted color** (1) mourning garments of black (2) dark melancholy   **69 Denmark** the King of Denmark

Do not forever with thy vailèd lids°   70
Seek for thy noble father in the dust.
Thou know'st 'tis common,° all that lives must die,
Passing through nature to eternity.
HAMLET Ay, madam, it is common.
QUEEN   If it be,
Why seems it so particular° with thee?   75
HAMLET Seems, madam? Nay, it is. I know not "seems."
'Tis not alone my inky cloak, good mother,
Nor customary° suits of solemn black,
Nor windy suspiration° of forced breath,
No, nor the fruitful° river in the eye,   80
Nor the dejected havior° of the visage,
Together with all forms, moods,° shapes of grief,
That can denote me truly. These indeed seem,
For they are actions that a man might play.
But I have that within which passes show;   85
These but the trappings and the suits of woe.
KING 'Tis sweet and commendable in your nature, Hamlet,
To give these mourning duties to your father.
But you must know your father lost a father,
That father lost, lost his, and the survivor bound   90
In filial obligation for some term
To do obsequious° sorrow. But to persever
In obstinate condolement° is a course
Of impious stubbornness. 'Tis unmanly grief.
It shows a will most incorrect to heaven,   95
A heart unfortified,° a mind impatient,
An understanding simple° and unschooled.
For what we know must be and is as common
As any the most vulgar thing to sense,°
Why should we in our peevish opposition   100
Take it to heart? Fie, 'tis a fault to heaven,
A fault against the dead, a fault to nature,

---

70 vailèd lids lowered eyes **72 common** of universal occurrence (but Hamlet plays on the sense of "vulgar" in line 74) **75 particular** personal **78 customary** customary to mourning **79 suspiration** sighing **80 fruitful** abundant **81 havior** expression **82 moods** outward expression of feeling **92 obsequious** suited to obsequies or funerals **93 condolement** sorrowing **96 unfortified** against adversity **97 simple** ignorant **99 As . . . sense** as the most ordinary experience

To reason most absurd, whose common theme
Is death of fathers, and who still° hath cried,
From the first corpse° till he that died today,   105
"This must be so." We pray you, throw to earth
This unprevailing° woe and think of us
As of a father; for let the world take note,
You are the most immediate° to our throne,
And with no less nobility of love   110
Than that which dearest father bears his son
Do I impart toward° you. For° your intent
In going back to school° in Wittenberg,°
It is most retrograde° to our desire,
And we beseech you bend you° to remain   115
Here in the cheer and comfort of our eye,
Our chiefest courtier, cousin, and our son.
QUEEN Let not thy mother lose her prayers, Hamlet.
I pray thee, stay with us, go not to Wittenberg.
HAMLET I shall in all° my best° obey you, madam.   120
KING Why, 'tis a loving and a fair reply.
Be as ourself in Denmark. Madam, come.
This gentle and unforced accord of Hamlet
Sits smiling to° my heart, in grace° whereof
No jocund° health that Denmark drinks today   125
But the great cannon to the clouds shall tell,
And the King's rouse° the heaven shall bruit again,°
Respeaking earthly thunder.° Come away.
                    Flourish. Exeunt all but Hamlet
HAMLET Oh, that this too too sullied° flesh would melt,
Thaw, and resolve itself into a dew!   130
Or that the Everlasting had not fixed
His canon° 'gainst self-slaughter! Oh, God, God,
How weary, stale, flat, and unprofitable

---

104 still always **105 the first corpse** (Abel's) **107 unprevailing** unavailing, useless
109 most immediate next in succession **112 impart toward** liberally bestow on |
For as for **113 to school** to your studies | **Wittenberg** famous German university
founded in 1502 **114 retrograde** contrary **115 bend you** incline yourself **120 in all
my best** to the best of my ability **124 to** at | **grace** thanksgiving **125 jocund** merry
127 rouse drinking of a draft of liquor | **bruit again** loudly echo **128 thunder** of
trumpet and kettledrum, sounded when the King drinks; see 1.4.8–12 **129 sullied**
defiled (the early quartos read "sallied"; the Folio, "solid") **132 canon** law

Seem to me all the uses of this world!
Fie on't, ah fie! 'Tis an unweeded garden   135
That grows to seed. Things rank and gross in nature
Possess it merely.° That it should come to this!
But two months dead—nay, not so much, not two.
So excellent a king, that was to° this
Hyperion° to a satyr,° so loving to my mother   140
That he might not beteem° the winds of heaven
Visit her face too roughly. Heaven and earth,
Must I remember? Why, she would hang on him
As if increase of appetite had grown
By what it fed on, and yet within a month—   145
Let me not think on't; frailty, thy name is woman!—
A little month, or ere° those shoes were old
With which she followed my poor father's body,
Like Niobe,° all tears, why she, even she—
Oh, God, a beast, that wants discourse of reason,°   150
Would have mourned longer—married with my uncle,
My father's brother, but no more like my father
Than I to Hercules. Within a month,
Ere yet the salt of most unrighteous tears
Had left the flushing in her gallèd° eyes,   155
She married. Oh, most wicked speed, to post°
With such dexterity to incestuous° sheets!
It is not, nor it cannot come to good.
But break, my heart, for I must hold my tongue.

Enter Horatio, Marcellus, and Bernardo

HORATIO   Hail to Your Lordship!
HAMLET   I am glad to see you well.   160
Horatio!—or I do forget myself.

---

137 merely completely   **139 to** in comparison to   **140 Hyperion** Titan sun-god,
father of Helios | **satyr** a lecherous creature of classical mythology, half-human
but with a goat's legs, tail, ears, and horns   **141 beteem** allow   **147 or ere** even
before   **149 Niobes** Tantalus's daughter, Queen of Thebes, who boasted that she
had more sons and daughters than Leto; for this, Apollo and Artemis, children of
Leto, slew her fourteen children; she was turned by Zeus into a stone that
continually dropped tears   **150 wants . . . reason** lacks the faculty of reason
155 gallèd irritated, inflamed   **156 post** hasten   **157 incestuous** (in Shakespeare's
day, the marriage of a man like Claudius to his deceased brother's wife was
considered incestuous)

8 ### The Doome, vvarning

Also there are certain men which haue no heads, but their eyes, nose, and mouth, are fixed in their breastes, so that their belly is close vnder the chin, supposed of those people that haunte ye seas to be *Polantines*, who in times past calling Mariners by their names, did in the nighte season deuoure them that came a shore.

Scipodes and Cathani.

Scipodes and *Monomeri*, are people hauing but one foote, without bending their knee at any time, and yet very swift. Plinie reporteth that in the great heate of the yeare, they lye vpon their backes and with the bignesse of their foote they shadow their bodies from the Sun.

Cathaini are a kinde of people of *Scithia*, betwéene *Gedrosa* and the riuer *Indus*: they say that no man liuing but themselues, haue the vse or sighte in both their eyes, but that all other mortall men are cleane voyde of sight, or else that they sée but with one eye, and the other to be blinde: they are of colour very white, their eyes are small and little, they are by nature without haire on their faces, their religion is nothing but mere superstition : they worship the Sun and Moone, and other fonde creatures, and some of them worship an Ore.

Satiri.

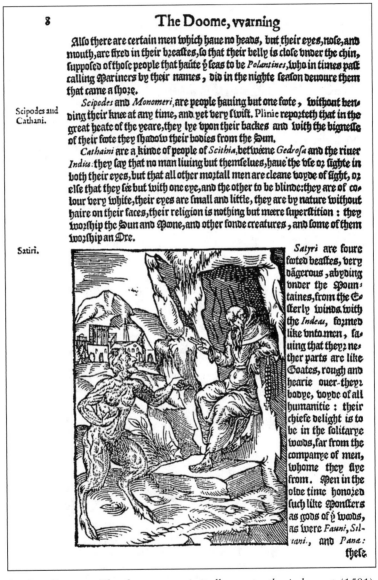

Satyri are foure footed beastes, very dágerous, abyding vnder the Mountaines, from the Easterly winds with the *Indeas*, formed like vnto men, saying that theyr nether parts are like Goates, rough and hearie ouer-theyr bodye, voyde of all humanitie : their chiefe delight is to be in the solitarye woods, far from the companye of men, whome they flye from. Men in the olde time honored suchlike Monsters as gods of ye woods, as were *Fauni, Siltani.*, and *Panæ*: these

Stephen Batman, *The doome warning all men to the judgment* (1581). When Hamlet likens Claudius to a satyr (1.2.140), he refers to legendary monsters. As described by Stephen Batman, they are "foore footed beastes, very dangerous, abyding under the Mountaines . . . formed like to men, saving that theyr nether parts are like Goates." Here one converses with St. Jerome. (By permission of the Folger Shakespeare Library.)

HORATIO   The same, my lord, and your poor servant ever.
HAMLET   Sir, my good friend; I'll change that name° with you.
  And what make you from° Wittenberg, Horatio?—
  Marcellus.
MARCELLUS   My good lord.   165
HAMLET
  I am very glad to see you. [*To Bernardo*] Good even, sir.—
  But what in faith make you from Wittenberg?
HORATIO   A truant disposition, good my lord.
HAMLET   I would not hear your enemy say so,
  Nor shall you do my ear that violence   170
  To make it truster of° your own report
  Against yourself. I know you are no truant.
  But what is your affair in Elsinore?
  We'll teach you to drink deep ere you depart.
HORATIO   My lord, I came to see your father's funeral.   175
HAMLET   I prithee, do not mock me, fellow student;
  I think it was to see my mother's wedding.
HORATIO   Indeed, my lord, it followed hard° upon.
HAMLET   Thrift, thrift, Horatio! The funeral baked meats°
  Did coldly° furnish forth the marriage tables.   180
  Would I had met my dearest° foe in heaven
  Or ever° I had seen that day, Horatio!
  My father!—Methinks I see my father.
HORATIO   Where, my lord?
HAMLET   In my mind's eye, Horatio.
HORATIO   I saw him once. 'A was a goodly king.   185
HAMLET   'A° was a man. Take him for all in all,
  I shall not look upon his like again.
HORATIO   My lord, I think I saw him yesternight.
HAMLET   Saw? Who?
HORATIO   My lord, the King your father.
HAMLET   The King my father?   190

---

163 **change that name** give and receive reciprocally the name of "friend" rather than
talk of "servant;" or Hamlet may be saying, "no, I am *your* servant"   164 **what
make you from** what are you doing away from   171 **To . . . of** to make it trust
178 **hard** close   179 **baked meats** meat pies   180 **coldly** as cold leftovers
181 **dearest** closest (and therefore deadliest)   182 **Or ever** ere, before   186 **'A** he

HORATIO Season your admiration° for a while
With an attent° ear till I may deliver,
Upon the witness of these gentlemen,
This marvel to you.
HAMLET   For God's love, let me hear!
HORATIO Two nights together had these gentlemen,   195
Marcellus and Bernardo, on their watch,
In the dead waste° and middle of the night,
Been thus encountered. A figure like your father,
Armèd at point° exactly, cap-à-pie,°
Appears before them, and with solemn march   200
Goes slow and stately by them. Thrice he walked
By their oppressed and fear-surprisèd eyes
Within his truncheon's° length, whilst they, distilled°
Almost to jelly with the act° of fear,
Stand dumb and speak not to him. This to me   205
In dreadful° secrecy impart they did,
And I with them the third night kept the watch,
Where, as they had delivered, both in time,
Form of the thing, each word made true and good,
The apparition comes. I knew your father;   210
These hands are not more like.
HAMLET   But where was this?
MARCELLUS My lord, upon the platform where we watch.
HAMLET Did you not speak to it?
HORATIO   My lord, I did,
But answer made it none. Yet once methought
It lifted up it° head and did address   215
Itself to motion, like as it would speak;°
But even then° the morning cock crew loud,
And at the sound it shrunk in haste away
And vanished from our sight.
HAMLET   'Tis very strange.

191 **Season your admiration** moderate your astonishment 192 **attent** attentive
197 **dead waste** desolate stillness 199 **at point** correctly in every detail | **cap-à-pie**
from head to foot 203 **truncheon** officer's staff | **distilled** dissolved 204 **act**
action, operation 206 **dreadful** full of dread 215 **it** its 215–16 **did . . . speak**
prepared to move as though it was about to speak 217 **even then** at that very
instant

HORATIO   As I do live, my honored lord, 'tis true,   220
And we did think it writ down in our duty
To let you know of it.
HAMLET   Indeed, indeed, sirs. But this troubles me.
Hold you the watch tonight?
ALL   We do, my lord.
HAMLET   Armed, say you?   225
ALL   Armed, my lord.
HAMLET   From top to toe?
ALL   My lord, from head to foot.
HAMLET   Then saw you not his face?
HORATIO   Oh, yes, my lord, he wore his beaver° up.
HAMLET   What° looked he, frowningly?   230
HORATIO   A countenance more in sorrow than in anger.
HAMLET   Pale or red?
HORATIO   Nay, very pale.
HAMLET   And fixed his eyes upon you?
HORATIO   Most constantly.
HAMLET   I would I had been there.
HORATIO   It would have much amazed you.   235
HAMLET   Very like, very like. Stayed it long?
HORATIO   While one with moderate haste might tell° a hundred.
MARCELLUS, BERNARDO   Longer, longer.
HORATIO   Not when I saw't.
HAMLET   His beard was grizzled—no?
HORATIO   It was, as I have seen it in his life,   240
A sable silvered.
HAMLET   I will watch tonight.
Perchance 'twill walk again.
HORATIO   I warr'nt it will.
HAMLET   If it assume my noble father's person,
I'll speak to it though hell itself should gape
And bid me hold my peace. I pray you all,   245
If you have hitherto concealed this sight,
Let it be tenable° in your silence still,
And whatsomever else shall hap tonight,

---

229 beaver visor on the helmet   **230 What** how   **237 tell** count   **247 tenable** held

Give it an understanding but no tongue.
I will requite your loves. So, fare you well. 250
Upon the platform twixt eleven and twelve
I'll visit you.

ALL   Our duty to Your Honor.

HAMLET   Your loves,° as mine to you. Farewell.

                       Exeunt [all but Hamlet]

My father's spirit in arms! All is not well.
I doubt° some foul play. Would the night were come! 255
Till then sit still, my soul. Foul deeds will rise,
Though all the earth o'erwhelm them, to men's eyes.

                             Exit

♣

ACT 1
SCENE 3

Location: Polonius's chambers

Enter Laertes and Ophelia, his sister

LAERTES   My necessaries are embarked. Farewell.
And, sister, as the winds give benefit
And convoy is assistant,° do not sleep
But let me hear from you.

OPHELIA   Do you doubt that?

LAERTES   For° Hamlet, and the trifling of his favor, 5
Hold it a fashion and a toy in blood,°
A violet in the youth of primy° nature,
Forward,° not permanent, sweet, not lasting,
The perfume and suppliance° of a minute—
No more.

OPHELIA   No more but so?

LAERTES   Think it no more. 10
For nature crescent does not grow alone
In thews and bulk, but as this temple waxes

---

253 **Your loves** say "your loves" to me, not just your "duty"   255 **doubt** suspect
3 **convoy is assistant** means of conveyance are available   5 **For** as for   6 **toy in blood** passing amorous fancy   7 **primy** in its prime, springtime   8 **Forward** precocious   9 **suppliance** pastime, something to fill the time   11–14 **For nature . . .**

The inward service of the mind and soul
Grows wide withal.° Perhaps he loves you now,
And now no soil nor cautel° doth besmirch   15
The virtue of his will;° but you must fear,
His greatness weighed,° his will is not his own.
For he himself is subject to his birth.
He may not, as unvalued persons do,
Carve° for himself, for on his choice depends   20
The safety and health of this whole state,
And therefore must his choice be circumscribed
Unto the voice and yielding° of that body
Whereof he is the head. Then if he says he loves you,
It fits your wisdom so far to believe it   25
As he in his particular act and place°
May give his saying deed, which is no further
Than the main voice° of Denmark goes withal.°
Then weigh what loss your honor may sustain
If with too credent° ear you list° his songs,   30
Or lose your heart, or your chaste treasure open
To his unmastered° importunity.
Fear it, Ophelia, fear it, my dear sister,
And keep you in the rear of your affection,°
Out of the shot and danger of desire.   35
The chariest° maid is prodigal enough
If she unmask° her beauty to the moon.°
Virtue itself scapes not calumnious strokes.
The canker galls° the infants of the spring
Too oft before their buttons be disclosed,°   40
And in the morn and liquid dew° of youth

---

withal for nature, as it ripens, does not grow only in physical strength, but as the body matures the inner qualities of mind and soul grow along with it (Laertes warns Ophelia that the mature Hamlet may not cling to his youthful interests)   **15 soil nor cautel** blemish nor deceit   **16 The . . . will** the purity of his desire   **17 His greatness weighed** taking into account his high fortune   **20 Carve** choose   **23 voice and yielding** assent, approval   **26 in . . . place** in his particular restricted circumstances   **28 main voice** general assent **| withal** along with   **30 credent** credulous **| list** listen to   **32 unmastered** uncontrolled   **34 keep . . . affection** don't advance as far as your affection might lead you (a military metaphor)   **36 chariest** most scrupulously modest   **37 if she unmask** if she does no more than show **| moon** (symbol of chastity)   **39 canker galls** cankerworm destroys   **40 buttons be disclosed** buds be opened   **41 liquid dew** time when dew is fresh and bright

Contagious blastments° are most imminent.
Be wary then; best safety lies in fear.
Youth to itself rebels,° though none else near.

OPHELIA   I shall the effect of this good lesson keep   45
As watchman to my heart. But, good my brother,
Do not, as some ungracious° pastors do,
Show me the steep and thorny way to heaven,
Whiles like a puffed° and reckless libertine
Himself the primrose path of dalliance treads,   50
And recks° not his own rede.°

                                          Enter Polonius

LAERTES   Oh, fear me not.°
I stay too long. But here my father comes.
A double blessing is a double grace;
Occasion smiles upon a second leave.°

POLONIUS   Yet here, Laertes? Aboard, aboard, for shame!   55
The wind sits in the shoulder of your sail,
And you are stayed for. There—my blessing with thee!
And these few precepts in thy memory
Look thou character.° Give thy thoughts no tongue,
Nor any unproportioned° thought his° act.   60
Be thou familiar,° but by no means vulgar.°
Those friends thou hast, and their adoption tried,°
Grapple them unto thy soul with hoops of steel,
But do not dull thy palm° with entertainment
Of each new-hatched, unfledged courage.° Beware   65
Of entrance to a quarrel, but being in,
Bear't that° th'opposèd may beware of thee.
Give every man thy ear, but few thy voice;
Take each man's censure,° but reserve thy judgment.

42 **blastments** blights   44 **Youth . . . rebels** youth yields to the rebellion of the flesh
47 **ungracious** ungodly   49 **puffed** bloated or swollen with pride   51 **recks** heeds |
rede counsel | **fear me not** don't worry on my account   53–54 **A double . . . leave**
the goddess Occasion or Opportunity smiles on the happy circumstance of being
able to say good-bye twice and thus receive a second blessing   59 **Look thou**
character see to it that you inscribe   60 **unproportioned** badly calculated,
intemperate | **his** its   61 **familiar** sociable | **vulgar** common   62 **and . . . tried**
and their suitability to be your friends having been put to the test   64 **dull thy palm**
shake hands so often as to make the gesture meaningless   65 **courage** swashbuckler
67 **Bear't that** manage it so that   69 **censure** opinion, judgment

Costly thy habit° as thy purse can buy, 70
But not expressed in fancy;° rich, not gaudy,
For the apparel oft proclaims the man,
And they in France of the best rank and station
Are of a most select and generous chief in that.°
Neither a borrower nor a lender be, 75
For loan oft loses both itself and friend,
And borrowing dulleth edge of husbandry.°
This above all: to thine own self be true,
And it must follow, as the night the day,
Thou canst not then be false to any man. 80
Farewell. My blessing season° this in thee!

LAERTES Most humbly do I take my leave, my lord.

POLONIUS The time invests° you. Go, your servants tend.°

LAERTES Farewell, Ophelia, and remember well
What I have said to you.

OPHELIA   'Tis in my memory locked, 85
And you yourself shall keep the key of it.

LAERTES Farewell.   *Exit Laertes*

POLONIUS What is't, Ophelia, he hath said to you?

OPHELIA So please you, something touching the Lord Hamlet.

POLONIUS Marry,° well bethought. 90
'Tis told me he hath very oft of late
Given private time to you, and you yourself
Have of your audience been most free and bounteous.
If it be so—as so 'tis put on° me,
And that in way of caution—I must tell you 95
You do not understand yourself so clearly
As it behooves° my daughter and your honor.
What is between you? Give me up the truth.

OPHELIA He hath, my lord, of late made many tenders°
Of his affection to me. 100

POLONIUS Affection? Pooh! You speak like a green girl,
Unsifted° in such perilous circumstance.
Do you believe his tenders, as you call them?

70 **habit** clothing   71 **fancy** excessive ornament, decadent fashion   74 **Are . . . that**
are of a most refined and well-bred preeminence in choosing what to wear
77 **husbandry** thrift   81 **season** mature   83 **invests** besieges, presses upon | **tend**
attend, wait   90 **Marry** by the Virgin Mary (a mild oath)   94 **put on** impressed on,
told to   97 **behooves** befits   99 **tenders** offers   102 **Unsifted** untried

OPHELIA   I do not know, my lord, what I should think.

POLONIUS   Marry, I will teach you. Think yourself a baby   105
That you have ta'en these tenders for true pay
Which are not sterling.° Tender yourself more dearly,°
Or—not to crack the wind° of the poor phrase,
Running it thus—you'll tender me a fool.°

OPHELIA   My lord, he hath importuned me with love   110
In honorable fashion.

POLONIUS   Ay, fashion° you may call it. Go to, go to.°

OPHELIA   And hath given countenance° to his speech, my lord,
With almost all the holy vows of heaven.

POLONIUS   Ay, springes° to catch woodcocks.° I do know,   115
When the blood burns, how prodigal° the soul
Lends the tongue vows. These blazes, daughter,
Giving more light than heat, extinct in both
Even in their promise as it° is a-making,
You must not take for fire. From this time   120
Be something° scanter of your maiden presence.
Set your entreatments at a higher rate
Than a command to parle.° For° Lord Hamlet,
Believe so much in him° that he is young,
And with a larger tether may he walk   125
Than may be given you. In few,° Ophelia,
Do not believe his vows, for they are brokers,°
Not of that dye° which their investments° show,
But mere implorators° of unholy suits,
Breathing° like sanctified and pious bawds,   130
The better to beguile. This is for all:°

---

107 **sterling** legal currency | **Tender . . . dearly** (1) bargain for your favors at a higher rate—hold out for marriage (2) show greater care of yourself   108 **crack the wind** run it until it is broken-winded   109 **tender . . . fool** (1) make a fool of me (2) present me with a *fool* or baby   112 **fashion** mere form, pretense | **Go to** (an expression of impatience)   113 **countenance** credit, confirmation   115 **springes** snares | **woodcocks** birds easily caught; here used to connote gullibility   116 **prodigal** prodigally   119 **it** the promise   121 **something** somewhat   122–23 **Set . . . parle** as defender of your chastity, negotiate for something better than a surrender simply because the besieger requests an interview   123 **For** as for   124 **so . . . him** this much concerning him   126 **In few** briefly   127 **brokers** go-betweens, procurers   129 **dye** color or sort | **investments** clothes (the vows are not what they seem)   129 **mere implorators** out-and-out solicitors   130 **Breathing** speaking   131 **for all** once for all, in sum

I would not, in plain terms, from this time forth
Have you so slander° any moment° leisure
As to give words or talk with the Lord Hamlet.
Look to't, I charge you. Come your ways.° 135
OPHELIA   I shall obey, my lord.

Exeunt

❖

ACT 1
SCENE 4

Location: The guard platform

Enter Hamlet, Horatio, and Marcellus

HAMLET   The air bites shrewdly;° it is very cold.
HORATIO   It is a nipping and an eager° air.
HAMLET   What hour now?
HORATIO   I think it lacks of° twelve.
MARCELLUS   No, it is struck.
HORATIO   Indeed? I heard it not.
It then draws near the season°   5
Wherein the spirit held his wont° to walk.
      A flourish of trumpets, and two pieces° go off [within]
What does this mean, my lord?
HAMLET   The King doth wake° tonight and takes his rouse,°
Keeps wassail, and the swagg'ring upspring reels;°
And as he drains his drafts of Rhenish° down,   10
The kettledrum and trumpet thus bray out
The triumph of his pledge.°
HORATIO   Is it a custom?
HAMLET   Ay, marry, is't,
But to my mind, though I am native here

---

133 **slander** abuse, misuse | **moment** moment's   135 **Come your ways** come along

1 **shrewdly** keenly, sharply   2 **eager** biting   3 **lacks of** is just short of   5 **season** time   6 **held his wont** was accustomed   6.1 s.d. *pieces* of ordnance, cannon   8 **wake** stay awake and hold revel | **takes his rouse** carouses   9 **Keeps . . . reels** carouses, and riotously dances a German dance called the upspring   10 **Rhenish** Rhine wine 12 **The triumph . . . pledge** the celebration of his offering a toast

And to the manner° born, it is a custom   15
More honored in the breach than the observance.°
This heavy-headed revel east and west°
Makes us traduced and taxed of° other nations.
They clepe° us drunkards, and with swinish phrase°
Soil our addition;° and indeed it takes   20
From our achievements, though performed at height,°
The pith and marrow of our attribute.°
So, oft it chances in particular men,
That for some vicious mole° of nature in them,
As in their birth—wherein they are not guilty,   25
Since nature cannot choose his° origin—
By their o'ergrowth of some complexion,°
Oft breaking down the pales° and forts of reason,
Or by some habit that too much o'erleavens
The form of plausive manners,° that these men,   30
Carrying, I say, the stamp of one defect,
Being nature's livery or fortune's star,°
His virtues else,° be they as pure as grace,
As infinite as man may undergo,°
Shall in the general censure° take corruption   35
From that particular fault. The dram of evil
Doth all the noble substance often dout
To his own scandal.°

                                                    Enter Ghost

HORATIO   Look, my lord, it comes!

15 **manner** custom (of drinking)   16 **More . . . observance** better neglected than
followed   17 **east and west** everywhere   18 **taxed of** censured by   19 **clepe** call |
with swinish phrase by calling us swine   20 **addition** reputation   21 **at height**
outstandingly   22 **The pith . . . attribute** the most essential part of the esteem that
should be attributed to us   24 **for . . . mole** on account of some natural defect in
their constitutions   26 **his** its   27 **their o'ergrowth . . . complexion** the excessive
growth in individuals of some natural trait   28 **pales** palings, fences (as of a
fortification)   29–30 **o'erleavens . . . manners** infects the way we should behave
(much as bad yeast spoils the dough); *plausive* means "pleasing"   32 **Being . . . star**
(that stamp of defect) being a sign identifying one as wearing the livery of, and hence
being the servant to, nature (unfortunate inherited qualities) or fortune (mischance)
33 **His virtues else** the other qualities of *these men* (line 30)   34 **may undergo** can
sustain   35 **in . . . censure** in overall appraisal, in people's opinion generally
36–38 **The dram . . . scandal** the small drop of evil blots out or works against the
noble substance of the whole and brings it into disrepute (to *dout* is to blot out; a
famous crux)

HAMLET   Angels and ministers of grace° defend us!
  Be thou a spirit of health° or goblin damned,   40
  Bring° with thee airs from heaven or blasts from hell,
  Be thy intents° wicked or charitable,
  Thou com'st in such a questionable° shape
  That I will speak to thee. I'll call thee Hamlet,
  King, father, royal Dane. Oh, answer me!   45
  Let me not burst in ignorance, but tell
  Why thy canonized° bones, hearsèd° in death,
  Have burst their cerements;° why the sepulcher
  Wherein we saw thee quietly inurned°
  Hath oped his ponderous and marble jaws   50
  To cast thee up again. What may this mean,
  That thou, dead corpse, again in complete steel,°
  Revisits thus the glimpses of the moon,°
  Making night hideous, and we fools of nature°
  So horridly to shake our disposition°   55
  With thoughts beyond the reaches of our souls?
  Say, why is this? Wherefore? What should we do?
                      [*The Ghost*] *beckons* [*Hamlet*]
HORATIO   It beckons you to go away with it,
  As if it some impartment° did desire
  To you alone.
MARCELLUS   Look with what courteous action   60
  It wafts you to a more removèd ground.
  But do not go with it.
HORATIO   No, by no means.
HAMLET   It will not speak. Then I will follow it.
HORATIO   Do not, my lord!
HAMLET   Why, what should be the fear?
  I do not set my life at a pin's fee,°   65

---

39 ministers of grace messengers of God   **40 Be . . . health** whether you are a good
angel   **41 Bring** whether you bring   **42 Be thy intents** whether your intentions are
43 questionable inviting question   **47 canonized** buried according to the canons
of the church | **hearsèd** coffined   **48 cerements** grave clothes   **49 inurned**
entombed   **52 complete steel** full armor   **53 the glimpses . . . moon** the sublunary
world, all that is beneath the moon   **54 fools of nature** mere mortals, limited to
natural knowledge and subject to nature   **55 So . . . disposition** to distress our
mental composure so violently   **59 impartment** communication   **65 fee** value

And for° my soul, what can it do to that,
Being a thing immortal as itself?
It waves me forth again. I'll follow it.

HORATIO   What if it tempt you toward the flood,° my lord,
Or to the dreadful summit of the cliff   70
That beetles o'er° his° base into the sea,
And there assume some other horrible form
Which might deprive your sovereignty of reason°
And draw you into madness? Think of it.
The very place puts toys of desperation,°   75
Without more motive, into every brain
That looks so many fathoms to the sea
And hears it roar beneath.

HAMLET   It wafts me still.—Go on, I'll follow thee.

MARCELLUS   You shall not go, my lord.   [*They try to stop him*]

HAMLET   Hold off your hands!   80

HORATIO   Be ruled. You shall not go.

HAMLET   My fate cries out,°
And makes each petty° artery° in this body
As hardy as the Nemean lion's nerve.°
Still am I called. Unhand me, gentlemen.
By heaven, I'll make a ghost of him that lets° me!   85
I say, away!—Go on, I'll follow thee.

                              Exeunt Ghost and Hamlet

HORATIO   He waxes desperate with imagination.

MARCELLUS   Let's follow. 'Tis not fit thus to obey him.

HORATIO   Have after.° To what issue° will this come?

MARCELLUS   Something is rotten in the state of Denmark.   90

HORATIO   Heaven will direct it.°

MARCELLUS   Nay, let's follow him.

                                        Exeunt

❧

66 **for** as for   69 **flood** sea   71 **beetles o'er** overhangs threateningly (like bushy
eyebrows) | **his** its   73 **deprive . . . reason** take away the rule of reason over your
mind   75 **toys of desperation** fancies of desperate acts, suicide   81 **My fate cries out**
my destiny summons me   82 **petty** weak | **artery** blood vessel system through
which the vital spirits were thought to have been conveyed   83 **as the Nemean lion's
nerve** as a sinew of the huge lion slain by Hercules as the first of his twelve labors
85 **lets** hinders   89 **Have after** let's go after him | **issue** outcome   91 **it** the outcome

ACT 1
SCENE 5

Location: The battlements of the castle

Enter Ghost and Hamlet

HAMLET Whither wilt thou lead me? Speak. I'll go no further.
GHOST Mark me.
HAMLET   I will.
GHOST   My hour is almost come,
  When I to sulf'rous and tormenting flames
  Must render up myself.
HAMLET   Alas, poor ghost!
GHOST Pity me not, but lend thy serious hearing   5
  To what I shall unfold.
HAMLET   Speak. I am bound° to hear.
GHOST So art thou to revenge, when thou shalt hear.
HAMLET What?
GHOST   I am thy father's spirit,
  Doomed for a certain term to walk the night,
  And for the day confined to fast° in fires,   10
  Till the foul crimes° done in my days of nature°
  Are burnt and purged away. But that° I am forbid
  To tell the secrets of my prison house,
  I could a tale unfold whose lightest word
  Would harrow up° thy soul, freeze thy young blood,   15
  Make thy two eyes like stars start from their spheres,°
  Thy knotted and combinèd locks° to part,
  And each particular hair to stand on end
  Like quills upon the fretful porcupine.
  But this eternal blazon° must not be   20
  To ears of flesh and blood. List, list, oh, list!
  If thou didst ever thy dear father love—
HAMLET Oh, God!

6 bound (1) ready (2) obligated by duty and fate (the ghost, in line 8, answers in the
second sense) 10 fast do penance by fasting 11 crimes sins | of nature as a
mortal 12 But that were it not that 15 harrow up lacerate, tear 16 spheres
eye-sockets, here compared to the orbits or transparent revolving spheres in which,
according to Ptolemaic astronomy, the heavenly bodies were fixed 17 knotted . . .
locks hair neatly arranged and confined 20 eternal blazon revelation of the secrets
of eternity

GHOST   Revenge his foul and most unnatural murder.

HAMLET   Murder?   25

GHOST   Murder most foul, as in the best° it is,
But this most foul, strange, and unnatural.

HAMLET   Haste me to know't, that I, with wings as swift
As meditation or the thoughts of love,
May sweep to my revenge.

GHOST   I find thee apt;   30
And duller shouldst thou be° than the fat° weed
That roots itself in ease on Lethe° wharf,
Wouldst thou not stir in this. Now, Hamlet, hear.
'Tis given out that, sleeping in my orchard,°
A serpent stung me. So the whole ear of Denmark   35
Is by a forgèd process° of my death
Rankly abused.° But know, thou noble youth,
The serpent that did sting thy father's life
Now wears his crown.

HAMLET   Oh, my prophetic soul! My uncle!

GHOST   Ay, that incestuous, that adulterate° beast,   40
With witchcraft of his wit, with traitorous gifts—°
Oh, wicked wit and gifts, that have the power
So to seduce!—won to his shameful lust
The will of my most seeming-virtuous queen.
Oh, Hamlet, what a falling off was there!   45
From me, whose love was of that dignity
That it went hand in hand even with the vow°
I made to her in marriage, and to decline
Upon a wretch whose natural gifts were poor
To° those of mine!   50
But virtue, as it° never will be moved,
Though lewdness court it in a shape of heaven,°
So lust, though to a radiant angel linked,
Will sate itself in a celestial bed°

---

26 in the best even at best   **31 shouldst thou be** you would have to be | **fat**
torpid, lethargic   **32 Lethe** the river of forgetfulness in Hades   **34 orchard** garden
36 forgèd process falsified account   **37 abused** deceived   **40 adulterate** adulterous
41 gifts (1) talents (2) presents   **47 even with the vow** with the very vow   **50 To**
compared with   **51 virtue, as it** just as virtue   **52 shape of heaven** heavenly form
54 sate . . . bed gratify its lustful appetite to the point of revulsion or ennui, even in
a virtuously lawful marriage

And prey on garbage.   55
But soft, methinks I scent the morning air.
Brief let me be. Sleeping within my orchard,
My custom always of the afternoon,
Upon my secure hour° thy uncle stole,
With juice of cursèd hebona° in a vial,   60
And in the porches° of my ears did pour
The leprous distillment,° whose effect
Holds such an enmity with blood of man
That swift as quicksilver it courses through
The natural gates° and alleys of the body,   65
And with a sudden vigor it doth posset
And curd,° like eager° droppings into milk,
The thin and wholesome blood. So did it mine,
And a most instant tetter° barked° about,
Most lazar-like,° with vile and loathsome crust,   70
All my smooth body.
Thus was I, sleeping, by a brother's hand
Of life, of crown, of queen at once dispatched,°
Cut off even in the blossoms of my sin,
Unhouseled, disappointed, unaneled,°   75
No reck'ning° made, but sent to my account
With all my imperfections on my head.
Oh, horrible! Oh, horrible, most horrible!
If thou hast nature° in thee, bear it not.
Let not the royal bed of Denmark be   80
A couch for luxury° and damnèd incest.
But, howsomever thou pursues this act,
Taint not thy mind nor let thy soul contrive
Against thy mother aught. Leave her to heaven
And to those thorns that in her bosom lodge,   85

---

59 **secure hour** time of being free from worries 60 **hebona** a poison (the word seems to be a form of *ebony*, though it is thought perhaps to be related to *henbane*, a poison, or to *ebenus*, "yew") 61 **porches** gateways 62 **leprous distillment** distillation causing leprosylike disfigurement 65 **gates** entryways 66–67 **posset . . . curd** coagulate and curdle 67 **eager** sour, acid 69 **tetter** eruption of scabs | **barked** covered with a rough covering, like bark on a tree 70 **lazar-like** leperlike 73 **dispatched** suddenly deprived 75 **Unhouseled . . . unaneled** without having received the Sacrament or other last rites including confession, absolution, and the holy oil of extreme unction 76 **reck'ning** settling of accounts 79 **nature** the promptings of a son 81 **luxury** lechery

To prick and sting her. Fare thee well at once.
The glowworm shows the matin° to be near,
And 'gins to pale his° uneffectual fire.
Adieu, adieu, adieu! Remember me.   [*Exit*]

HAMLET   O all you host of heaven! O earth! What else?   90
And shall I couple° hell? Oh, fie! Hold, hold,° my heart,
And you, my sinews, grow not instant° old,
But bear me stiffly up. Remember thee?
Ay, thou poor ghost, whiles memory holds a seat
In this distracted globe.° Remember thee?   95
Yea, from the table° of my memory
I'll wipe away all trivial fond° records,
All saws of books, all forms, all pressures past°
That youth and observation copied there,
And thy commandment all alone shall live   100
Within the book and volume of my brain,
Unmixed with baser matter. Yes, by heaven!
Oh, most pernicious woman!
Oh, villain, villain, smiling, damnèd villain!
My tables—meet it is I set it down°   105
That one may smile, and smile, and be a villain.
At least I am sure it may be so in Denmark.
So, uncle, there you are.° Now to my word:
It is "Adieu, adieu! Remember me."
I have sworn't.   110

                    Enter Horatio and Marcellus

HORATIO   My lord, my lord!
MARCELLUS   Lord Hamlet!
HORATIO   Heavens secure him!°
HAMLET   So be it.
MARCELLUS   Hillo, ho, ho, my lord!

---

87 matin morning   **88 his** its   **91 couple** add | **Hold** hold together   **92 instant**
instantly   **95 globe** (1) head (2) world (3) Globe Theater   **96 table** tablet, slate
97 fond foolish   **98 All . . . past** all wise sayings, all shapes or images imprinted on
the tablets of my memory, all past impressions   **105 My tables . . . down** editors
often specify that Hamlet makes a note in his writing tablet, but he may simply
mean that he is making a mental observation of lasting impression   **108 there you
are** there, I've noted that against you   **111 secure him** keep him safe

HAMLET   Hillo, ho, ho, boy! Come, bird, come.°
MARCELLUS   How is't, my noble lord?
HORATIO   What news, my lord?   115
HAMLET   Oh, wonderful!
HORATIO   Good my lord, tell it.
HAMLET   No, you will reveal it.
HORATIO   Not I, my lord, by heaven.
MARCELLUS   Nor I, my lord.
HAMLET   How say you, then, would heart of man once° think it?
     But you'll be secret?
HORATIO, MARCELLUS   Ay, by heaven, my lord.   120
HAMLET   There's never a villain dwelling in all Denmark
     But he's an arrant knave.°
HORATIO   There needs no ghost, my lord, come from the grave
     To tell us this.
HAMLET   Why, right, you are in the right.
     And so, without more circumstance° at all,   125
     I hold it fit that we shake hands and part,
     You as your business and desire shall point you—
     For every man hath business and desire,
     Such as it is—and for my own poor part,
     Look you, I'll go pray.   130
HORATIO   These are but wild and whirling words, my lord.
HAMLET   I am sorry they offend you, heartily;
     Yes, faith, heartily.
HORATIO   There's no offense, my lord.
HAMLET   Yes, by Saint Patrick,° but there is, Horatio,
     And much offense° too. Touching this vision here,   135
     It is an honest° ghost, that let me tell you.
     For your desire to know what is between us,
     O'ermaster't as you may. And now, good friends,
     As you are friends, scholars, and soldiers,
     Give me one poor request.   140
HORATIO   What is't, my lord? We will.

---

114 Hillo . . . come (a falconer's call to a hawk in air; Hamlet mocks the hallooing
as though it were a part of hawking) **119 once** ever **122 But . . . knave** (Hamlet
jokingly gives a self-evident answer: every villain is a thoroughgoing knave)
125 circumstance ceremony, elaboration **134 Saint Patrick** the keeper of
Purgatory **135 offense** (Hamlet deliberately changes Horatio's "no offense taken"
to "an offense against all decency") **136 honest** genuine

HAMLET Never make known what you have seen tonight.

HORATIO, MARCELLUS My lord, we will not.

HAMLET   Nay, but swear't.

HORATIO In faith, my lord, not I.°

MARCELLUS   Nor I, my lord, in faith.

HAMLET Upon my sword.°   [*He holds out his sword*]

MARCELLUS   We have sworn, my lord, already.°   145

HAMLET Indeed, upon my sword, indeed.

GHOST (*cries under the stage*)   Swear.

HAMLET Ha, ha, boy, say'st thou so? Art thou there, truepenny?°
Come on, you hear this fellow in the cellarage.
Consent to swear.

HORATIO   Propose the oath, my lord.

HAMLET Never to speak of this that you have seen,   150
Swear by my sword.

GHOST [*beneath*]   Swear.   [*They swear*°]

HAMLET *Hic et ubique?*° Then we'll shift our ground.
                                  [*He moves to another spot*]
Come hither, gentlemen,
And lay your hands again upon my sword.
Swear by my sword   155
Never to speak of this that you have heard.

GHOST [*beneath*] Swear by his sword.   [*They swear*]

HAMLET Well said, old mole. Canst work i'th'earth so fast?
A worthy pioneer!°—Once more remove, good friends.
                                          [*He moves again*]

HORATIO Oh, day and night, but this is wondrous strange!   160

HAMLET And therefore as a stranger° give it welcome.
There are more things in heaven and earth, Horatio,
Than are dreamt of in your philosophy.°
But come;

---

144 In faith . . . I I swear not to tell what I have seen (Horatio is not refusing to swear) **145 sword** the hilt in the form of a cross | **We . . . already** we swore *in faith* **147 truepenny** honest old fellow **151 s.d.** *They swear* (seemingly they swear here, and at lines 157 and 177, as they lay their hands on Hamlet's sword; triple oaths would have particular force; these three oaths deal with what they have seen, what they have heard, and what they promise about Hamlet's *antic disposition*) **152 *Hic et ubique?*** here and everywhere? (Latin) **159 pioneer** foot soldier assigned to dig tunnels and excavations **161 as a stranger** needing your hospitality **163 your philosophy** this subject that is called "natural philosophy" or "science" (*your* is not personal)

Here, as before, never, so help you mercy,°   165
How strange or odd some'er I bear myself—
As I perchance hereafter shall think meet
To put an antic° disposition on—
That you, at such times seeing me, never shall,
With arms encumbered° thus, or this headshake,   170
Or by pronouncing of some doubtful phrase
As "Well, we know," or "We could, an if° we would,"
Or "If we list° to speak," or "There be, an if they might,"°
Or such ambiguous giving out, to note°
That you know aught° of me—this do swear,   175
So grace and mercy at your most need help you.
GHOST [*beneath*]   Swear.   [*They swear*]
HAMLET   Rest, rest, perturbèd spirit!—So, gentlemen,
With all my love I do commend me to you;°
And what so poor a man as Hamlet is   180
May do t'express his love and friending° to you,
God willing, shall not lack.° Let us go in together,
And still° your fingers on your lips, I pray.
The time is out of joint.° Oh, cursèd spite
That ever I was born to set it right!   185
                         [*They wait for him to leave first*]
Nay, come, let's go together.°   *Exeunt*

♣

ACT 2
SCENE 1

Location: Polonius's chambers

Enter old Polonius with his man [Reynaldo]

POLONIUS   Give him this money and these notes, Reynaldo.
                    [*He gives money and papers*]

165 so help you mercy as you hope for God's mercy when you are judged
168 antic grotesque, strange   **170 encumbered** folded   **172 an if** if   **173 list**
wished | **There . . . might** there are those who could talk if they were at liberty to
do so   **174 note** indicate   **175 aught** anything   **179 commend . . . you** give you
my best wishes   **181 friending** friendliness   **182 lack** be lacking   **183 still** always
184 out of joint in utter disorder   **186 let's go together** (probably they wait for him
to leave first, but he refuses this ceremoniousness)

REYNALDO   I will, my lord.

POLONIUS   You shall do marvelous° wisely, good Reynaldo,
Before you visit him, to make inquire°
Of his behavior.

REYNALDO   My lord, I did intend it.   5

POLONIUS   Marry, well said, very well said. Look you, sir,
Inquire me first what Danskers° are in Paris,
And how, and who, what means,° and where they keep,°
What company, at what expense; and finding
By this encompassment and drift of question°   10
That they do know my son, come you more nearer
Than your particular demands will touch it.°
Take you,° as 'twere, some distant knowledge of him,
As thus, "I know his father and his friends,
And in part him." Do you mark this, Reynaldo?   15

REYNALDO   Ay, very well, my lord.

POLONIUS   "And in part him, but," you may say, "not well.
But if't be he I mean, he's very wild,
Addicted so and so," and there put on° him
What forgeries° you please—marry, none so rank°   20
As may dishonor him, take heed of that,
But, sir, such wanton,° wild, and usual slips
As are companions noted and most known
To youth and liberty.

REYNALDO   As gaming, my lord.

POLONIUS   Ay, or drinking, fencing, swearing,   25
Quarreling, drabbing°—you may go so far.

REYNALDO   My lord, that would dishonor him.

POLONIUS   Faith, no, as you may season° it in the charge.
You must not put another scandal on him
That he is open to incontinency;°   30
That's not my meaning. But breathe his faults so quaintly°

---

3 marvelous marvelously   **4 inquire** inquiry   **7 Danskers** Danes   **8 what means**
what wealth (they have) | **keep** dwell   **10 encompassment . . . question** roundabout
way of questioning   **11–12 come . . . it** you will find out more this way than by
asking pointed questions (*particular demands*)   **13 Take you** assume, pretend
19 put on impute to   **20 forgeries** invented tales | **rank** gross   **22 wanton**
sportive, unrestrained   **26 drabbing** whoring   **28 season** temper, soften
30 incontinency habitual sexual excess   **31 quaintly** artfully, subtly

That they may seem the taints of liberty,°
The flash and outbreak of a fiery mind,
A savageness in unreclaimèd blood,
Of general assault.°
REYNALDO   But, my good lord—   35
POLONIUS   Wherefore should you do this?
REYNALDO   Ay, my lord, I would know that.
POLONIUS   Marry, sir, here's my drift,
And I believe it is a fetch of warrant.°
You laying these slight sullies on my son,   40
As 'twere a thing a little soiled wi'th' working,°
Mark you,
Your party in converse,° him you would sound,°
Having ever° seen in the prenominate crimes°
The youth you breathe° of guilty, be assured   45
He closes with you in this consequence:°
"Good sir," or so, or "friend," or "gentleman,"
According to the phrase or the addition°
Of man and country.
REYNALDO   Very good, my lord.
POLONIUS   And then, sir, does 'a this—'a does—what was I about   50
to say? By the Mass, I was about to say something. Where did
I leave?
REYNALDO   At "closes in the consequence."
POLONIUS   At "closes in the consequence," ay, marry.
He closes thus: "I know the gentleman,   55
I saw him yesterday," or "th'other day,"
Or then, or then, with such or such, "and as you say,
There was 'a gaming," "there o'ertook in 's rouse,"°
"There falling out° at tennis," or perchance
"I saw him enter such a house of sale,"   60
Videlicet° a brothel, or so forth. See you now,

32 **taints of liberty** faults resulting from free living   34–35 **A savageness . . . assault**
a wildness in untamed youth that assails all indiscriminately   39 **fetch of warrant**
legitimate trick   41 **wi'th' working** in the process of being made, in everyday
experience   43 **Your . . . converse** the person you are conversing with | **sound**
sound out   44 **Having ever** if he has ever | **prenominate crimes** aforenamed offenses
45 **breathe** speak   46 **closes . . . consequence** takes you into his confidence as
follows   48 **addition** title   58 **o'ertook in 's rouse** overcome by drink   59 **falling
out** quarreling   61 **Videlicet** namely

Your bait of falsehood takes this carp° of truth;
And thus do we of wisdom and of reach,°
With windlasses° and with assays of bias,°
By indirections find directions° out.   65
So by my former lecture° and advice
Shall you my son. You have° me, have you not?

REYNALDO   My lord, I have.

POLONIUS   God b'wi'ye; fare ye well.

REYNALDO   Good my lord.

POLONIUS   Observe his inclination in yourself.°   70

REYNALDO   I shall, my lord.

POLONIUS   And let him ply his music.

REYNALDO   Well, my lord.

POLONIUS   Farewell.   *Exit Reynaldo*

                                        Enter Ophelia

                        How now, Ophelia, what's the matter?

OPHELIA   Oh, my lord, my lord, I have been so affrighted!

POLONIUS   With what, i'th' name of God?   75

OPHELIA   My lord, as I was sewing in my closet,°
Lord Hamlet, with his doublet° all unbraced,°
No hat upon his head, his stockings fouled,
Ungartered, and down-gyvèd° to his ankle,
Pale as his shirt, his knees knocking each other,   80
And with a look so piteous in purport°
As if he had been loosèd out of hell
To speak of horrors—he comes before me.

POLONIUS   Mad for thy love?

OPHELIA   My lord, I do not know,
But truly I do fear it.

POLONIUS   What said he?   85

OPHELIA   He took me by the wrist and held me hard.
Then goes he to the length of all his arm,

---

62 **carp** a fish   63 **reach** capacity, ability   64 **windlasses** circuitous paths (literally, circuits made to head off the game in hunting) | **assays of bias** attempts through indirection (like the curving path of the bowling ball, which is biased or weighted to one side)   65 **directions** the way things really are   66 **former lecture** just-ended set of instructions   67 **have** understand   70 **in yourself** in your own person (as well as by asking questions of others)   76 **closet** private chamber   77 **doublet** close-fitting jacket | **unbraced** unfastened   79 **down-gyvèd** fallen to the ankles (like gyves or fetters)   81 **in purport** in what it expressed

And, with his other hand thus o'er his brow
He falls to such perusal of my face
As° 'a would draw it. Long stayed he so. 90
At last, a little shaking of mine arm
And thrice his head thus waving up and down,
He raised a sigh so piteous and profound
As° it did seem to shatter all his bulk°
And end his being. That done, he lets me go, 95
And with his head over his shoulder turned
He seemed to find his way without his eyes,
For out o' doors he went without their helps,
And to the last bended their light on me.

POLONIUS   Come, go with me. I will go seek the King. 100
This is the very ecstasy° of love,
Whose violent property fordoes° itself
And leads the will to desperate undertakings
As oft as any passion under heaven
That does afflict our natures. I am sorry. 105
What, have you given him any hard words of late?

OPHELIA   No, my good lord, but as you did command
I did repel his letters and denied
His access to me.

POLONIUS   That hath made him mad.
I am sorry that with better heed and judgment 110
I had not quoted° him. I feared he did but trifle
And meant to wrack° thee. But beshrew my jealousy!°
By heaven, it is as proper to our age°
To cast beyond° ourselves in our opinions
As it is common for the younger sort 115
To lack discretion. Come, go we to the King.
This must be known,° which, being kept close,° might move
More grief to hide than hate to utter love.°
Come.   *Exeunt*

---

90 **As** as if   94 **As** that | **bulk** body   101 **ecstasy** madness   102 **property fordoes**
nature destroys   111 **quoted** observed   112 **wrack** ruin, seduce | **beshrew my
jealousy!** a plague upon my suspicious nature!   113 **proper . . . age** characteristic of
us (old) men   114 **cast beyond** overshoot, miscalculate (a metaphor from hunting)
117 **known** made known (to the King) | **close** secret   117–18 **might . . . love** might
cause more grief (because of what Hamlet might do) by hiding the knowledge of
Hamlet's strange behavior to Ophelia than unpleasantness by telling it

❦

ACT 2
SCENE 2

Location: The castle

Flourish. Enter King and Queen,
Rosencrantz, and Guildenstern [with others]

KING Welcome, dear Rosencrantz and Guildenstern.
 Moreover that° we much did long to see you,
 The need we have to use you did provoke
 Our hasty sending. Something have you heard
 Of Hamlet's transformation—so call it,   5
 Sith nor° th'exterior nor the inward man
 Resembles that° it was. What it should be,
 More than his father's death, that thus hath put him
 So much from th'understanding of himself,
 I cannot dream of. I entreat you both   10
 That, being of so young days brought up with him,
 And sith so neighbored to his youth and havior,°
 That you vouchsafe·your rest° here in our court
 Some little time, so by your companies
 To draw him on to pleasures, and to gather   15
 So much as from occasion° you may glean,
 Whether aught to us unknown afflicts him thus
 That, opened,° lies within our remedy.
QUEEN Good gentlemen, he hath much talked of you,
 And sure I am two men there is not living   20
 To whom he more adheres. If it will please you
 To show us so much gentry° and good will
 As to expend your time with us awhile
 For the supply and profit of our hope,°
 Your visitation shall receive such thanks   25

2 **Moreover that** besides the fact that   6 **Sith nor** since neither   7 **that** what
11–12 **That . . . havior** that, seeing as you were brought up with him from early youth
(see 3.4.204, where Hamlet refers to Rosencrantz and Guildenstern as "my two
schoolfellows"), and since you have been intimately acquainted with his youthful
ways   13 **vouchsafe your rest** consent to stay   16 **occasion** opportunity   18 **opened**
being revealed   22 **gentry** courtesy   24 **supply . . . hope** aid and furtherance of what
we hope for

As fits a kings's remembrance.°

ROSENCRANTZ   Both Your Majesties

Might, by the sovereign power you have of° us,
Put your dread° pleasures more into command
Than to entreaty.

GUILDENSTERN   But we both obey,
And here give up ourselves in the full bent°   30
To lay our service freely at your feet,
To be commanded.

KING   Thanks, Rosencrantz and gentle Guildenstern.

QUEEN   Thanks, Guildenstern and gentle Rosencrantz.
And I beseech you instantly to visit   35
My too much changèd son.—Go, some of you,
And bring these gentlemen where Hamlet is.

GUILDENSTERN   Heavens make our presence and our practices°
Pleasant and helpful to him!

QUEEN   Ay, amen!

Exeunt Rosencrantz and Guildenstern [with some attendants]

Enter Polonius

POLONIUS   Th'ambassadors from Norway, my good lord,   40
Are joyfully returned.

KING   Thou still° hast been the father of good news.

POLONIUS   Have I, my lord? I assure my good liege
I hold my duty, as I hold my soul,
Both to my God and to my gracious king;   45
And I do think, or else this brain of mine
Hunts not the trail of policy° so sure
As it hath used to do, that I have found
The very cause of Hamlet's lunacy.

KING   Oh, speak of that! That do I long to hear.   50

POLONIUS   Give first admittance to th'ambassadors.
My news shall be the fruit° to that great feast.

KING   Thyself do grace° to them and bring them in.

[Exit Polonius]

---

26 As fits . . . remembrance as would be a fitting gift of a king who rewards true service   **27 of** over   **28 dread** inspiring awe   **30 in . . . bent** to the utmost degree of our capacity (an archery metaphor)   **38 practices** doings   **42 still** always   **47 policy** statecraft   **52 fruit** dessert   **53 grace** honor (punning on *grace* said before a *feast,* line 52)

He tells me, my dear Gertrude, he hath found
The head and source of all your son's distemper.   55
QUEEN   I doubt° it is no other but the main,
His father's death and our o'erhasty marriage.

Enter Ambassadors [Voltimand and Cornelius, with Polonius]

KING   Well, we shall sift him.°—Welcome, my good friends!
Say, Voltimand, what from our brother° Norway?
VOLTIMAND   Most fair return of greetings and desires.°   60
Upon our first,° he sent out to suppress
His nephew's levies, which to him appeared
To be a preparation 'gainst the Polack,
But, better looked into, he truly found
It was against Your Highness. Whereat grieved   65
That so his sickness, age, and impotence°
Was falsely borne in hand,° sends out arrests°
On Fortinbras, which he, in brief, obeys,
Receives rebuke from Norway, and in fine°
Makes vow before his uncle never more   70
To give th'assay° of arms against Your Majesty.
Whereon old Norway, overcome with joy,
Gives him three thousand crowns in annual fee
And his commission to employ those soldiers,
So levied as before, against the Polack,   75
With an entreaty, herein further shown,

[*giving a paper*]

That it might please you to give quiet pass
Through your dominions for this enterprise
On such regards of safety and allowance°
As therein are set down.
KING   It likes° us well,   80
And at our more considered° time we'll read,
Answer, and think upon this business.

---

56 **doubt** fear, suspect 58 **sift him** question Polonius (or Hamlet) closely
59 **brother** fellow king 60 **desires** good wishes 61 **Upon our first** at our first
words on the business 66 **impotence** weakness 67 **borne in hand** deluded, taken
advantage of | **arrests** orders to desist 69 **in fine** in conclusion 71 **give th'assay**
make trial of strength, challenge 79 **On . . . allowance** with such considerations for
the safety of Denmark and permission for Fortinbras 80 **likes** pleases
81 **considered** suitable for deliberation

Meantime we thank you for your well-took labor.
Go to your rest; at night we'll feast together.
Most welcome home! *Exeunt Ambassadors*
POLONIUS   This business is well ended.   85
My liege, and madam, to expostulate°
What majesty should be, what duty is,
Why day is day, night night, and time is time,
Were nothing but to waste night, day, and time.
Therefore, since brevity is the soul of wit,°   90
And tediousness the limbs and outward flourishes,
I will be brief. Your noble son is mad.
Mad call I it, for, to define true madness,
What is't but to be nothing else but mad?
But let that go.
QUEEN   More matter, with less art.   95
POLONIUS   Madam, I swear I use no art at all.
That he's mad, 'tis true; 'tis true 'tis pity,
And pity 'tis 'tis true—a foolish figure,°
But farewell it, for I will use no art.
Mad let us grant him, then, and now remains   100
That we find out the cause of this effect,
Or rather say, the cause of this defect,
For this effect defective comes by cause.°
Thus it remains, and the remainder thus.
Perpend.°   105
I have a daughter—have while she is mine—
Who, in her duty and obedience, mark,
Hath given me this. Now gather and surmise.°

[*He reads the letter*] "To the celestial and my soul's idol, the
most beautified Ophelia"—That's an ill phrase, a vile   110
phrase; "beautified" is a vile phrase. But you shall hear.
Thus: [*He reads*]
    "In her excellent white bosom, these, etc."°

---

86 expostulate expound, inquire into   **90 wit** sense or judgment   **98 figure** figure
of speech   **103 For . . . cause** for this defective behavior, this madness, must have a
cause   **105 Perpend** consider   **108 gather and surmise** draw your own conclusions
113 "In . . . etc." (the letter is poetically addressed to her heart, where a letter would
be kept by a young lady)

QUEEN   Came this from Hamlet to her?

POLONIUS   Good madam, stay awhile, I will be faithful.°   115

[*He reads*]

"Doubt° thou the stars are fire,
    Doubt that the sun doth move,
Doubt truth to be a liar,
    But never doubt I love.

O dear Ophelia, I am ill° at these numbers. I have not art   120
to reckon° my groans. But that I love thee best, O most
best, believe it. Adieu.
    Thine evermore, most dear lady, whilst this
        machine° is to him, Hamlet."
This in obedience hath my daughter shown me,   125
And, more above, hath his solicitings,
As they fell out by time, by means, and place,
All given to mine ear.°

KING   But how hath she
Received his love?

POLONIUS   What do you think of me?

KING   As of a man faithful and honorable.   130

POLONIUS   I would fain° prove so. But what might you think,
When I had seen this hot love on the wing—
As I perceived it, I must tell you that,
Before my daughter told me—what might you,
Or my dear Majesty your queen here, think,   135
If I had played the desk or table book,
Or given my heart a winking, mute and dumb,°
Or looked upon this love with idle sight?°
What might you think? No, I went round° to work,
And my young mistress thus I did bespeak:°   140
"Lord Hamlet is a prince out of thy star;°

---

115 stay . . . faithful hold on, I will do as you wish   **116 Doubt** suspect   **120 ill . . .
numbers** unskilled at writing verses   **121 reckon** (1) count (2) number metrically,
scan   **124 machine** body   **126–28 And . . . ear** and moreover she has told me
when, how, and where his solicitings of her occurred   **131 fain** gladly   **136–37 If
. . . dumb** if I had acted as go-between, passing love notes, or if I had refused to let my
heart acknowledge what my eyes could see   **138 with idle sight** complacently or
incomprehendingly   **139 round** roundly, plainly   **140 bespeak** address   **141 out of
thy star** above your sphere, position

This must not be." And then I prescripts° gave her,
That she should lock herself from his resort,
Admit no messengers, receive no tokens.
Which done, she took the fruits of my advice;   145
And he, repellèd—a short tale to make—
Fell into a sadness, then into a fast,
Thence to a watch,° thence into a weakness,
Thence to a lightness,° and by this declension°
Into the madness wherein now he raves,   150
And all we mourn for.
KING [*to the Queen*]   Do you think 'tis this?
QUEEN   It may be, very like.
POLONIUS
   Hath there been such a time—I would fain know that—
   That I have positively said "'Tis so,"
   When it proved otherwise?
KING   Not that I know.   155
POLONIUS   Take this from this,° if this be otherwise.
   If circumstances lead me, I will find
   Where truth is hid, though it were hid indeed
   Within the center.°
KING   How may we try° it further?
POLONIUS   You know sometimes he walks four hours together   160
   Here in the lobby.
QUEEN   So he does indeed.
POLONIUS   At such a time I'll loose° my daughter to him.
   Be you and I behind an arras° then.
   Mark the encounter. If he love her not
   And be not from his reason fall'n thereon,°   165
   Let me be no assistant for a state,
   But keep a farm and carters.°
KING   We will try it.

---

142 **prescripts** orders   148 **watch** state of sleeplessness   149 **lightness** light-
headedness | **declension** decline, deterioration (with a pun on the grammatical
sense)   156 **Take this from this** (the actor probably gestures, indicating that he means
his head from his shoulders, or his staff of office or chain from his hands or neck, or
something similar)   159 **center** center of the earth, traditionally an extraordinarily
inaccessible place | **try** test   162 **loose** (as one might release an animal that is being
mated)   163 **arras** hanging, tapestry   165 **thereon** on that account   167 **carters**
wagon drivers

Enter Hamlet [reading on a book]

QUEEN   But look where sadly the poor wretch comes reading.

POLONIUS   Away, I do beseech you both, away.

I'll board him presently. Oh, give me leave.°   170

Exeunt King and Queen [with attendants]

How does my good Lord Hamlet?

HAMLET   Well, God-a-mercy.°

POLONIUS   Do you know me, my lord?

HAMLET   Excellent well. You are a fishmonger.°

POLONIUS   Not I, my lord.   175

HAMLET   Then I would you were so honest a man.

POLONIUS   Honest, my lord?

HAMLET   Ay, sir. To be honest, as this world goes, is to be one
man picked out of ten thousand.

POLONIUS   That's very true, my lord.   180

HAMLET   For if the sun breed maggots in a dead dog, being a
good kissing carrion°—Have you a daughter?

POLONIUS   I have, my lord.

HAMLET   Let her not walk i'th' sun.° Conception° is a blessing,
but as your daughter may conceive, friend, look to't.   185

POLONIUS   [*aside*]   How say you by that? Still harping on my
daughter. Yet he knew me not at first; 'a said I was a
fishmonger. 'A is far gone. And truly in my youth I suffered
much extremity for love, very near this. I'll speak to him
again.—What do you read, my lord?   190

HAMLET   Words, words, words.

POLONIUS   What is the matter, my lord?

HAMLET   Between who?

POLONIUS   I mean, the matter° that you read, my lord.

HAMLET   Slanders, sir; for the satirical rogue says here that old   195
men have gray beards, that their faces are wrinkled, their
eyes purging° thick amber° and plum-tree gum, and that
they have a plentiful lack of wit,° together with most weak

170 **I'll . . . leave** I'll accost him at once; please leave us alone; leave him to me
172 **God-a-mercy** God have mercy, thank you   174 **fishmonger** fish merchant
182 **a good kissing carrion** a good piece of flesh for kissing, or for the sun to kiss
184 **i'th' sun** in public (with additional implication of the sunshine of princely favors) |
Conception (1) understanding (2) pregnancy   194 **matter** substance (but Hamlet
plays on the sense of "basis for a dispute")   197 **purging** discharging | **amber**
resin, like the resinous *plum-tree gum*   198 **wit** understanding

hams. All which, sir, though I most powerfully and potently
believe, yet I hold it not honesty° to have it thus set down, 200
for yourself, sir, shall grow old° as I am, if like a crab you
could go backward.

POLONIUS [*aside*]   Though this be madness, yet there is method
in't.—Will you walk out of the air,° my lord?

HAMLET   Into my grave. 205

POLONIUS   Indeed, that's out of the air. [*Aside*] How pregnant°
sometimes his replies are! A happiness° that often madness
hits on, which reason and sanity could not so prosperously°
be delivered of. I will leave him and suddenly° contrive the
means of meeting between him and my daughter.—My 210
honorable lord, I will most humbly take my leave of you.

HAMLET   You cannot, sir, take from me anything that I will
more willingly part withal°—except my life, except my life,
except my life.

Enter Guildenstern and Rosencrantz

POLONIUS   Fare you well, my lord. 215

HAMLET   These tedious old fools!

POLONIUS   You go to seek the Lord Hamlet. There he is.

ROSENCRANTZ [*to Polonius*]   God save you, sir!

[*Exit Polonius*]

GUILDENSTERN   My honored lord!

ROSENCRANTZ   My most dear lord! 220

HAMLET   My excellent good friends! How dost thou, Guildenstern? Ah, Rosencrantz! Good lads, how do you both?

ROSENCRANTZ   As the indifferent° children of the earth.

GUILDENSTERN   Happy in that we are not overhappy.
On Fortune's cap we are not the very button. 225

HAMLET   Nor the soles of her shoe?

ROSENCRANTZ   Neither, my lord.

HAMLET   Then you live about her waist, or in the middle of her
favors?°

---

200 honesty decency, decorum   **201 old** as old   **204 out of the air** (the open air
was considered dangerous for sick people)   **206 pregnant** quick-witted, full of
meaning   **207 happiness** felicity of expression   **208 prosperously** successfully
209 suddenly immediately   **213 withal** with   **223 indifferent** ordinary, at neither
extreme of fortune or misfortune   **232–33 the middle . . . favors** her genitals

GUILDENSTERN   Faith, her privates we.°   230

HAMLET   In the secret parts of Fortune? Oh, most true, she is a
strumpet.° What news?

ROSENCRANTZ   None, my lord, but the world's grown honest.

HAMLET   Then is doomsday near. But your news is not true. Let
me question more in particular. What have you, my good   235
friends, deserved at the hands of Fortune that she sends you
to prison hither?

GUILDENSTERN   Prison, my lord?

HAMLET   Denmark's a prison.

ROSENCRANTZ   Then is the world one.   240

HAMLET   A goodly one, in which there are many confines,°
wards, and dungeons, Denmark being one o'th' worst.

ROSENCRANTZ   We think not so, my lord.

HAMLET   Why then 'tis none to you, for there is nothing either
good or bad but thinking makes it so. To me it is a prison.   245

ROSENCRANTZ   Why then, your ambition makes it one. 'Tis too
narrow for your mind.

HAMLET   Oh, God, I could be bounded in a nutshell and count
myself a king of infinite space, were it not that I have bad
dreams.   250

GUILDENSTERN   Which dreams indeed are ambition, for the very
substance of the ambitious° is merely the shadow of a dream.

HAMLET   A dream itself is but a shadow.

ROSENCRANTZ   Truly, and I hold ambition of so airy and light a
quality that it is but a shadow's shadow.   255

HAMLET   Then are our beggars bodies, and our monarchs and
outstretched heroes the beggars' shadows.° Shall we to th'
court? For, by my fay,° I cannot reason.

ROSENCRANTZ, GUILDENSTERN   We'll wait upon° you.

---

230 her privates we (1) we dwell in her privates, her genitals, in the middle of her
favors (2) we are her ordinary footsoldiers   **232 strumpet** (fortune was proverbially
thought of as fickle)   **241 confines** places of confinement   **251–52 the very . . .
ambitious** that seemingly very substantial thing that the ambitious pursue
256–57 Then . . . shadows (Hamlet pursues their argument about ambition to its
absurd extreme: if ambition is only a shadow of a shadow, then beggars (who are
presumably without ambition) must be real, whereas monarchs and heroes are only
their shadows—*outstretched* like elongated shadows, made to look bigger than they
are)   **258 fay** faith   **259 wait upon** accompany, attend (but Hamlet uses the
phrase in the sense of providing menial service)

HAMLET   No such matter. I will not sort° you with the rest of   260
my servants, for, to speak to you like an honest man, I am
most dreadfully attended.° But, in the beaten way° of
friendship, what make° you at Elsinore?

ROSENCRANTZ   To visit you, my lord, no other occasion.

HAMLET   Beggar that I am, I am even poor in thanks; but I   265
thank you, and sure, dear friends, my thanks are too dear a
halfpenny.° Were you not sent for? Is it your own inclining?
Is it a free° visitation? Come, come, deal justly with me.
Come, come. Nay, speak.

GUILDENSTERN   What should we say, my lord?   270

HAMLET   Anything but to th' purpose.° You were sent for, and
there is a kind of confession in your looks which your
modesties have not craft enough to color.° I know the good
King and Queen have sent for you.

ROSENCRANTZ   To what end, my lord?   275

HAMLET   That you must teach me. But let me conjure° you, by
the rights of our fellowship, by the consonancy of our
youth,° by the obligation of our ever-preserved love, and by
what more dear a better° proposer could charge° you withal,
be even° and direct with me whether you were sent for or no.   280

ROSENCRANTZ   [*aside to Guildenstern*]   What say you?

HAMLET   [*aside*]   Nay, then, I have an eye of° you.—If you love
me, hold not off.°

GUILDENSTERN   My lord, we were sent for.

HAMLET   I will tell you why; so shall my anticipation prevent   285
your discovery,° and your secrecy to the King and Queen
molt no feather.° I have of late—but wherefore I know not—
lost all my mirth, forgone all custom of exercises; and
indeed it goes so heavily with my disposition that this

<hr>

260 **sort** class, categorize 262 **dreadfully attended** waited upon in slovenly fashion | **beaten way** familiar path, tried-and-true course 263 **make** do 266–67 **too dear a halfpenny** (1) too expensive at even a halfpenny, of little worth (2) too expensive *by* a halfpenny in return for worthless kindness 268 **free** voluntary 271 **Anything but to th' purpose** anything except a straightforward answer (said ironically) 273 **color** disguise 276 **conjure** adjure, entreat 277–78 **the consonancy of our youth** our closeness in our younger days 279 **better** more skillful | **charge** urge 280 **even** straight, honest 282 **of** on 283 **hold not off** don't hold back 285–86 **so . . . discovery** in that way my saying it first will spare you from having to reveal the truth 287 **molt no feather** not diminish in the least

goodly frame, the earth, seems to me a sterile promontory; 290
this most excellent canopy, the air, look you, this brave°
o'erhanging firmament, this majestical roof fretted° with
golden fire, why, it appeareth nothing to me but a foul and
pestilent congregation° of vapors. What a piece of work° is a
man! How noble in reason, how infinite in faculties, in form 295
and moving how express° and admirable, in action how like
an angel, in apprehension° how like a god! The beauty of
the world, the paragon of animals! And yet, to me, what is
this quintessence° of dust? Man delights not me—no, nor
woman neither, though by your smiling you seem to say so. 300

ROSENCRANTZ My lord, there was no such stuff in my
thoughts.

HAMLET Why did you laugh, then, when I said man delights
not me?

ROSENCRANTZ To think, my lord, if you delight not in man, 305
what Lenten entertainment° the players shall receive from
you. We coted° them on the way, and hither are they coming
to offer you service.

HAMLET He that plays the king shall be welcome; His Majesty
shall have tribute° of° me. The adventurous knight shall use 310
his foil and target,° the lover shall not sigh gratis,° the
humorous man° shall end his part in peace,° the clown shall
make those laugh whose lungs are tickle o'th'° sear, and the
lady shall say her mind freely, or the blank verse shall halt°
for't. What players are they? 315

ROSENCRANTZ Even those you were wont to take such delight
in, the tragedians° of the city.

HAMLET How chances it they travel? Their residence,° both in
reputation and profit, was better both ways.

---

291 **brave** splendid   292 **fretted** adorned (with fretwork, as in a vaulted ceiling)
294 **congregation** mass | **piece of work** masterpiece   296 **express** well-framed,
exact, expressive   297 **apprehension** power of comprehending   299 **quintessence**
very essence (literally, the fifth essence beyond earth, water, air, and fire, supposed
to be extractable from them)   306 **Lenten entertainment** meager reception
(appropriate to Lent)   307 **coted** overtook and passed by   310 **tribute** (1) applause
(2) homage paid in money | **of** from   311 **foil and target** sword and shield |
gratis for nothing   312 **humorous man** eccentric character, dominated by one trait
or "humor" | **in peace** with full license   313 **tickle o'th' sear** hair trigger, ready to
laugh easily (a *sear* is part of a gun-lock)   314 **halt** limp   317 **tragedians** actors
318 **residence** remaining in their usual place, in the city

ROSENCRANTZ   I think their inhibition° comes by the means of   320
the late innovation.°

HAMLET   Do they hold the same estimation they did when I
was in the city? Are they so followed?

ROSENCRANTZ   No, indeed are they not.

HAMLET   How comes it? Do they grow rusty?°   325

ROSENCRANTZ   Nay, their endeavor keeps in the wonted° pace.
But there is, sir, an aerie° of children, little eyases,° that cry
out on the top of question° and are most tyrannically°
clapped for't. These are now the fashion, and so berattle the
common stages°—so they call them—that many wearing   330
rapiers° are afraid of goose quills° and dare scarce come
thither.

HAMLET   What, are they children? Who maintains 'em? How
are they escotted?° Will they pursue the quality° no longer
than they can sing?° Will they not say afterwards, if they   335
should grow themselves to common° players—as it is most
like,° if their means are no better°—their writers do them
wrong to make them exclaim against their own succession?°

ROSENCRANTZ   Faith, there has been much to-do° on both sides,
and the nation holds it no sin to tar° them to controversy.   340
There was for a while no money bid for argument unless the
poet and the player went to cuffs in the question.°

HAMLET   Is't possible?

320 **inhibition** formal prohibition (from acting plays in the city)   321 **late innovation**
recent new fashion in satirical plays performed by boy actors in the "private" theaters;
or the Earl of Essex's abortive rebellion in 1601 against Elizabeth's government (a
much debated passage of seemingly topical reference)   325 **How . . . rusty?** have they
lost their polish, gone out of fashion? (this passage, through line 348, alludes to the
rivalry between the children's companies and the adult actors, given strong impetus by
the reopening of the Children of the Chapel at the Blackfriars Theater in late 1600)
326 **keeps . . . wonted** continues in the usual   327 **aerie** nest | **eyases** young hawks
327–28 **cry . . . question** speak shrilly, dominating the controversy (in decrying the
public theaters)   328 **tyrannically** vehemently   329–30 **berattle . . . stages** clamor
against the public theaters   330–31 **many wearing rapiers** many men of fashion,
afraid to patronize the common players for fear of being satirized by the poets writing
for the boy actors   331 **goose quills** pens of satirists   334 **escotted** maintained |
quality (acting) profession   334–35 **no longer . . . sing** only until their voices change
336 **common** regular, adult   337 **like** likely | **if . . . better** if they find no better way
to support themselves   338 **succession** future careers   339 **to-do** ado   340 **tar** incite
(as in inciting dogs to attack a chained bear)   341–42 **There . . . question** for a while,
no money was offered by the acting companies to playwrights for the plot to a play
unless the satirical poets who wrote for the boys and the adult actors came to blows in
the play itself

GUILDENSTERN   Oh, there has been much throwing about of
brains.   345

HAMLET   Do the boys carry it away?°

ROSENCRANTZ   Ay, that they do, my lord—Hercules and his
load° too.

HAMLET   It is not very strange; for my uncle is King of
Denmark, and those that would make mouths° at him while   350
my father lived give twenty, forty, fifty, a hundred ducats°
apiece for his picture in little.° 'Sblood,° there is something
in this more than natural, if philosophy could find it out.

A flourish [of trumpets within]

GUILDENSTERN   There are the players.

HAMLET   Gentlemen, you are welcome to Elsinore. Your hands,   355
come then. Th'appurtenance° of welcome is fashion and
ceremony. Let me comply° with you in this garb,° lest my
extent° to the players, which, I tell you, must show fairly
outwards,° should more appear like entertainment° than
yours. You are welcome. But my uncle-father and aunt-   360
mother are deceived.

GUILDENSTERN   In what, my dear lord?

HAMLET   I am but mad north-north-west.° When the wind is
southerly I know a hawk from a handsaw.°

Enter Polonius

POLONIUS   Well be with you, gentlemen!   365

HAMLET   Hark you, Guildenstern, and you too; at each ear a
hearer. That great baby you see there is not yet out of his
swaddling clouts.°

ROSENCRANTZ   Haply° he is the second time come to them, for
they say an old man is twice a child.   370

---

346 carry it away win the day   **347–48 Hercules . . . load** (thought to be an allusion
to the sign of the Globe Theatre, which allegedly was Hercules bearing the world on
his shoulders)   **350 mouths** faces   **351 ducats** gold coins   **352 in little** in
miniature | **'Sblood** by God's (Christ's) blood   **356 Th'appurtenance** the proper
accompaniment   **357 comply** observe the formalities of courtesy | **garb** manner
357–58 my extent that which I extend, my polite behavior   **358–59 show fairly
outwards** show every evidence of cordiality   **359 entertainment** a (warm) reception
363 north-north-west just off true north, only partly   **364 I . . . handsaw** (speaking
in his mad guise, Hamlet perhaps suggests that he can tell true from false; a *handsaw*
may be a *hernshaw* or heron; still, a supposedly mad disposition might compare
hawks and handsaws)   **368 swaddling clouts** cloths in which to wrap a newborn
baby   **369 Haply** perhaps

HAMLET I will prophesy he comes to tell me of the players.
Mark it.—You say right, sir, o' Monday morning, 'twas then
indeed.°
POLONIUS My lord, I have news to tell you.
HAMLET My lord, I have news to tell you. When Roscius° was   375
an actor in Rome—
POLONIUS The actors are come hither, my lord.
HAMLET Buzz, buzz!°
POLONIUS Upon my honor—
HAMLET Then came each actor on his ass.   380
POLONIUS The best actors in the world, either for tragedy,
comedy, history, pastoral, pastoral-comical, historical-
pastoral, tragical-historical, tragical-comical-historical-
pastoral, scene individable, or poem unlimited.° Seneca°
cannot be too heavy, nor Plautus° too light. For the law of   385
writ and the liberty,° these° are the only men.
HAMLET O Jephthah, judge of Israel,° what a treasure hadst
thou!
POLONIUS What a treasure had he, my lord?
HAMLET Why,   390
    "One fair daughter, and no more,
    The which he lovèd passing° well."
POLONIUS [*aside*] Still on my daughter.
HAMLET Am I not i'th' right, old Jephthah?
POLONIUS If you call me Jephthah, my lord, I have a daughter   395
that I love passing well.
HAMLET Nay, that follows not.°
POLONIUS What follows then, my lord?°

372–73 You say . . . then indeed (said to impress upon Polonius the idea that
Hamlet is in serious conversation with his friends) **375 Roscius** a famous Roman
actor who died in 62 B.C. **378 buzz** (an interjection used to denote stale news)
384 scene . . . unlimited plays that are unclassifiable and all-inclusive (an absurdly
catchall conclusion to Polonius's pompous list of categories) | **Seneca** writer of
Latin tragedies **385 Plautus** writer of Latin comedies **385–86 law . . . liberty**
dramatic composition both according to the rules and disregarding the rules |
these the actors **387 Jephthah . . . Israel** (Jephthah had to sacrifice his daughter; see
Judges 11; Hamlet goes on to quote from a ballad on the theme) **392 passing**
surpassingly **397 that follows not** just because you resemble Jephthah in having a
daughter does not logically prove that you love her **398 What . . . lord?** what does
follow logically? (but Hamlet, pretending madness, answers with a fragment of a
ballad, as if Polonius had asked, "what comes next?" see 403n)

HAMLET Why,

     "As by lot,° God wot,"°   400

and then, you know,

     "It came to pass, as most like° it was"—

the first row of the pious chanson will show you more,° for
look where my abridgement° comes.

Enter the Players

You are welcome, masters;° welcome, all. I am glad to see 405
thee well. Welcome, good friends. Oh, old friend! Why, thy
face is valanced° since I saw thee last. Com'st thou to beard°
me in Denmark? What, my young lady° and mistress! By'r
Lady,° Your Ladyship is nearer to heaven° than when I saw
you last, by the altitude of a chopine.° Pray God your voice, 410
like a piece of uncurrent° gold, be not cracked within the
ring.° Masters, you are all welcome. We'll e'en to't° like
French falconers, fly at anything we see. We'll have a speech
straight.° Come, give us a taste of your quality.° Come, a
passionate speech.   415

FIRST PLAYER What speech, my good lord?

HAMLET I heard thee speak me a speech once, but it was never
acted, or if it was, not above once, for the play, I remember,
pleased not the million; 'twas caviar to the general.° But it
was—as I received it, and others, whose judgments in such 420
matters cried in the top of° mine—an excellent play, well
digested° in the scenes, set down with as much modesty° as
cunning.° I remember one said there were no sallets° in the

---

400 lot chance | **wot** knows **402 like** likely, probable **403 the first . . . more** the
first stanza of this biblically based ballad will satisfy your stated desire to know
what follows (line 398) **404 my abridgment** something that cuts short my
conversation; also, a diversion **405 masters** good sirs **407 valanced** fringed (with
a beard) | **beard** confront, challenge (with obvious pun) **408 young lady** boy
playing women's parts | **By'r Lady** by our Lady **409 nearer to heaven** taller
410 chopine thick-soled shoe of Italian fashion **411 uncurrent** not passable as
lawful coinage **411–12 cracked . . . ring** changed from adolescent to male voice,
no longer suitable for women's roles (coins featured rings enclosing the sovereign's
head; if the coin was sufficiently clipped to invade within this ring, it was unfit for
currency) **412 e'en to't** go at it **414 straight** at once | **quality** professional skill
419 caviar to the general an expensive delicacy not generally palatable to
uneducated tastes **421 cried in the top of** spoke with greater authority than
422 digested arranged, ordered | **modesty** moderation, restraint **423 cunning**
skill | **sallets** something savory, spicy improprieties

lines to make the matter savory, nor no matter in the phrase
that might indict° the author of affectation, but called it an   425
honest method, as wholesome as sweet, and by very much
more handsome° than fine.° One speech in't I chiefly loved:
'twas Aeneas' tale to Dido, and there-about of it especially
when he speaks of Priam's slaughter.° If it live in your
memory, begin at this line: let me see, let me see—   430

"The rugged Pyrrhus,° like th' Hyrcanian beast"°—

'Tis not so. It begins with Pyrrhus:

"The rugged° Pyrrhus, he whose sable° arms,
Black as his purpose, did the night resemble
When he lay couchèd° in th' ominous horse,°   435
Hath now this dread and black complexion smeared
With heraldry more dismal.° Head to foot
Now is he total gules,° horridly tricked°
With blood of fathers, mothers, daughters, sons,
Baked and impasted with the parching streets,°   440
That lend a tyrannous° and a damnèd light
To their lord's° murder. Roasted in wrath and fire,
And thus o'ersizèd° with coagulate gore,
With eyes like carbuncles,° the hellish Pyrrhus
Old grandsire Priam seeks."   445

So proceed you.

425 indict convict 427 handsome well-proportioned | fine elaborately
ornamented, showy 429 Priam's slaughter the slaying of the ruler of Troy, when
the Greeks finally took the city 431 Pyrrhus a Greek hero in the Trojan War, also
known as Neoptolemus, son of Achilles—another avenging son | th' Hyrcanian
beast the tiger (on the death of Priam, see Virgil, *Aeneid*, 2.506 ff.; compare the
whole speech with Marlowe's *Dido Queen of Carthage*, 2.1.214 ff; on the
Hyrcanian tiger, see *Aeneid*, 4.366–367; Hyrcania is on the Caspian Sea)
433 rugged shaggy, savage | sable black (for reasons of camouflage during the
episode of the Trojan horse) 435 couchèd concealed | ominous horse fateful
Trojan horse, by which the Greeks gained access to Troy 437 dismal calamitous
438 total gules entirely red (a heraldic term) | tricked spotted and smeared
(heraldic) 440 Baked . . . streets roasted and encrusted, like a thick paste, by the
parching heat of the streets (because of the fires everywhere) 441 tyrannous cruel
442 their lord's Priam's 443 o'ersizèd covered as with size or glue 444 carbuncles
large fiery-red precious stones thought to emit their own light

POLONIUS 'Fore God, my lord, well spoken, with good accent
and good discretion.

FIRST PLAYER "Anon he finds him
Striking too short at Greeks. His antique° sword,   450
Rebellious to his arm, lies where it falls,
Repugnant° to command. Unequal matched,
Pyrrhus at Priam drives, in rage strikes wide,
But with the whiff and wind of his fell° sword
Th'unnervèd° father falls. Then senseless Ilium,°   455
Seeming to feel this blow, with flaming top
Stoops to his° base, and with a hideous crash
Takes prisoner Pyrrhus' ear. For, lo! His sword,
Which was declining° on the milky° head
Of reverend Priam, seemed i'th'air to stick.   460
So as a painted° tyrant Pyrrhus stood,
And, like a neutral to his will and matter,°
Did nothing.
But as we often see against° some storm
A silence in the heavens, the rack° stand still,   465
The bold winds speechless, and the orb° below
As hush as death, anon the dreadful thunder
Doth rend the region,° so, after Pyrrhus' pause,
A rousèd vengeance sets him new a-work,
And never did the Cyclops'° hammers fall   470
On Mars's armor forged for proof° eterne
With less remorse° than Pyrrhus' bleeding sword
Now falls on Priam.
Out, out, thou strumpet Fortune! All you gods
In general synod° take away her power!   475
Break all the spokes and fellies° from her wheel,
And bowl the round nave° down the hill of heaven°

---

450 antique ancient, long-used   452 Repugnant disobedient, resistant   454 fell
cruel   455 th' unnervèd the strengthless | senseless Ilium inanimate citadel of
Troy   457 his its   459 declining descending | milky white-haired   461 painted
motionless, as in a painting   462 like . . . matter as though suspended between his
intention and its fulfillment   464 against just before   465 rack mass of clouds
466 orb globe, earth   468 region sky   470 Cyclops giant armor makers in the
smithy of Vulcan   471 proof proven or tested resistance to assault   472 remorse
pity   475 synod assembly   476 fellies pieces of wood forming the rim of a wheel
477 nave hub | hill of heaven Mount Olympus

As low as to the fiends!"
POLONIUS   This is too long.
HAMLET   It shall to the barber's with your beard.—Prithee, say
   on. He's for a jig° or a tale of bawdry, or he sleeps. Say on; 480
   come to Hecuba.°
FIRST PLAYER   "But who, ah woe! had° seen the moblèd° queen"—
HAMLET   "The moblèd queen?"
POLONIUS   That's good. "Moblèd queen" is good.
FIRST PLAYER   "Run barefoot up and down, threat'ning the flames° 485
   With bisson rheum,° a clout° upon that head
   Where late° the diadem stood, and, for a robe,
   About her lank and all o'erteemèd° loins
   A blanket, in the alarm of fear caught up—
   Who this had seen, with tongue in venom steeped, 490
   'Gainst Fortune's state° would treason have pronounced.°
   But if the gods themselves did see her then
   When she saw Pyrrhus make malicious sport
   In mincing with his sword her husband's limbs,
   The instant burst of clamor that she made, 495
   Unless things mortal move them not at all,
   Would have made milch° the burning eyes of heaven,°
   And passion° in the gods."
POLONIUS   Look whe'er° he has not turned his color and has
   tears in 's eyes. Prithee, no more. 500
HAMLET   'Tis well; I'll have thee speak out the rest of this
   soon.—Good my lord, will you see the players well
   bestowed?° Do you hear, let them be well used, for they are
   the abstract° and brief chronicles of the time. After your
   death you were better have a bad epitaph than their ill 505
   report while you live.
POLONIUS   My lord, I will use them according to their desert.

---

480 jig comic song and dance often given at the end of a play   **481 Hecuba** wife
of Priam   **482 who . . . had** anyone who had (also in line 490) | **moblèd** muffled
485 threat'ning the flames weeping hard enough to dampen the flames
486 bisson rheum blinding tears | **clout** cloth   **487 late** lately   **488 all
o'erteemèd** utterly worn out with bearing children   **491 state** rule, managing |
pronounced proclaimed   **497 milch** milky, moist with tears | **burning eyes of
heaven** stars, heavenly bodies   **498 passion** overpowering emotion   **499 whe'er**
whether   **503 bestowed** lodged   **504 abstract** summary account

Guillaume de La Perrière, *La Morosophie* (1553). Fortune was often described as a fatal figure whose ever-turning wheel signified the rise and fall of
persons, families, and states (see 2.2.491). But she was also a devious figure
whose music could both charm and tempt the listener: "blest are those /
Whose blood and judgment are so well commeddled [i.e., commingled] /
That they are not a pipe for Fortune's finger / To sound what stop she
please" (3.2.62–65). (By permission of the Folger Shakespeare Library.)

HAMLET   God's bodikin,° man, much better. Use every man
after° his desert, and who shall scape whipping? Use them
after your own honor and dignity. The less they deserve, the   510
more merit is in your bounty. Take them in.

POLONIUS   Come, sirs.   [Exit]

HAMLET   Follow him, friends. We'll hear a play tomorrow. [As
they start to leave, Hamlet detains the First Player] Dost
thou hear me, old friend? Can you play The Murder of   515
Gonzago?

FIRST PLAYER   Ay, my lord.

HAMLET   We'll ha 't° tomorrow night. You could, for a need,
study° a speech of some dozen or sixteen lines which I
would set down and insert in 't, could you not?   520

FIRST PLAYER   Ay, my lord.

HAMLET   Very well. Follow that lord, and look you mock him
not.   Exeunt players
My good friends, I'll leave you till night. You are welcome
to Elsinore.   525

ROSENCRANTZ   Good my lord!

                          Exeunt [Rosencrantz and Guildenstern]

HAMLET   Ay, so, goodbye to you.—Now I am alone.
Oh, what a rogue and peasant slave am I!
Is it not monstrous that this player here,
But° in a fiction, in a dream of passion,   530
Could force his soul so to his own conceit°
That from her working° all his visage wanned,°
Tears in his eyes, distraction in his aspect,°
A broken voice, and his whole function suiting
With forms to his conceit?° And all for nothing!   535
For Hecuba!
What's Hecuba to him, or he to Hecuba,
That he should weep for her? What would he do
Had he the motive and the cue for passion

---

508 God's bodikin by God's (Christ's) little body, *bodykin* (not to be confused with
bodkin, "dagger")   **509 after** according to   **518 ha 't** have it   **519 study** memorize
530 But merely   **531 force . . . conceit** bring his innermost being so entirely into
accord with his conception (of the role)   **532 from her working** as a result of, or in
response to, his soul's activity | **wanned** grew pale   **533 aspect** look, glance
534–35 his whole . . . conceit all his bodily powers responding with actions to suit
his thought

That I have? He would drown the stage with tears   540
And cleave the general ear° with horrid° speech,
Make mad the guilty and appall° the free,°
Confound the ignorant,° and amaze° indeed
The very faculties of eyes and ears. Yet I,
A dull and muddy-mettled° rascal, peak   545
Like John-a-dreams, unpregnant of my cause,°
And can say nothing—no, not for a king
Upon whose property° and most dear life
A damned defeat° was made. Am I a coward?
Who calls me villain? Breaks my pate° across?   550
Plucks off my beard and blows it in my face?
Tweaks me by the nose? Gives me the lie i'th' throat°
As deep as to the lungs? Who does me this?
Ha, 'swounds,° I should take it; for it cannot be
But I am pigeon-livered° and lack gall   555
To make oppression bitter,° or ere this
I should ha' fatted all the region kites°
With this slave's offal.° Bloody, bawdy villain!
Remorseless,° treacherous, lecherous, kindless° villain!
Oh, vengeance!   560
Why, what an ass am I! This is most brave,°
That I, the son of a dear father murdered,
Prompted to my revenge by heaven and hell,
Must like a whore unpack my heart with words
And fall a-cursing, like a very drab,°   565
A scullion!° Fie upon't, foh! About,° my brains!
Hum, I have heard
That guilty creatures sitting at a play

---

541 the general ear everyone's ear | **horrid** horrible   **542 appall** (literally, make pale) | **free** innocent   **543 Confound the ignorant** dumbfound those who know nothing of the crime that has been committed | **amaze** stun   **545 muddy-mettled** dull-spirited   **545–46 peak . . . cause** mope, like a dreaming idler, not quickened by my cause   **548 property** person and function   **549 damned defeat** damnable act of destruction   **550 pate** head   **552 Gives . . . throat** calls me an out-and-out liar   **554 'swounds** by his (Christ's) wounds   **555 pigeon-livered** (the pigeon or dove was popularly supposed to be mild because it secreted no gall)   **556 To . . . bitter** to make things bitter for oppressors   **557 region kites** kites (birds of prey) of the air   **558 offal** entrails   **559 Remorseless** pitiless | **kindless** unnatural   **561 brave** fine, admirable (said ironically)   **565 drab** whore   **566 scullion** menial kitchen servant (apt to be foul-mouthed) | **about** about it, to work

Have by the very cunning° of the scene°
Been struck so to the soul that presently°   570
They have proclaimed their malefactions;
For murder, though it have no tongue, will speak
With most miraculous organ. I'll have these players
Play something like the murder of my father
Before mine uncle. I'll observe his looks;   575
I'll tent° him to the quick.° If 'a do blench,°
I know my course. The spirit that I have seen
May be the devil, and the devil hath power
T'assume a pleasing shape; yea, and perhaps,
Out of my weakness and my melancholy,   580
As he is very potent with such spirits,°
Abuses° me to damn me. I'll have grounds
More relative° than this. The play's the thing
Wherein I'll catch the conscience of the King.

Exit

❖

ACT 3
SCENE 1

Location: The castle

Enter King, Queen, Polonius, Ophelia,
Rosencrantz, Guildenstern, lords

KING   And can you by no drift of conference°
Get from him why he puts on this confusion,
Grating so harshly all his days of quiet
With turbulent and dangerous lunacy?
ROSENCRANTZ   He does confess he feels himself distracted,   5
But from what cause 'a will by no means speak.
GUILDENSTERN   Nor do we find him forward° to be sounded,°
But with a crafty madness keeps aloof

---

569 **cunning** art, skill | **scene** dramatic presentation   570 **presently** at once
576 **tent** probe | **the quick** the tender part of a wound, the core | **blench** quail,
flinch   581 **spirits** humors (of melancholy)   582 **Abuses** deludes | 583 **relative**
cogent, pertinent

1 **drift of conference** course of talk   7 **forward** willing | **sounded** questioned

When we would bring him on to some confession
Of his true state.

QUEEN   Did he receive you well?   10

ROSENCRANTZ   Most like a gentleman.

GUILDENSTERN   But with much forcing of his disposition.°

ROSENCRANTZ   Niggard of question,° but of our demands°
Most free in his reply.

QUEEN   Did you assay° him
To any pastime?   15

ROSENCRANTZ   Madam, it so fell out that certain players
We o'erraught° on the way. Of these we told him,
And there did seem in him a kind of joy
To hear of it. They are here about the court,
And, as I think, they have already order   20
This night to play before him.

POLONIUS   'Tis most true,
And he beseeched me to entreat Your Majesties
To hear and see the matter.

KING   With all my heart, and it doth much content me
To hear him so inclined.   25
Good gentlemen, give him a further edge°
And drive his purpose into these delights.

ROSENCRANTZ   We shall, my lord.

                   Exeunt Rosencrantz and Guildenstern

KING   Sweet Gertrude, leave us too,
For we have closely° sent for Hamlet hither,
That he, as 'twere by accident, may here   30
Affront° Ophelia.
Her father and myself, lawful espials,°
Will so bestow ourselves that seeing, unseen,
We may of their encounter frankly judge,
And gather by him, as he is behaved,   35
If't be th'affliction of his love or no
That thus he suffers for.

QUEEN   I shall obey you.
And for your part, Ophelia, I do wish

---

12 disposition inclination   **13 Niggard of question** laconic | **demands** questions
14 assay try to win   **17 o'erraught** overtook   **26 edge** incitement   **29 closely**
privately   **31 affront** confront, meet   **32 espials** spies

That your good beauties be the happy cause
Of Hamlet's wildness. So shall I hope your virtues 40
Will bring him to his wonted way again,
To both your honors.

OPHELIA   Madam, I wish it may.

[*Exit Queen*]

POLONIUS   Ophelia, walk you here.—Gracious,° so please you,
We will bestow° ourselves. [*To Ophelia*] Read on this book,

[*giving her a book*]

That show of such an exercise° may color° 45
Your loneliness.° We are oft to blame in this—
'Tis too much proved°—that with devotion's visage
And pious action we do sugar o'er
The devil himself.

KING [*aside*]   Oh, 'tis too true!
How smart a lash that speech doth give my conscience! 50
The harlot's cheek, beautied with plast'ring art,
Is not more ugly to the thing that helps it°
Than is my deed to my most painted word.°
Oh, heavy burden!

POLONIUS   I hear him coming. Let's withdraw, my lord. 55

[*The King and Polonius withdraw°*]

Enter Hamlet. [*Ophelia pretends to read a book*]

HAMLET   To be, or not to be, that is the question:
Whether 'tis nobler in the mind to suffer
The slings and arrows of outrageous fortune,
Or to take arms against a sea of troubles
And by opposing end them. To die, to sleep— 60
No more—and by a sleep to say we end
The heartache and the thousand natural shocks
That flesh is heir to. 'Tis a consummation
Devoutly to be wished. To die, to sleep;

---

43 Gracious Your Grace (the King)   **44 bestow** conceal   **45 exercise** religious
exercise (the book she reads is one of devotion) | **color** give a plausible appearance
to   **46 loneliness** being alone   **47 too much proved** too often shown to be true, too
often practiced   **52 to . . . helps it** in comparison with the cosmetic that fashions the
cheek's false beauty   **53 painted word** deceptive utterances   **56.1 s.d. *withdraw***
(the King and Polonius may retire behind an arras; the stage directions specify that
they "enter" again near the end of the scene)

To sleep, perchance to dream. Ay, there's the rub,°   65
For in that sleep of death what dreams may come,
When we have shuffled° off this mortal coil,°
Must give us pause. There's the respect°
That makes calamity of so long life.°
For who would bear the whips and scorns of time,   70
Th'oppressor's wrong, the proud man's contumely,°
The pangs of disprized° love, the law's delay,
The insolence of office,° and the spurns°
That patient merit of th'unworthy takes,°
When he himself might his quietus° make   75
With a bare bodkin?° Who would fardels° bear,
To grunt and sweat under a weary life,
But that the dread of something after death,
The undiscovered country from whose bourn°
No traveler returns, puzzles the will,   80
And makes us rather bear those ills we have
Than fly to others that we know not of?
Thus conscience does make cowards of us all;
And thus the native hue° of resolution
Is sicklied o'er with the pale cast° of thought,   85
And enterprises of great pitch° and moment°
With this regard° their currents° turn awry
And lose the name of action.—Soft you° now,
The fair Ophelia.—Nymph, in thy orisons
Be all my sins remembered.°

OPHELIA   Good my lord,   90
How does Your Honor for this many a day?
HAMLET   I humbly thank you; well, well, well.
OPHELIA   My lord, I have remembrances of yours,
That I have longèd long to redeliver.

---

65 rub (literally, an obstacle in the game of bowls) **67 shuffled** sloughed, cast | **coil** turmoil **68 respect** consideration **69 of . . . life** so long-lived, something we willingly endure for so long (also suggesting that long life is itself a calamity) **71 contumely** insolent abuse **72 disprized** unvalued **73 office** officialdom | **spurns** insults **74 of . . . takes** receives from unworthy persons **75 quietus** acquittance; here, death **76 a bare bodkin** a mere dagger, unsheathed | **fardels** burdens **79 bourn** frontier, boundary **84 native hue** natural color, complexion **85 cast** tinge, shade of color **86 pitch** height (as of a falcon's flight) | **moment** importance **87 regard** respect, consideration | **currents** courses **88 Soft you** wait a minute, gently **89–90 in . . . remembered** pray for me, sinner that I am

I pray you, now receive them.   [*She offers tokens*]   95
HAMLET   No, not I, I never gave you aught.
OPHELIA   My honored lord, you know right well you did,
And with them words of so sweet breath composed
As made the things more rich. Their perfume lost,
Take these again, for to the noble mind   100
Rich gifts wax poor when givers prove unkind.
There, my lord.   [*She gives tokens*]
HAMLET   Ha, ha! Are you honest?°
OPHELIA   My lord?
HAMLET   Are you fair?
OPHELIA   What means Your Lordship?
HAMLET   That if you be honest and fair,° your honesty° should   105
admit no discourse to° your beauty.
OPHELIA   Could beauty, my lord, have better commerce° than
with honesty?
HAMLET   Ay, truly, for the power of beauty will sooner
transform honesty from what it is to a bawd than the force   110
of honesty can translate beauty into his° likeness. This was
sometime a paradox, but now the time gives it proof.° I did
love you once.
OPHELIA   Indeed, my lord, you made me believe so.
HAMLET   You should not have believed me, for virtue cannot so   115
inoculate our old stock but we shall relish of it.° I loved you
not.
OPHELIA   I was the more deceived.
HAMLET   Get thee to a nunnery.° Why wouldst thou be a
breeder of sinners? I am myself indifferent honest,° but yet I   120
could accuse me of such things that it were better my
mother had not borne me: I am very proud, revengeful,
ambitious, with more offenses at my beck° than I have
thoughts to put them in, imagination to give them shape, or

---

102 honest (1) truthful (2) chaste   **105 fair** (1) beautiful (2) just, honorable | **your honesty** your chastity   **106 discourse to** familiar dealings with   **107 commerce** dealings, intercourse   **111 his** its   **111–12 This . . . proof** this was formerly an unfashionable view, but now the present age confirms how true it is.   **115–16 virtue . . . of it** virtue cannot be grafted onto our sinful condition without our retaining some taste of the old stock.   **119 nunnery** convent (with an awareness that the word was also used derisively to denote a brothel)   **120 indifferent honest** reasonably virtuous   **123 beck** command

time to act them in. What should such fellows as I do 125
crawling between earth and heaven? We are arrant knaves
all; believe none of us. Go thy ways to a nunnery. Where's
your father?

OPHELIA   At home, my lord.

HAMLET   Let the doors be shut upon him, that he may play the 130
fool nowhere but in 's own house. Farewell.

OPHELIA   Oh, help him, you sweet heavens!

HAMLET   If thou dost marry, I'll give thee this plague for thy
dowry: be thou as chaste as ice, as pure as snow, thou shalt
not escape calumny. Get thee to a nunnery, farewell. Or, if 135
thou wilt needs marry, marry a fool, for wise men know well
enough what monsters° you° make of them. To a nunnery,
go, and quickly too. Farewell.

OPHELIA   Heavenly powers, restore him!

HAMLET   I have heard of your paintings° too, well enough. God 140
hath given you one face, and you make yourselves another.
You jig, you amble, and you lisp, you nickname God's
creatures, and make your wantonness your ignorance.° Go
to, I'll no more on't;° it hath made me mad. I say we will
have no more marriage. Those that are married already—all 145
but one—shall live. The rest shall keep as they are. To a
nunnery, go.   *Exit*

OPHELIA   Oh, what a noble mind is here o'erthrown!
The courtier's, soldier's, scholar's, eye, tongue, sword,
Th'expectancy and rose° of the fair state,   150
The glass of fashion and the mold of form,°
Th'observed° of all observers, quite, quite down!
And I, of ladies most deject and wretched,
That sucked the honey of his music° vows,
Now see that noble and most sovereign reason   155
Like sweet bells jangled out of tune and harsh,
That unmatched form and feature of blown° youth

137 **monsters** (an illusion to the horns of a cuckold) | **you** you women
140 **paintings** use of cosmetics | 142–43 **You jig . . . ignorance** you prance about
frivolously and speak with affected coynesss, you put new labels on God's creatures
(by your use of cosmetics), and you excuse your affectations on the grounds of
pretended ignorance   144 **on't** of it   150 **Th'expectancy and rose** the hope and
ornament   151 **The glass . . . form** the mirror of true self-fashioning and the pattern
of courtly behavior   152 **Th'observed . . . observers** the center of attention and
honor in the court   154 **music** musical, sweetly uttered   157 **blown** blossoming

Blasted with ecstasy.° Oh, woe is me,
T'have seen what I have seen, see what I see!

Enter King and Polonius

KING   Love? His affections° do not that way tend;   160
Nor what he spake, though it lacked form a little,
Was not like madness. There's something in his soul
O'er which his melancholy sits on brood,°
And I do doubt° the hatch and the disclose°
Will be some danger; which for to prevent,   165
I have in quick determination
Thus set it down:° he shall with speed to England
For the demand of our neglected tribute.
Haply the seas and countries different
With variable objects° shall expel   170
This something-settled matter in his heart,°
Whereon his brains still° beating puts him thus
From fashion of himself.° What think you on't?
POLONIUS   It shall do well. But yet do I believe
The origin and commencement of his grief   175
Sprung from neglected love.—How now, Ophelia?
You need not tell us what Lord Hamlet said;
We heard it all.—My lord, do as you please,
But, if you hold it fit, after the play
Let his queen-mother all alone entreat him   180
To show his grief. Let her be round° with him;
And I'll be placed, so please you, in the ear
Of all their conference. If she find him not,°
To England send him, or confine him where
Your wisdom best shall think.   KING   It shall be so.   185
Madness in great ones must not unwatched go.

Exeunt

---

158 **Blasted with ecstasy** blighted with madness   160 **affections** emotions, feelings
163 **sits on brood** sits like a bird on a nest, about to *hatch* mischief (line 164)
164 **doubt** suspect, fear | **disclose** disclosure, hatching   167 **set it down** resolved
170 **variable objects** various sights and surroundings to divert him   171 **This
something . . . heart** the strange matter settled in his heart   172 **still** continually
173 **From . . . himself** out of his natural manner   181 **round** blunt   183 **find him
not** fails to discover what is troubling him

❖

ACT 3
SCENE 2

Location: The castle

Enter Hamlet and three of the Players

HAMLET   Speak the speech, I pray you, as I pronounced it to you, trippingly on the tongue. But if you mouth it, as many of our players° do, I had as lief° the town crier spoke my lines. Nor do not saw the air too much with your hand, thus, but use all gently; for in the very torrent, tempest, and,   5
as I may say, whirlwind of your passion, you must acquire and beget a temperance that may give it smoothness. Oh, it offends me to the soul to hear a robustious° periwig-pated° fellow tear a passion to tatters, to very rags, to split the ears of the groundlings,° who for the most part are capable of°   10
nothing but inexplicable dumb shows and noise.° I would have such a fellow whipped for o'erdoing Termagant.° It out-Herods Herod.° Pray you, avoid it.

FIRST PLAYER   I warrant Your Honor.

HAMLET   Be not too tame neither, but let your own discretion   15
be your tutor. Suit the action to the word, the word to the action, with this special observance, that you o'erstep not the modesty° of nature. For anything so o'erdone is from° the purpose of playing, whose end, both at the first and now, was and is to hold as 'twere the mirror up to nature, to show   20
virtue her feature, scorn° her own image, and the very age and body of the time his form and pressure.° Now this overdone or come tardy off,° though it makes the unskillful°

---

3 **our players** players nowadays | **I had as lief** I would just as soon   8 **robustious**
violent, boisterous | **periwig-pated** wearing a wig   10 **groundlings** spectators who
paid least and stood in the yard of the theater | **capable of** able to understand
11 **dumb shows and noise** noisy spectacle (rather than thoughtful drama)
12 **Termagant** a supposed deity of the Mohammedans, not found in any English
medieval play but elsewhere portrayed as violent and blustering   13 **Herod** Herod
of Jewry (a character in *The Slaughter of the Innocents* and other cycle plays; the part
was played with great noise and fury)   18 **modesty** restraint, moderation | **from**
contrary to   21 **scorn** something foolish and deserving of scorn   21–22 **and the . . .
pressure** and the present state of affairs its likeness as seen in an impression, such as
wax   23 **come tardy off** falling short | **the unskillful** those lacking in judgment

laugh, cannot but make the judicious grieve, the censure of
the which one° must in your allowance° o'erweigh a whole   25
theater of others. Oh, there be players that I have seen play,
and heard others praise, and that highly, not to speak it
profanely,° that, neither having th'accent of Christians° nor
the gait of Christian, pagan, nor man,° have so strutted and
bellowed that I have thought some of nature's journeymen°   30
had made men and not made them well, they imitated
humanity so abominably.°
FIRST PLAYER I hope we have reformed that indifferently° with
us, sir.
HAMLET Oh, reform it altogether. And let those that play your   35
clowns speak no more than is set down for them; for there
be of them° that will themselves laugh, to set on some
quantity of barren° spectators to laugh too, though in the
meantime some necessary question of the play be then to be
considered. That's villainous, and shows a most pitiful   40
ambition in the fool that uses it. Go make you ready.

                       [*Exeunt Players*]

    Enter Polonius, Guildenstern, and Rosencrantz

How now, my lord, will the King hear this piece of work?
POLONIUS And the Queen too, and that presently.°
HAMLET Bid the players make haste.   [*Exit Polonius*]
Will you two help to hasten them?   45
ROSENCRANTZ Ay, my lord.   *Exeunt they two*
HAMLET   What ho, Horatio!

                Enter Horatio

HORATIO Here, sweet lord, at your service.
HAMLET Horatio, thou art e'en as just a man
As e'er my conversation coped withal.°

24–25 the censure . . . one the judgment of even one of whom   25 your allowance
your scale of values   27–28 not . . . profanely (Hamlet anticipates his idea in lines
30–31 that some men were not made by God at all)   28 Christians ordinary decent
folk   29 nor man nor any human being at all   30 journeymen common workmen
32 abominably (Shakespeare's usual spelling, "abhominably," suggests a literal
though etymologically incorrect meaning, "removed from human nature")
33 indifferently tolerably   37 of them some among them   38 barren of wit
43 presently at once   49 my . . . withal my dealings encountered

HORATIO   Oh, my dear lord—
HAMLET   Nay, do not think I flatter,   50
For what advancement may I hope from thee
That no revenue hast but thy good spirits
To feed and clothe thee? Why should the poor be flattered?
No, let the candied° tongue lick absurd pomp,
And crook the pregnant° hinges of the knee   55
Where thrift° may follow fawning. Dost thou hear?
Since my dear soul was mistress of her choice
And could of men distinguish her election,°
Sh' hath sealed thee° for herself, for thou hast been
As one, in suffering all, that suffers nothing,   60
A man that Fortune's buffets and rewards
Hast ta'en with equal thanks; and blest are those
Whose blood° and judgment are so well commeddled°
That they are not a pipe for Fortune's finger
To sound what stop° she please. Give me that man   65
That is not passion's slave, and I will wear him
In my heart's core, ay, in my heart of heart,
As I do thee.—Something too much of this.—
There is a play tonight before the King.
One scene of it comes near the circumstance   70
Which I have told thee of my father's death.
I prithee, when thou see'st that act afoot,
Even with the very comment of thy soul°
Observe my uncle. If his occulted° guilt
Do not itself unkennel° in one speech,   75
It is a damnèd ghost that we have seen,
And my imaginations are as foul
As Vulcan's stithy.° Give him heedful note,
For I mine eyes will rivet to his face,
And after we will both our judgments join   80

---

54 candied sugared, flattering   **55 pregnant** compliant   **56 thrift** profit   **58 could
. . . election** could make distinguishing choices among persons   **59 sealed thee**
(literally, as one would seal a legal document to mark possession)   **63 blood**
passion | **commeddled** commingled   **65 stop** hole in a wind instrument for
controlling the sound   **73 very . . . soul** your most penetrating observation and
consideration   **74 occulted** hidden   **75 unkennel** (as one would say of a fox driven
from its lair)   **78 Vulcan's stithy** the smithy, the place of stiths (anvils) of the
Roman god of fire and metalworking

In censure of his seeming.°

HORATIO   Well, my lord.
If 'a steal aught° the whilst this play is playing
And scape detecting, I will pay the theft.

> [*Flourish.*] *Enter trumpets and kettledrums, King,*
> *Queen, Polonius, Ophelia, [Rosencrantz, Guildenstern,*
> *and other lords, with guards carrying torches]*

HAMLET   They are coming to the play. I must be idle.°
Get you a place.   [*The King, Queen, and courtiers sit*]

KING   How fares our cousin° Hamlet?   85

HAMLET   Excellent, i'faith, of the chameleon's dish:° I eat the
air, promise-crammed. You cannot feed capons° so.

KING   I have nothing with° this answer, Hamlet. These words
are not mine.°

HAMLET   No, nor mine now.° [*To Polonius*] My lord, you   90
played once i'th'university, you say?

POLONIUS   That did I, my lord, and was accounted a good
actor.

HAMLET   What did you enact?

POLONIUS   I did enact Julius Caesar. I was killed i'th' Capitol;°   95
Brutus killed me.

HAMLET   It was a brute° part° of him to kill so capital a calf°
there.—Be the players ready?

ROSENCRANTZ   Ay, my lord. They stay upon° your patience.

QUEEN   Come hither, my dear Hamlet, sit by me.   100

HAMLET   No, good mother, here's metal° more attractive.

POLONIUS [*to the King*]   O ho, do you mark that?

---

81 censure of his seeming judgment of his appearance or behavior   **82 If 'a steal
aught** if he gets away with anything   **84 idle** (1) unoccupied (2) mad   **85 cousin**
close relative   **86 chameleon's dish** (chameleons were supposed to feed on air;
Hamlet deliberately misinterprets the King's *fares* as "feeds;" by his phrase *eat the
air* he also plays on the idea of feeding himself with the promise of succession, of
being the *heir*)   **87 capons** roosters castrated and *crammed* with feed to make them
succulent   **88 have . . . with** make nothing of, or gain nothing from   **89 are not
mine** do not respond to what I asked   **90 nor mine now** (once spoken, words are
proverbially no longer the speaker's own—and hence should be uttered warily)
95 i'th' capitol (where Caesar was assassinated, according to *Julius Caesar*, 3.1)
97 brute (the Latin meaning of *brutus*, "stupid," was often used punningly with
the name Brutus | **part** (1) deed (2) role | **calf** fool   **99 stay upon** await
101 metal substance that is *attractive*, magnetic, but with suggestion also of *mettle*,
"disposition"

HAMLET   Lady,° shall I lie in your lap?

                 [*Lying down at Ophelia's feet*]

OPHELIA   No, my lord.

HAMLET   I mean, my head upon your lap?   105

OPHELIA   Ay, my lord.

HAMLET   Do you think I meant country matters?°

OPHELIA   I think nothing, my lord.

HAMLET   That's a fair thought to lie between maids' legs.

OPHELIA   What is, my lord?   110

HAMLET   Nothing.°

OPHELIA   You are merry, my lord.

HAMLET   Who, I?

OPHELIA   Ay, my lord.

HAMLET   Oh, God, your only jig maker.° What should a man 115
do but be merry? For look you how cheerfully my mother
looks, and my father died within 's° two hours.

OPHELIA   Nay, 'tis twice two months, my lord.

HAMLET   So long? Nay then, let the devil wear black, for I'll
have a suit of sables.° O heavens! Die two months ago, and 120
not forgotten yet? Then there's hope a great man's memory
may outlive his life half a year. But, by'r Lady, 'a must build
churches, then, or else shall 'a suffer not thinking on,° with
the hobbyhorse, whose epitaph is "For oh, for oh, the
hobbyhorse is forgot."°   125

    The trumpets sound. Dumb show follows.

    *Enter a King and a Queen [very lovingly]; the
    Queen embracing him, and he her. [She kneels,*

---

103 Lady . . . lap? (onstage, Hamlet often lies at Ophelia's feet, but he could instead offer to do this and continue to stand) **107 country matters** sexual intercourse (with a bawdy pun on the first syllable of *country*) **111 Nothing** the figure zero or naught, suggesting the female sexual anatomy (*thing* not infrequently has a bawdy connotation of male or female anatomy, and the reference here could be male) **115 only jig maker** very best composer of jigs, pointless merriment (Hamlet replies sardonically to Ophelia's observation that he is merry by saying, "If you're looking for someone who is really merry, you've come to the right person") **117 within 's** within this (these) **120 suit of sables** garments trimmed with the dark fur of the sable and hence suited for a person in mourning **123 suffer . . . on** undergo oblivion **124–25 "For . . . forgot"** (verse of a song occurring also in *Love's Labor's Lost*, 3.1.27–28; the hobbyhorse was a character made up to resemble a horse and rider, appearing in the morris dance and such May-game sports; this song laments the disappearance of such customs under pressure from the Puritans) *and makes show of protestation unto him.] He takes her up, and declines his head upon her neck. He lies him down upon a bank of flowers. She, seeing him asleep, leaves him. Anon comes in another man, takes off his crown, kisses it, pours poison in the sleeper's ears, and leaves him. The Queen returns, finds the King dead, makes passionate action. The Poisoner with some three or four come in again, seem to condole with° her. The dead body is carried away. The Poisoner woos the Queen with gifts; she seems harsh awhile, but in the end accepts love.*

[Exeunt players]

OPHELIA   What means this, my lord?

HAMLET   Marry, this' miching mallico;° it means mischief.

OPHELIA   Belike° this show imports the argument° of the play.

Enter Prologue

HAMLET   We shall know by this fellow. The players cannot keep counsel;° they'll tell all.   130

OPHELIA   Will 'a tell us what this show meant?

HAMLET   Ay, or any show that you will show him. Be not you° ashamed to show, he'll not shame to tell you what it means.

OPHELIA   You are naught,° you are naught. I'll mark the play.

PROLOGUE   For us, and for our tragedy,   135
        Here stooping° to your clemency,
        We beg your hearing patiently.   *[Exit]*

HAMLET   Is this a prologue, or the posy of a ring?°

OPHELIA   'Tis brief, my lord.

HAMLET   As woman's love.

Enter [two Players as] King and Queen

PLAYER KING   Full thirty times hath Phoebus' cart° gone round   140

125.13 s.d. *condole with* offer sympathy to   127 **this' miching mallico** this is sneaking mischief   128 **Belike** probably | **argument** plot   130 **counsel** secret   132 **Be not you** provided you are not   134 **naught** indecent (Ophelia is reacting to Hamlet's pointed remarks about not being ashamed to show all)   136 **stooping** bowing   138 **posy . . . ring** brief motto in verse inscribed in a ring   140 **Phoebus' cart** the sun-god's chariot, making its yearly cycle

Neptune's salt wash° and Tellus'° orbèd ground,
And thirty dozen moons with borrowed° sheen
About the world have times twelve thirties been,
Since love our hearts and Hymen° did our hands
Unite commutual° in most sacred bands.°   145
PLAYER QUEEN   So many journeys may the sun and moon
Make us again count o'er ere love be done!
But, woe is me, you are so sick of late,
So far from cheer and from your former state,
That I distrust you. Yet, though I distrust,°   150
Discomfort you, my lord, it nothing must.°
For women's fear and love hold quantity;°
In neither aught, or in extremity.°
Now, what my love is, proof° hath made you know,
And as my love is sized, my fear is so.   155
Where love is great, the littlest° doubts are fear;
Where little fears grow great, great love grows there.
PLAYER KING   Faith, I must leave thee, love, and shortly too;
My operant powers their functions leave to do.°
And thou shalt live in this fair world behind,°   160
Honored, beloved; and haply one as kind
For husband shalt thou—
PLAYER QUEEN   Oh, confound the rest!
Such love must needs be treason in my breast.
In second husband let me be accurst!
None° wed the second but who° killed the first.   165
HAMLET   Wormwood,° wormwood.
PLAYER QUEEN   The instances° that second marriage move°
Are base respects of thrift,° but none of love.

---

141 salt wash the sea | **Tellus** goddess of the earth, of the *orbèd* ground
142 borrowed reflected   **144 Hymen** god of matrimony   **145 commutual** mutually
| **bands** bonds   **150 distrust** am anxious about   **151 Discomfort . . . must** it must
not distress you at all   **152 hold quantity** keep proportion with one another
153 In . . . extremity (women feel) either no anxiety if they do not love or extreme
anxiety if they do love   **154 proof** experience   **156 the littlest** even the littlest
159 My . . . to do my vital functions are shutting down   **160 behind** after I have
gone   **165 None** (1) let no woman; or (2) no woman does | **but who** except the
one who   **166 Wormwood** how bitter (literally, a bitter-tasting plant)
167 instances motives | **move** motivate   **168 base . . . thrift** ignoble
considerations of material prosperity

A second time I kill my husband dead
When second husband kisses me in bed.   170
PLAYER KING   I do believe you think what now you speak,
But what we do determine oft we break.
Purpose is but the slave to memory,°
Of violent birth, but poor validity,°
Which° now, like fruit unripe, sticks on the tree,   175
But fall unshaken when they mellow be.
Most necessary 'tis that we forget
To pay ourselves what to ourselves is debt.°
What to ourselves in passion we propose,
The passion ending, doth the purpose lose.   180
The violence of either grief or joy
Their own enactures° with themselves destroy.
Where joy most revels, grief doth most lament;
Grief joys, joy grieves, on slender accident.°
This world is not for aye,° nor 'tis not strange   185
That even our loves should with our fortunes change;
For 'tis a question left us yet to prove,
Whether love lead fortune, or else fortune love.
The great man down,° you mark his favorite flies;
The poor advanced makes friends of enemies.°   190
And hitherto° doth love on fortune tend;°
For who not needs° shall never lack a friend,
And who in want° a hollow friend doth try°
Directly seasons him° his enemy.
But, orderly to end where I begun,   195
Our wills and fates do so contrary run°
That our devices° still° are overthrown;

---

173 **Purpose . . . memory** our good intentions are subject to forgetfulness
174 **validity** strength, durability   175 **Which** purpose   177–78 **Most . . . debt**
it's inevitable that in time we forget the obligations we have imposed on ourselves
182 **enactures** fulfillments   183–84 **Where . . . accident** the capacity for extreme
joy and grief go together, and often one extreme is instantly changed into its
opposite on the slightest provocation   185 **aye** ever   189 **down** fallen in fortune
190 **The poor . . . enemies** when one of humble station is promoted, you see his
enemies suddenly becoming his friends   191 **hitherto** up to this point in the
argument, or, to this extent │ **tend** attend   192 **who not needs** he who is not in
need (of wealth)   193 **who in want** he who, being in need │ **try** test (his
generosity)   194 **seasons him** ripens him into   196 **Our . . . run** what we want
and what we get go so contrarily   197 **devices** intentions │ **still** continually

Our thoughts are ours, their ends° none of our own.
So think thou wilt no second husband wed,
But die thy thoughts when thy first lord is dead.   200
PLAYER QUEEN   Nor° earth to me give food, nor heaven light,
Sport and repose lock from me day and night,°
To desperation turn my trust and hope,
An anchor's cheer° in prison be my scope!°
Each opposite that blanks the face of joy   205
Meet what I would have well and it destroy!°
Both here and hence° pursue me lasting strife
If, once a widow, ever I be wife!
HAMLET   If she should break it now!
PLAYER KING   'Tis deeply sworn. Sweet, leave me here awhile;   210
My spirits° grow dull, and fain I would beguile
The tedious day with sleep.
PLAYER QUEEN   Sleep rock thy brain,
And never come mischance between us twain!
                              [*He sleeps.*] *Exit* [*Player Queen*]

HAMLET   Madam, how like you this play?
QUEEN   The lady doth protest too much,° methinks.   215
HAMLET   Oh, but she'll keep her word.
KING   Have you heard the argument?° Is there no offense in't?
HAMLET   No, no, they do but jest, poison in jest.° No offense°
i'th' world.
KING   What do you call the play?   220
HAMLET   *The Mousetrap.* Marry, how? Tropically.° This play is
the image of a murder done in Vienna. Gonzago is the
Duke's° name, his wife, Baptista. You shall see anon. 'Tis a

198 ends results   **201 Nor** let neither   **202 Sport . . . night** may day deny me its
pastimes and night its repose   **204 anchor's cheer** anchorite's or hermit's fare |
my scope the extent of my happiness   **205–6 Each . . . destroy!** may every adverse
thing that causes the face of joy to turn pale meet and destroy everything that I
desire to see prosper!   **207 hence** in the life hereafter   **211 spirits** vital spirits
215 doth . . . much makes too many promises and protestations   **217 argument**
plot   **218 jest** make believe | **offense** crime, injury (Hamlet playfully alters the
King's use of the word in line 217 to mean "cause for objection")   **221 Tropically**
figuratively (the First Quarto reading, "trapically," suggests a pun on *trap* in
Mousetrap)   **223 Duke's** King's (an inconsistency that may be due to Shakespeare's
possible acquaintance with a historical incident, the alleged murder of the Duke of
Urbino by Luigi Gonzaga in 1538)

knavish piece of work, but what of that? Your Majesty, and
we that have free° souls, it touches us not. Let the galled jade° 225
wince, our withers° are unwrung.°

Enter Lucianus

This is one Lucianus, nephew to the King.
OPHELIA   You are as good as a chorus,° my lord.
HAMLET   I could interpret° between you and your love, if I
could see the puppets dallying° 230
OPHELIA   You are keen,° my lord, you are keen.
HAMLET   It would cost you a groaning to take off mine edge.
OPHELIA   Still better, and worse.°
HAMLET   So° you mis-take° your husbands.—Begin, murderer;
leave thy damnable faces and begin. Come, the croaking 235
raven doth bellow for revenge.

LUCIANUS

Thoughts black, hands apt, drugs fit, and time agreeing,
Confederate season, else no creature seeing,°
Thou mixture rank, of midnight weeds collected,
With Hecate's ban° thrice blasted, thrice infected, 240
Thy natural magic and dire property°
On wholesome life usurp immediately.

[He pours the poison into the sleeper's ear]
HAMLET   'A poisons him i'th' garden for his estate.° His° name's
Gonzago. The story is extant, and written in very choice

---

225 free guiltless | **galled jade** horse whose hide is rubbed by saddle or harness
226 withers the part between the horse's shoulder blades | **unwrung** not rubbed
sore   **228 chorus** (in many Elizabethan plays, the forthcoming action was explained
by an actor known as the "chorus"; at a puppet show, the actor who spoke the
dialogue was known as an "interpreter," as indicated by the lines following)
229 interpret (1) ventriloquize the dialogue, as in puppet show (2) act as pander
230 puppets dallying (with suggestion of sexual play, continued in *keen,* "sexually
aroused," *groaning,* "moaning in pregnancy," and *edge,* "sexual desire" or
"impetuosity")   **231 keen** sharp, bitter   **233 Still . . . worse** more keen, always
bettering what other people say with witty wordplay, but at the same time more
offensive   **234 So** even thus (in marriage) | **mis-take** take falseheartedly and cheat
on (the marriage vows say "for better, for worse.")   **238 Confederate . . . seeing** the
time and occasion conspiring (to assist me), and also no one seeing me   **240 Hecate's
ban** the curse of Hecate, the goddess of witchcraft   **241 dire property** baleful quality
243 estate the kingship | **His** the King's

Italian. You shall see anon how the murderer gets the love of   245
Gonzago's wife.

[*Claudius rises*]

OPHELIA   The King rises.

HAMLET   What, frighted with false fire?°

QUEEN   How fares my lord?

POLONIUS   Give o'er the play.

KING   Give me some light. Away!

POLONIUS   Lights, lights, lights!   250

Exeunt all but Hamlet and Horatio

HAMLET

    "Why, let the strucken deer go weep,
        The hart ungallèd° play.
    For some must watch,° while some must sleep;
        Thus runs the world away."°

Would not this,° sir, and a forest of feathers°—if the rest of   255
my fortunes turn Turk with° me—with two Provincial roses°
on my razed° shoes, get me a fellowship in a cry° of players?°

HORATIO   Half a share.

HAMLET   A whole one, I.

    "For thou dost know, O Damon° dear,   260
        This realm dismantled° was
    Of Jove himself, and now reigns here
        A very, very—pajock."°

---

248 false fire the blank discharge of a gun loaded with powder but no shot
251–54 Why . . . away (perhaps this comes from an old ballad, with allusion to the
popular belief that a wounded deer retires to weep and die; compare with *As You
Like It*, 2.1.33–66)   **252 ungallèd** unafflicted   **253 watch** remain awake   **254 Thus
. . . away** thus the world goes   **255 this** this success with the play I have just
presented | **feathers** (allusion to the plumes that Elizabethan actors were fond of
wearing)   **256 turn Turk with** turn renegade against, go back on | **Provincial
roses** rosettes of ribbon, named for roses grown in a part of France   **257 razed** with
ornamental slashing | **fellowship . . . players** partnership in a theatrical company |
cry pack (of hounds, etc.)   **260 Damon** the friend of Pythias, as Horatio is friend of
Hamlet; or, a traditional pastoral name   **261–63 This realm . . . pajock** Jove,
representing divine authority and justice, has abandoned this realm to its own
devices, leaving in his stead only a peacock or vain pretender to virtue (though the
rhyme-word expected in place of *pajock* or "peacock" suggests that the realm is
now ruled over by an "ass")   **261 dismantled** stripped, divested

HORATIO   You might have rhymed.

HAMLET   Oh, good Horatio, I'll take the ghost's word for a   265
thousand pound. Didst perceive?

HORATIO   Very well, my lord.

HAMLET   Upon the talk of the poisoning?

HORATIO   I did very well note him.

Enter Rosencrantz and Guildenstern

HAMLET   Aha! Come, some music! Come, the recorders.   270

"For if the King like not the comedy,
Why then, belike, he likes it not, perdy."°

Come, some music.

GUILDENSTERN   Good my lord, vouchsafe me a word with you.

HAMLET   Sir, a whole history.   275

GUILDENSTERN   The King, sir—

HAMLET   Ay, sir, what of him?

GUILDENSTERN   Is in his retirement° marvelous distempered.°

HAMLET   With drink, sir?

GUILDENSTERN   No, my lord, with choler.°   280

HAMLET   Your wisdom should show itself more richer to
signify this to the doctor, for for me to put him to his
purgation° would perhaps plunge him into more choler.

GUILDENSTERN   Good my lord, put your discourse into some
frame° and start° not so wildly from my affair.   285

HAMLET   I am tame, sir. Pronounce.

GUILDENSTERN   The Queen, your mother, in most great affliction of spirit, hath sent me to you.

HAMLET   You are welcome.

GUILDENSTERN   Nay, good my lord, this courtesy is not of the   290
right breed.° If it shall please you to make me a wholesome

---

272 **perdy** (a corruption of the French *par dieu*, "by God")   278 **retirement**
withdrawal to his chambers | **distempered** out of humor (but Hamlet deliberately
plays on the wider application to any illness of mind or body, as in lines 311–14,
especially to drunkenness)   280 **choler** anger (but Hamlet takes the word in its
more basic humoral sense of "bilious disorder")   283 **purgation** (Hamlet hints at
something going beyond medical treatment to bloodletting and the extraction of
confession)   285 **frame** order | **start** shy or jump away (like a horse; the opposite
of *tame* in line 286)   291 **breed** (1) kind (2) breeding, manners

answer, I will do your mother's commandment; if not, your pardon° and my return shall be the end of my business.

HAMLET Sir, I cannot.

ROSENCRANTZ What, my lord?   295

HAMLET Make you a wholesome answer; my wit's diseased. But, sir, such answer as I can make, you shall command, or rather, as you say, my mother. Therefore no more, but to the matter. My mother, you say—

ROSENCRANTZ Then thus she says: your behavior hath struck   300
her into amazement and admiration.°

HAMLET Oh, wonderful son, that can so 'stonish a mother! But is there no sequel at the heels of this mother's admiration? Impart.

ROSENCRANTZ She desires to speak with you in her closet° ere   305
you go to bed.

HAMLET We shall obey, were she ten times our mother. Have you any further trade with us?

ROSENCRANTZ My lord, you once did love me.

HAMLET And do still, by these pickers and stealers.°   310

ROSENCRANTZ Good my lord, what is your cause of distemper? You do surely bar the door upon your own liberty° if you deny° your griefs to your friend.

HAMLET Sir, I lack advancement.

ROSENCRANTZ How can that be, when you have the voice of   315
the King himself for your succession in Denmark?

HAMLET Ay, sir, but "While the grass grows"°—the proverb is something° musty.

Enter the Players° with recorders

Oh, the recorders. Let me see one. [*He takes a recorder*] To withdraw° with you: why do you go about to recover the   320
wind° of me, as if you would drive me into a toil?°

---

293 **pardon** permission to depart 301 **admiration** bewilderment 305 **closet** private chamber 310 **pickers and stealers** hands (so called from the catechism, "to keep my hands from picking and stealing") 312 **liberty** being freed from *distemper*, line 311; but perhaps with a veiled threat as well 313 **deny** refuse to share 317 **"While . . . grows"** (the rest of the proverb is "the silly horse starves"; Hamlet implies that his hopes of succession are distant in time at best) 318 **something** somewhat 318.1 s.d. *Players* actors 320 **withdraw** speak privately 320–21 **recover the wind** get to the windward side (thus allowing the game to scent the hunter and thereby be driven in the opposite direction into the *toil* or net) 321 **toil** snare

GUILDENSTERN   Oh, my lord, if my duty be too bold, my love is too unmannerly.°

HAMLET   I do not well understand that.° Will you play upon this pipe?   325

GUILDENSTERN   My lord, I cannot.

HAMLET   I pray you.

GUILDENSTERN   Believe me, I cannot.

HAMLET   I do beseech you.

GUILDENSTERN   I know no touch of it, my lord.   330

HAMLET   It is as easy as lying. Govern these ventages° with your fingers and thumb, give it breath with your mouth, and it will discourse most eloquent music. Look you, these are the stops.

GUILDENSTERN   But these cannot I command to any utterance of   335
harmony. I have not the skill.

HAMLET   Why, look you now, how unworthy a thing you make of me! You would play upon me, you would seem to know my stops, you would pluck out the heart of my mystery, you would sound° me from my lowest note to the top of my   340
compass,° and there is much music, excellent voice, in this little organ,° yet cannot you make it speak. 'Sblood, do you think I am easier to be played on than a pipe? Call me what instrument you will, though you can fret° me, you cannot play upon me.   345

Enter Polonius

God bless you, sir!

POLONIUS   My lord, the Queen would speak with you, and presently.°

HAMLET   Do you see yonder cloud that's almost in shape of a camel?
                                                                                                           350

POLONIUS   By th' Mass and 'tis, like a camel indeed.

HAMLET   Methinks it is like a weasel.

322–23 if . . . unmannerly if I am using an unmannerly boldness, it is my love that occasions it   324 I . . . that I don't understand how genuine love can be unmannerly   331 ventages finger-holes or *stops* (line 334) of the recorder   340 sound (1) fathom (2) produce sound in   341 compass range (of voice)   342 organ musical instrument   344 fret irritate (with a quibble on the *frets* or ridges on the fingerboard of some stringed instruments to regulate the fingering)   348 presently at once

POLONIUS   It is backed like a weasel.

HAMLET   Or like a whale.

POLONIUS   Very like a whale.   355

HAMLET   Then I will come to my mother by and by. [*Aside*]
    They fool me to the top of my bent.°—I will come by and by.

POLONIUS   I will say so.   [*Exit*]

HAMLET   "By and by" is easily said. Leave me, friends.
                                              [*Exeunt all but Hamlet*]
    'Tis now the very witching time° of night,   360
    When churchyards yawn and hell itself breathes out
    Contagion to this world. Now could I drink hot blood
    And do such bitter business as the day
    Would quake to look on. Soft, now to my mother.
    O heart, lose not thy nature!° Let not ever   365
    The soul of Nero° enter this firm bosom.
    Let me be cruel, not unnatural;
    I will speak daggers to her, but use none.
    My tongue and soul in this be hypocrites:
    How in my words somever she be shent,   370
    To give them seals never my soul consent!°

                                                                Exit

                              ❧

                            ACT 3
                           SCENE 3

                    Location: The castle

            Enter King, Rosencrantz, and Guildenstern

KING   I like him° not, nor stands it safe with us
    To let his madness range. Therefore prepare you.
    I your commission will forthwith dispatch,°

---

357 They fool . . . bent they humor my odd behavior to the limit of my ability or
endurance (literally, the extent to which a bow may be bent)   **360 witching time**
time when spells are cast and evil is abroad   **365 nature** natural feeling   **366 Nero**
(this infamous Roman emperor put to death his mother, Agrippina, who had
murdered her husband, Claudius)   **370–71 How . . . consent!** however much she is
to be rebuked by my words, may my soul never consent to ratify those words with
deeds of violence!

1 him his behavior   **3 dispatch** prepare, cause to be drawn up

And he to England shall along with you.
The terms of our estate° may not endure   5
Hazard so near 's as doth hourly grow
Out of his brows.°

GUILDENSTERN   We will ourselves provide.°
Most holy and religious fear° it is
To keep those many many bodies safe
That live and feed upon Your Majesty.   10

ROSENCRANTZ   The single and peculiar° life is bound
With all the strength and armor of the mind
To keep itself from noyance,° but much more
That spirit upon whose weal° depends and rests
The lives of many. The cess° of majesty   15
Dies not alone, but like a gulf° doth draw
What's near it with it; or it is a massy° wheel
Fixed on the summit of the highest mount,
To whose huge spokes ten thousand lesser things
Are mortised° and adjoined, which, when it falls,°   20
Each small annexment, petty consequence,°
Attends° the boist'rous ruin. Never alone
Did the King sigh, but with a general groan.

KING   Arm° you, I pray you, to this speedy voyage,
For we will fetters put about this fear,   25
Which now goes too free-footed.

ROSENCRANTZ   We will haste us.
            Exeunt gentlemen [Rosencrantz and Guildenstern]

                                    Enter Polonius

POLONIUS   My lord, he's going to his mother's closet.
Behind the arras° I'll convey myself

---

5 **terms of our estate** circumstances of my royal position   7 **Out . . . brows** from his brain, in the form of plots and threats | **We . . . provide** we'll put ourselves in readiness   8 **religious fear** sacred concern   11 **single and peculiar** individual and private   13 **noyance** harm   14 **weal** well-being   15 **cess** decease, cessation   16 **gulf** whirlpool   17 **massy** massive   20 **mortised** fastened (as with a fitted joint) | **when it falls** when it descends, like the wheel of Fortune, bringing a king down with it   21 **Each . . . consequence** every hanger-on and unimportant person or thing connected with the King   22 **Attends** participates in   24 **Arm** provide, prepare   28 **arras** screen of tapestry placed around the walls of household apartments (on the Elizabethan stage, the arras was presumably over a door or aperture in the tiring-house façade)

To hear the process.° I'll warrant she'll tax him home,°
And, as you said—and wisely was it said—   30
'Tis meet° that some more audience than a mother,
Since nature makes them partial, should o'erhear
The speech of vantage.° Fare you well, my liege.
I'll call upon you ere you go to bed
And tell you what I know.

KING   Thanks, dear my lord.   35

Exit [Polonius]

Oh, my offense is rank! It smells to heaven.
It hath the primal eldest curse° upon't,
A brother's murder. Pray can I not,
Though inclination be as sharp as will;°
My stronger guilt defeats my strong intent,   40
And like a man to double business bound°
I stand in pause where I shall first begin,
And both neglect. What if this cursèd hand
Were thicker than itself with brother's blood,
Is there not rain enough in the sweet heavens   45
To wash it white as snow? Whereto serves mercy
But to confront the visage of offense?°
And what's in prayer but this twofold force,
To be forestallèd° ere we come to fall,
Or pardoned being down? Then I'll look up.   50
My fault is past. But oh, what form of prayer
Can serve my turn? "Forgive me my foul murder"?
That cannot be, since I am still possessed
Of those effects for which I did the murder:
My crown, mine own ambition, and my queen.   55
May one be pardoned and retain th'offense?°
In the corrupted currents° of this world
Offense's gilded hand° may shove by° justice,

29 **process** proceedings | **tax him home** reprove him severely   31 **meet** fitting
33 **of vantage** from an advantageous place, or, in addition   37 **the primal eldest
curse** the curse of Cain, the first murderer, who killed his brother Abel   39 **Though
. . . will** though my desire is as strong as my determination   41 **bound** (1) destined
(2) obliged (the King wants to repent and still enjoy what he has gained)
46–47 **Whereto . . . offense?** what function does mercy serve other than to meet sin
face to face?   49 **forestallèd** prevented (from sinning)   56 **th'offense** the thing for
which one offended   57 **currents** courses of events   58 **gilded hand** hand offering
gold as a bribe | **shove by** thrust aside

And oft 'tis seen the wicked prize° itself
Buys out the law. But 'tis not so above.   60
There is no shuffling, there the action lies°
In his° true nature, and we ourselves compelled,
Even to the teeth and forehead° of our faults,
To give in° evidence. What then? What rests?°
Try what repentance can. What can it not?   65
Yet what can it, when one cannot repent?
O wretched state, O bosom black as death,
O limèd° soul that, struggling to be free,
Art more engaged!° Help, angels! Make assay.°
Bow, stubborn knees, and heart with strings of steel,   70
Be soft as sinews of the newborn babe!
All may be well.   [He kneels]

                                                         Enter Hamlet

HAMLET   Now might I do it pat,° now 'a is a-praying;
And now I'll do't. [He draws his sword] And so 'a goes to
    heaven,
And so am I revenged. That would be scanned:°   75
A villain kills my father, and for that,
I, his sole son, do this same villain send
To heaven.
Why, this is hire and salary, not revenge.
'A took my father grossly, full of bread,°   80
With all his crimes broad blown,° as flush° as May;
And how his audit° stands who knows save° heaven?
But in our circumstance and course of thought°
'Tis heavy with him. And am I then revenged,
To take him in the purging of his soul,   85
When he is fit and seasoned° for his passage?

---

59 **wicked prize** prize won by wickedness   61 **There . . . lies** there in heaven can be
no evasion, there the deed lies exposed to view   62 **his** its   63 **to the teeth and
forehead** face to face, concealing nothing   64 **give in** provide | **rests** remains
68 **limèd** caught as with birdlime, a sticky substance used to ensnare birds   69 **engaged**
entangled | **assay** trial (said to himself, or to the angels to try him)   73 **pat**
opportunely   75 **would be scanned** needs to be looked into, or, would be
interpreted as follows   80 **grossly, full of bread** enjoying his worldly pleasures
rather than fasting (see Ezekiel 16.49)   81 **crimes broad blown** sins in full bloom |
flush vigorous   82 **audit** account | **save** except for   83 **in . . . thought** as we see it
from our mortal perspective   86 **seasoned** matured, readied

No!
Up, sword, and know thou a more horrid hent.°

[*He puts up his sword*]

When he is drunk asleep, or in his rage,°
Or in th'incestuous pleasure of his bed,   90
At game,° a-swearing, or about some act
That has no relish° of salvation in't—
Then trip him, that his heels may kick at heaven,
And that his soul may be as damned and black
As hell, whereto it goes. My mother stays.°   95
This physic° but prolongs thy sickly days.   *Exit*
KING   My words fly up, my thoughts remain below.
Words without thoughts never to heaven go.

Exit

❧

ACT 3
SCENE 4

Location: The Queen's private chamber

Enter [Queen] Gertrude and Polonius

POLONIUS   'A will come straight. Look you lay home° to him.
Tell him his pranks have been too broad° to bear with,
And that Your Grace hath screened and stood between
Much heat° and him. I'll silence me° even here.
Pray you, be round° with him.   5
HAMLET (*within*)   Mother, mother, mother!
QUEEN   I'll warrant you, fear me not.
Withdraw, I hear him coming.

[*Polonius hides behind the arras*]

Enter Hamlet

88 know . . . hent await to be grasped by me on a more horrid occasion (*hent* means
"act of seizing")   89 drunk . . . rage dead drunk, or in a fit of sexual passion
91 game gambling   92 relish trace, savor   95 stays awaits (me)   96 physic
purging (by prayer), or, Hamlet's postponement of the killing

1 lay home reprove him soundly   2 broad unrestrained   4 Much heat the King's
anger | I'll silence me I'll quietly conceal myself (ironic, since it is his crying out at
line 23 that leads to his death; some editors emend *silence* to "sconce;" the First
Quarto's reading, "shroud," is attractive)   5 round blunt

HAMLET   Now, mother, what's the matter?

QUEEN   Hamlet, thou hast thy father° much offended.   10

HAMLET   Mother, you have my father much offended.

QUEEN   Come, come, you answer with an idle° tongue.

HAMLET   Go, go, you question with a wicked tongue.

QUEEN   Why, how now, Hamlet?

HAMLET   What's the matter now?

QUEEN   Have you forgot me?°

HAMLET   No, by the rood,° not so: 15
   You are the Queen, your husband's brother's wife,
   And—would it were not so!—you are my mother.

QUEEN   Nay, then, I'll set those to you that can speak.°

HAMLET   Come, come, and sit you down; you shall not budge.
   You go not till I set you up a glass   20
   Where you may see the inmost part of you.

QUEEN   What wilt thou do? Thou wilt not murder me?
   Help, ho!

POLONIUS [*behind the arras*]   What ho! Help!

HAMLET [*drawing*]   How now? A rat? Dead for a ducat,° dead!
          [*He thrusts his rapier through the arras*]

POLONIUS [*behind the arras*]

   Oh, I am slain!   [*He falls and dies*]

QUEEN   Oh, me, what hast thou done?   25

HAMLET   Nay, I know not. Is it the King?

QUEEN   Oh, what a rash and bloody deed is this!

HAMLET   A bloody deed—almost as bad, good mother,
   As kill a king, and marry with his brother.

QUEEN   As kill a king!

HAMLET   Ay, lady, it was my word.   30
       [*He parts the arras and discovers Polonius*]
   Thou wretched, rash, intruding fool, farewell!
   I took thee for thy better. Take thy fortune.
   Thou find'st to be too busy° is some danger.—
   Leave wringing of your hands. Peace, sit you down,
   And let me wring your heart, for so I shall,   35
   If it be made of penetrable stuff,

10 thy father your stepfather, Claudius   **12 idle** foolish   **15 forgot me** forgotten
that I am your mother | **rood** cross of Christ   **18 speak** speak to someone so rude
24 Dead for a ducat I bet a ducat he's dead; or, a ducat is his life's fee   **33 busy**
nosey

If damnèd custom° have not brazed° it so
That it be proof° and bulwark against sense.°
QUEEN   What have I done, that thou dar'st wag thy tongue
In noise so rude against me?
HAMLET   Such an act   40
That blurs the grace and blush of modesty,
Calls virtue hypocrite, takes off the rose
From the fair forehead of an innocent love
And sets a blister° there, makes marriage vows
As false as dicers' oaths. Oh, such a deed   45
As from the body of contraction° plucks
The very soul, and sweet religion makes°
A rhapsody° of words. Heaven's face does glow
O'er this solidity and compound mass
With tristful visage, as against the doom,   50
Is thought-sick at the act.°
QUEEN   Ay me, what act,
That roars so loud and thunders in the index?°
HAMLET [*showing her two likenesses*]
Look here upon this picture, and on this,
The counterfeit presentment° of two brothers.
See what a grace was seated on this brow: 55
Hyperion's° curls, the front° of Jove himself,
An eye like Mars° to threaten and command,
A station° like the herald Mercury°
New-lighted° on a heaven-kissing° hill—
A combination and a form indeed   60
Where every god did seem to set his seal°
To give the world assurance of a man.
This was your husband. Look you now what follows:

---

37 **damnèd custom** habitual wickedness | **brazed** brazened, hardened   38 **proof** impenetrable, like *proof* or tested armor | **sense** feeling   44 **sets a blister** brands as a harlot   46 **contraction** the marriage contract   47 **sweet religion makes** makes marriage vows   48 **rhapsody** senseless string   48–51 **Heaven's . . . act** heaven's face blushes at this solid world compounded of the various elements, with sorrowful face as though the day of doom were near, and is sick with horror at the deed (Gertrude's marriage)   52 **index** table of contents, prelude or preface   54 **counterfeit presentment** representation in portraiture   56 **Hyperion's** the sun-god's | **front** brow   57 **Mars** god of war   58 **station** manner of standing | **Mercury** winged messenger of the gods   59 **New-lighted** newly alighted | **heaven-kissing** reaching to the sky   61 **set his seal** affix his approval

Here is your husband, like a mildewed ear,°
Blasting° his wholesome brother. Have you eyes?　　　　　65
Could you on this fair mountain leave° to feed
And batten° on this moor?° Ha, have you eyes?
You cannot call it love, for at your age
The heyday in the blood° is tame, it's humble,
And waits upon the judgment, and what judgment　　　　70
Would step from this to this? Sense,° sure, you have,
Else could you not have motion, but sure that sense
Is apoplexed,° for madness would not err,
Nor sense to ecstasy was ne'er so thralled,
But it reserved some quantity of choice　　　　　　　　75
To serve in such a difference.° What devil was't
That thus hath cozened° you at hoodman-blind?°
Eyes without feeling, feeling without sight,
Ears without hands or eyes, smelling sans° all,
Or but a sickly part of one true sense　　　　　　　　80
Could not so mope.° O shame, where is thy blush?
Rebellious hell,
If thou canst mutine° in a matron's bones,
To flaming youth let virtue be as wax
And melt in her own fire.° Proclaim no shame　　　　　85
When the compulsive ardor gives the charge,
Since frost itself as actively doth burn,
And reason panders will.°
QUEEN　　　　　　　　　　Oh, Hamlet, speak no more!

---

64 **ear** of grain　65 **Blasting** blighting　66 **leave** cease　67 **batten** gorge | **moor**
barren or marshy ground (suggesting also "dark-skinned")　69 **The heyday . . .
blood** (the blood was thought to be the source of sexual desire)　71 **sense**
perception through the five senses (the functions of the middle or sensible soul)
73 **apoplexed** paralyzed | **err** so err　74–76 **Nor . . . difference** nor could your
physical senses ever have been so enthralled to *ecstasy* or lunacy that they could not
distinguish to some degree between Hamlet Senior and Claudius　77 **cozened**
cheated | **hoodman-blind** blindman's buff (in this game, says Hamlet, the devil
must have pushed Claudius toward Gertrude while she was blindfolded)　79 **sans**
without　81 **mope** be dazed, act aimlessly　83 **mutine** mutiny　84–85 **To . . . fire**
when it comes to sexually passionate youth, let virtue melt like a candle or stick of
sealing wax held over a candle flame (there's no point in hoping for self-restraint
among young people when matronly women set such a bad example)
86–88 **Proclaim . . . will** call it no shameful business when the compelling ardor of
youth delivers the attack, commits lechery, since the *frost* of advanced age burns
with as active a fire of lust and reason perverts itself by fomenting lust rather than
restraining it

Thou turn'st mine eyes into my very soul,
And there I see such black and grainèd° spots   90
As will not leave their tinct.°

HAMLET   Nay, but to live
In the rank sweat of an enseamèd° bed,
Stewed° in corruption, honeying and making love
Over the nasty sty!°

QUEEN   Oh, speak to me no more!   95
These words like daggers enter in my ears.
No more, sweet Hamlet!

HAMLET   A murderer and a villain,
A slave that is not twentieth part the tithe°
Of your precedent lord,° a vice° of kings,
A cutpurse of the empire and the rule,   100
That from a shelf the precious diadem stole
And put it in his pocket!

QUEEN   No more!

Enter Ghost [in his nightgown°]

HAMLET   A king of shreds and patches—°
Save me, and hover o'er me with your wings,
You heavenly guards! What would your gracious figure?   105

QUEEN   Alas, he's mad!

HAMLET   Do you not come your tardy son to chide,
That, lapsed in time and passion,° lets go by
Th'important° acting of your dread command?
Oh, say!

GHOST   Do not forget. This visitation   110
Is but to whet° thy almost blunted purpose.
But look, amazement° on thy mother sits.
Oh, step between her and her fighting soul!
Conceit° in weakest bodies strongest works.

90 **grainèd** ingrained, indelible   91 **leave their tinct** surrender their dark stain
92 **enseamèd** saturated in the grease and filth of passionate lovemaking   93 **Stewed**
soaked, bathed (with a suggestion of "stew," brothel)   94 **over . . . sty** (like
barnyard animals)   98 **tithe** tenth part   99 **precedent lord** former husband │ **vice**
(from the morality plays, a model of iniquity and a buffoon)   103.1 s.d. ***nightgown***
a robe for indoor wear   103 **A king . . . patches** a king whose splendor is all sham;
a clown or fool dressed in motley   108 **lapsed . . . passion** having let time and
passion slip away   109 **Th'important** the importunate, urgent   111 **whet** sharpen
112 **amazement** distraction   114 **Conceit** imagination

Speak to her, Hamlet.

HAMLET   How is it with you, lady?   115

QUEEN   Alas, how is't with you,

That you do bend your eye on vacancy,

And with th'incorporal° air do hold discourse?

Forth at your eyes your spirits wildly peep,

And, as the sleeping soldiers in th'alarm,°   120

Your bedded° hair, like life in excrements,°

Start up and stand on end. O gentle son,

Upon the heat and flame of thy distemper°

Sprinkle cool patience. Whereon do you look?

HAMLET   On him, on him! Look you how pale he glares!   125

His form and cause conjoined,° preaching to stones,

Would make them capable.°—Do not look upon me,

Lest with this piteous action you convert

My stern effects.° Then what I have to do

Will want true color—tears perchance for blood.°   130

QUEEN   To whom do you speak this?

HAMLET   Do you see nothing there?

QUEEN   Nothing at all, yet all that is I see.

HAMLET   Nor did you nothing hear?

QUEEN   No, nothing but ourselves.   135

HAMLET   Why, look you there, look how it steals away!

My father, in his habit° as° he lived!

Look where he goes even now out at the portal!

Exit Ghost

QUEEN   This is the very° coinage of your brain.

This bodiless creation ecstasy   140

Is very cunning in.°

HAMLET   Ecstasy?

My pulse as yours doth temperately keep time,

---

118 **th'incorporal** the immaterial   120 **as . . . th'alarm** like soldiers called out of
sleep by an alarum   121 **bedded** laid flat | **like life in excrements** as though hair,
an outgrowth of the body, had a life of its own (hair was thought to be lifeless
because it lacks sensation, and so its standing on end would be unnatural and
ominous)   123 **distemper** disorder   126 **His . . . conjoined** his appearance joined to
his cause for speaking   127 **capable** capable of feeling, receptive   128–29 **convert
. . . effects** divert me from my stern duty   130 **want . . . blood** lack plausibility so
that (with a play on the normal sense of *color*) I shall shed colorless tears instead of
blood   137 **habit** clothes | **as** as when   139 **very** mere   140–41 **This . . . in**
madness is skillful in creating this kind of hallucination

V. 8. p. 335.   *Lud. Du Guernier inv. et Sculp. 20*

"Hamlet and the Ghost in Gertrude's Chamber." This eighteenth-century depiction of the scene in which Hamlet sees his father's ghost not in a night-gown (103.1 s.d.) but in full armor in Gertrude's chamber illustrates her confusion at Hamlet's apparent madness. Because the ghost is invisible to her, she can only exclaim: "Alas, how is't with you, / That you do bend your eye on vacancy" (3.4.116–17). (J. Tonson, *The Works of Shakespeare*, vol. VIII [London, 1728]. By permission of the Folger Shakespeare Library.)

And makes as healthful music. It is not madness
That I have uttered. Bring me to the test,
And I the matter will reword,° which madness   145
Would gambol° from. Mother, for love of grace,
Lay not that flattering unction° to your soul
That not your trespass but my madness speaks.
It will but skin° and film the ulcerous place,
Whiles rank corruption, mining° all within,   150
Infects unseen. Confess yourself to heaven,
Repent what's past, avoid what is to come,
And do not spread the compost° on the weeds
To make them ranker. Forgive me this my virtue;°
For in the fatness° of these pursy° times   155
Virtue itself of vice must pardon beg,
Yea, curb° and woo for leave° to do him good.
QUEEN   Oh, Hamlet, thou hast cleft my heart in twain.
HAMLET   Oh, throw away the worser part of it,
And live the purer with the other half.   160
Good night. But go not to my uncle's bed;
Assume a virtue, if you have it not.
That monster, custom, who all sense doth eat,°
Of habits devil,° is angel yet in this,
That to the use of actions fair and good   165
He likewise gives a frock or livery°
That aptly° is put on. Refrain tonight,
And that shall lend a kind of easiness
To the next abstinence; the next more easy;
For use° almost can change the stamp of nature,°   170
And either° . . . the devil, or throw him out
With wondrous potency. Once more, good night;

---

145 reword repeat word for word   **146 gambol** skip away   **147 unction** ointment
149 skin grow a skin over   **150 mining** working under the surface   **153 compost**
manure   **154 this my virtue** my virtuous talk in reproving you   **155 fatness**
grossness | **pursy** flabby, out of shape   **157 curb** bow, bend the knee | **leave**
permission   **163 who . . . eat** which consumes and overwhelms the physical senses
164 Of habits devil devil-like in prompting evil habits   **166 livery** an outer
appearance, a customary garb (and hence a predisposition easily assumed in time of
stress)   **167 aptly** readily   **170 use** habit | **the stamp of nature** our inborn traits
171 And either (a defective line, often emended by inserting the word "master" after
either, following the Third Quarto and early editors, or some other word such as
"shame," "lodge," "curb," or "house")

And when you are desirous to be blest,
I'll blessing beg of you.° For this same lord,

                          [*pointing to Polonius*]

I do repent; but heaven hath pleased it so   175
To punish me with this, and this with me,°
That I must be their scourge and minister.°
I will bestow° him, and will answer° well
The death I gave him. So, again, good night.
I must be cruel only to be kind.   180
This° bad begins, and worse remains behind.°
One word more, good lady.

QUEEN   What shall I do?

HAMLET   Not this by no means that I bid you do:
Let the bloat° king tempt you again to bed,
Pinch wanton° on your cheek, call you his mouse,   185
And let him, for a pair of reechy° kisses,
Or paddling° in your neck with his damned fingers,
Make you to ravel all this matter out°
That I essentially am not in madness,
But mad in craft.° 'Twere good° you let him know,   190
For who that's but a queen, fair, sober, wise,
Would from a paddock,° from a bat, a gib,°
Such dear concernings° hide? Who would do so?
No, in despite of sense and secrecy,°
Unpeg the basket° on the house's top,   195
Let the birds fly, and like the famous ape,°
To try conclusions,° in the basket creep

173–74 **when . . . you** when you are ready to be penitent and seek God's blessing, I will ask your blessing as a dutiful son should **176 To punish . . . with me** to seek retribution from me for killing Polonius, and from him through my means **177 their scourge and minister** agent of heavenly retribution **178 bestow** stow, dispose of | **answer** account or pay for **181 This** the killing of Polonius | **behind** to come **184 bloat** bloated **185 Pinch wanton** leave his love pinches on your cheeks, branding you as wanton **186 reechy** dirty, filthy **187 paddling** fingering amorously **188 ravel . . . out** unravel, disclose **190 in craft** by cunning | **good** (said sarcastically; also the following eight lines) **192 paddock** toad | **gib** tomcat **193 dear concernings** important affairs **194 sense and secrecy** secrecy that common sense requires **195 Unpeg the basket** open the cage, let out the secret **196 famous ape** (in a story now lost) **197 try conclusions** test the outcome (in which the ape apparently enters a cage from which birds have been released and then tries to fly out of the cage as they have done, falling to its death)

And break your own neck down.°
QUEEN   Be thou assured, if words be made of breath,
  And breath of life, I have no life to breathe   200
  What thou hast said to me.
HAMLET   I must to England. You know that?
QUEEN   Alack,
  I had forgot. 'Tis so concluded on.
HAMLET   There's letters sealed, and my two schoolfellows,
  Whom I will trust as I will adders fanged,   205
  They bear the mandate; they must sweep my way
  And marshal me to knavery.° Let it work.°
  For 'tis the sport to have the engineer°
  Hoist with° his own petard,° and 't shall go hard
  But I will° delve one yard below their mines°   210
  And blow them at the moon. Oh, 'tis most sweet
  When in one line° two crafts° directly meet.
  This man shall set me packing.°
  I'll lug the guts into the neighbor room.
  Mother, good night indeed. This counselor   215
  Is now most still, most secret, and most grave,
  Who was in life a foolish prating knave.—
  Come, sir, to draw toward an end° with you.—
  Good night, mother.
        Exeunt [separately, Hamlet dragging in Polonius]

❖

198 **down** in the fall   206–7 **sweep . . . knavery** sweep a path before me and
conduct me to some *knavery* or treachery prepared for me   207 **work** proceed
208 **engineer** maker of *engines* of war   209 **Hoist with** blown up by | **petard** an
explosive used to blow in a door or make a breach   209–10 **'t shall . . . will** unless
luck is against me, I will   210 **mines** tunnels used in warfare to undermine the
enemy's emplacements; Hamlet will countermine by going under their mines
212 **in one line** mines and countermines on a collision course, or the countermines
directly below the mines | **crafts** acts of guile, plots   213 **set me packing** set me to
making schemes, and set me to lugging (him), and, also, send me off in a hurry
218 **draw . . . end** finish up (with a pun on *draw*, "pull")

ACT 4
SCENE 1

Location: The castle

Enter King and Queen,° with Rosencrantz and Guildenstern

KING There's matter° in these sighs, these profound heaves.°
You must translate; 'tis fit we understand them.
Where is your son?

QUEEN Bestow this place on us a little while.

                [Exeunt Rosencrantz and Guildenstern]
Ah, mine own lord, what have I seen tonight!   5

KING What, Gertrude? How does Hamlet?

QUEEN Mad as the sea and wind when both contend
Which is the mightier. In his lawless fit,
Behind the arras hearing something stir,
Whips out his rapier, cries, "A rat, a rat!"   10
And in this brainish apprehension° kills
The unseen good old man.

KING   Oh, heavy° deed!
It had been so with us,° had we been there.
His liberty is full of threats to all—
To you yourself, to us, to everyone.   15
Alas, how shall this bloody deed be answered?°
It will be laid to us, whose providence°
Should have kept short,° restrained, and out of haunt°
This mad young man. But so much was our love,
We would not understand what was most fit,   20
But, like the owner of a foul disease,

0.1 s.d. *Enter . . . Queen* (some editors argue that Gertrude does not in fact exit at
the end of 3.4 and that the scene is continuous here; it is true that the Folio ends 3.4
with "*Exit Hamlet tugging in Polonius,*" not naming Gertrude, and opens 4.1 with
"*Enter King;*" yet the Second Quarto concludes 3.4 with a simple "*Exit,*" which
often stands ambiguously for a single exit or an exeunt in early modern texts, and
then starts 4.1 with "*Enter King, and Queene, with Rosencraus and
Guyldensterne*"; the King's opening lines in 4.1 suggest that he has had time, during
a brief intervening pause, to become aware of Gertrude's highly wrought emotional
state; in line 35, the King refers to Gertrude's *closet* as though it were elsewhere; the
differences between the Second Quarto and the Folio offer an alternative staging; in
either case, 4.1 follows swiftly upon 3.4) **1 matter** significance | **heaves** heavy
sighs **11 brainish apprehension** frenzied misapprehension **12 heavy** grievous
13 us me (the royal "we"; also in line 15) **16 answered** explained **17 providence**
foresight **18 short** on a short tether | **out of haunt** secluded

To keep it from divulging,° let it feed
Even on the pith of life. Where is he gone?
QUEEN   To draw apart the body he hath killed,
O'er whom his very madness, like some ore°   25
Among a mineral° of metals base,
Shows itself pure: 'a weeps for what is done.
KING   Oh, Gertrude, come away!
The sun no sooner shall the mountains touch
But we will ship him hence, and this vile deed   30
We must with all our majesty and skill
Both countenance and excuse.—Ho, Guildenstern!

Enter Rosencrantz and Guildenstern

Friends both, go join you with some further aid.
Hamlet in madness hath Polonius slain,
And from his mother's closet hath he dragged him.   35
Go seek him out, speak fair,° and bring the body
Into the chapel. I pray you, haste in this.

[Exeunt Rosencrantz and Guildenstern]

Come, Gertrude, we'll call up our wisest friends
And let them know both what we mean to do
And what's untimely done°   40
Whose whisper o'er the world's diameter,°
As level° as the cannon to his blank,°
Transports his poisoned shot, may miss our name
And hit the woundless° air. Oh, come away!
My soul is full of discord and dismay.   45

Exeunt

❖

22 **from divulging** from becoming publicly known   25 **ore** vein of gold   26 **mineral** mine   32 **countenance** put the best face on   36 **fair** gently, courteously   40 **And . . . done** (a defective line; conjectures as to the missing words include "so, haply, slander" [Capell and others]; "for, haply, slander" [Theobald and others]; and "so envious slander" [Jenkins])   41 **diameter** extent from side to side   42 **As level** with as direct aim | **his blank** its target at point-blank range   44 **woundless** invulnerable

ACT 4
SCENE 2

Location: The castle

Enter Hamlet

HAMLET　Safely stowed.

ROSENCRANTZ, GUILDENSTERN *(within)*　Hamlet! Lord Hamlet!

HAMLET　But soft, what noise? Who calls on Hamlet? Oh, here
they come.

Enter Rosencrantz and Guildenstern

ROSENCRANTZ

What have you done, my lord, with the dead body?　　　　5

HAMLET　Compounded it with dust, whereto 'tis kin.

ROSENCRANTZ　Tell us where 'tis, that we may take it thence
And bear it to the chapel.

HAMLET　Do not believe it.

ROSENCRANTZ　Believe what?　　　　10

HAMLET　That I can keep your counsel and not mine own.°
Besides, to be demanded of° a sponge, what replication°
should be made by the son of a king?

ROSENCRANTZ　Take you me for a sponge, my lord?

HAMLET　Ay, sir, that soaks up the King's countenance,° his　　15
rewards, his authorities.° But such officers do the King best
service in the end. He keeps them, like an ape, an apple, in
the corner of his jaw, first mouthed to be last swallowed.
When he needs what you have gleaned, it is but squeezing
you, and, sponge, you shall be dry again.　　　　20

ROSENCRANTZ　I understand you not, my lord.

HAMLET　I am glad of it. A knavish speech sleeps in° a foolish
ear.

ROSENCRANTZ　My lord, you must tell us where the body is and
go with us to the King.　　　　25

---

11 That . . . own don't expect me to do as you bid me and not follow my own
counsel　**12 demanded of** questioned by | **replication** reply　**15 countenance**
favor　**16 authorities** delegated power, influence　**22 sleeps in** has no meaning to

HAMLET   The body° is with the King, but the King is not with
the body. The King is a thing—
GUILDENSTERN   A thing, my lord?
HAMLET   Of nothing.° Bring me to him. Hide fox, and all after!°

Exeunt [running]

❖

ACT 4
SCENE 3

Location: The castle

Enter King, and two or three

KING   I have sent to seek him, and to find the body.
How dangerous is it that this man goes loose!
Yet must not we put the strong law on him.
He's loved of° the distracted° multitude,
Who like not in their judgment, but their eyes,°   5
And where 'tis so, th'offender's scourge is weighed,
But never the offense.° To bear all smooth and even,°
This sudden sending him away must seem
Deliberate pause.° Diseases desperate grown
By desperate appliance° are relieved,   10
Or not at all.

Enter Rosencrantz, [Guildenstern,] and all the rest

How now, what hath befall'n?

26–27 **The . . . body** (perhaps alludes to the legal commonplace of "the king's two
bodies," which drew a distinction between the sacred office of kingship and the
particular mortal who possessed it at any given time; hence, although Claudius's
body is necessarily a part of him, true kingship is not contained in it; similarly,
Claudius will have Polonius's body when it is found, but there is no kingship in this
business either)   29 **Of nothing** (1) of no account (2) lacking the essence of kingship,
as in lines 26–27 and note | **Hide . . . after** (an old signal cry in the game of
hide-and-seek, suggesting that Hamlet now runs away from them)

4 **of** by | **distracted** fickle, unstable   5 **Who . . . eyes** who choose not by judgment
but by appearance   6–7 **th'offender's . . . offense** the populace often takes umbrage
at the severity of a punishment without taking into account the gravity of the crime
7 **To . . . even** to manage the business in an unprovocative way   9 **Deliberate pause**
carefully considered action   10 **appliance** remedies

ROSENCRANTZ   Where the dead body is bestowed, my lord,
We cannot get from him.

KING   But where is he?

ROSENCRANTZ
Without,° my lord; guarded, to know your pleasure.

KING   Bring him before us.   15

ROSENCRANTZ [*calling*]   Ho! Bring in the lord.

                              They enter [with Hamlet]

KING   Now, Hamlet, where's Polonius?

HAMLET   At supper.

KING   At supper? Where?

HAMLET   Not where he eats, but where 'a is eaten. A certain   20
convocation of politic worms° are e'en° at him. Your worm°
is your only emperor for diet.° We fat all creatures else to fat
us, and we fat ourselves for maggots. Your fat king and your
lean beggar is but variable service°—two dishes, but to one
table. That's the end.   25

KING   Alas, alas!

HAMLET   A man may fish with the worm that hath eat° of a
king, and eat of the fish that hath fed of that worm.

KING   What dost thou mean by this?

HAMLET   Nothing but to show you how a king may go a   30
progress° through the guts of a beggar.

KING   Where is Polonius?

HAMLET   In heaven. Send thither to see. If your messenger find
him not there, seek him i'th'other place yourself. But if
indeed you find him not within this month, you shall nose°   35
him as you go up the stairs into the lobby.

KING [*to some attendants*]   Go seek him there.

HAMLET   'A will stay till you come.   [*Exeunt attendants*]

KING   Hamlet, this deed, for thine especial safety—
Which we do tender,° as we dearly° grieve   40

---

14 Without outside   **21 politic worms** crafty worms (suited to a master spy like
Polonius) | **e'en** even now | **Your worm** your average worm (compare *your fat
king and your lean beggar* in lines 23–24)   **22 diet** food, eating (with a punning
reference to the Diet of Worms, a famous *convocation* held in 1521)   **24 service**
food served at table (worms feed on kings and beggars alike)   **27 eat** eaten
(pronounced *et*)   **31 progress** royal journey of state   **35 nose** smell   **40 tender**
regard, hold dear | **dearly** intensely

For that which thou hast done—must send thee hence
With fiery quickness. Therefore prepare thyself.
The bark° is ready, and the wind at help,
Th'associates tend,° and everything is bent°
For England.

HAMLET   For England!

KING   Ay, Hamlet.

HAMLET   Good.   45

KING   So is it, if thou knew'st our purposes.

HAMLET   I see a cherub° that sees them. But come, for England!
Farewell, dear mother.

KING   Thy loving father, Hamlet.

HAMLET   My mother. Father and mother is man and wife, man   50
and wife is one flesh, and so, my mother. Come, for England!
                                                        Exit

KING   Follow him at foot;° tempt him with speed aboard.
Delay it not. I'll have him hence tonight.
Away! For everything is sealed and done
That else leans on° th'affair. Pray you, make haste.   55
                          [*Exeunt all but the King*]
And, England,° if my love thou hold'st at aught°—
As my great power thereof may give thee sense,°
Since yet thy cicatrice° looks raw and red
After the Danish sword, and thy free awe°
Pays homage to us—thou mayst not coldly set°   60
Our sovereign process,° which imports at full,°
By letters congruing° to that effect,
The present° death of Hamlet. Do it, England,
For like the hectic° in my blood he rages,
And thou must cure me. Till I know 'tis done,   65
Howe'er my haps, my joys were ne'er begun.°
                                                        Exit

---

43 bark sailing vessel   **44 tend** wait ǀ **bent** in readiness   **47 cherub** (cherubim are angels of knowledge; Hamlet hints that both he and heaven are onto Claudius's tricks)   **52 at foot** close behind, at heel   **55 leans on** bears upon, is related to   **56 England** King of England ǀ **at aught** at any value   **57 As . . . sense** for so my great power may give you a just appreciation of the importance of valuing my love   **58 cicatrice** scar   **59 free awe** unconstrained show of respect   **60 coldly set** regard with indifference   **61 process** command ǀ **imports at full** conveys specific directions for   **62 congruing** agreeing   **63 present** immediate   **64 hectic** persistent fever   **66 Howe'er . . . begun** whatever else happens, I cannot begin to be happy

❖

ACT 4
SCENE 4

Location: The coast of Denmark

Enter Fortinbras with his army over the stage

FORTINBRAS Go, Captain, from me greet the Danish king.
Tell him that by his license° Fortinbras
Craves the conveyance° of a promised march
Over his kingdom. You know the rendezvous.
If that His Majesty would aught with us,   5
We shall express our duty in his eye;°
And let him know so.

CAPTAIN   I will do't, my lord.

FORTINBRAS Go softly° on.   *[Exeunt all but the Captain]*

Enter Hamlet, Rosencrantz, [Guildenstern,] etc.

HAMLET Good sir, whose powers° are these?

CAPTAIN They are of Norway, sir.   10

HAMLET How purposed, sir, I pray you?

CAPTAIN Against some part of Poland.

HAMLET Who commands them, sir?

CAPTAIN The nephew to old Norway, Fortinbras.

HAMLET Goes it against the main° of Poland, sir,   15
Or for some frontier?

CAPTAIN Truly to speak, and with no addition,°
We go to gain a little patch of ground
That hath in it no profit but the name.
To pay° five ducats, five, I would not farm it;°   20
Nor will it yield to Norway or the Pole
A ranker° rate, should it be sold in fee.°

HAMLET Why, then the Polack never will defend it.

CAPTAIN Yes, it is already garrisoned.

---

2 **license** permission   3 **conveyance** unhindered passage   6 **We . . . eye** I will come pay my respects in person   8 **softly** slowly, circumspectly   9 **powers** forces   15 **main** main part   17 **addition** exaggeration   20 **To pay** for a yearly rental of | **farm it** take a lease of it   22 **ranker** higher | **in fee** fee simple, outright

HAMLET Two thousand souls and twenty thousand ducats   25
Will not debate the question of this straw.°
This is th'impostume° of much wealth and peace,
That inward breaks,° and shows no cause without°
Why the man dies. I humbly thank you, sir.
CAPTAIN God b'wi'you, sir.   [*Exit*]
ROSENCRANTZ   Will't please you go, my lord?   30
HAMLET I'll be with you straight. Go a little before.
                    [*Exeunt all except Hamlet*]
How all occasions do inform against° me
And spur my dull revenge! What is a man,
If his chief good and market of° his time
Be but to sleep and feed? A beast, no more.   35
Sure he that made us with such large discourse,°
Looking before and after,° gave us not
That capability and godlike reason
To fust° in us unused. Now, whether it be
Bestial oblivion,° or some craven° scruple   40
Of thinking too precisely° on th'event°—
A thought which, quartered, hath but one part wisdom
And ever three parts coward—I do not know
Why yet I live to say "This thing's to do,"
Sith° I have cause, and will, and strength, and means   45
To do't. Examples gross° as earth exhort me:
Witness this army of such mass and charge,°
Led by a delicate and tender° prince,
Whose spirit with divine ambition puffed
Makes mouths° at the invisible event,°   50
Exposing what is mortal and unsure
To all that fortune, death, and danger dare,°

---

26 **debate . . . straw** argue about this trifling matter   27 **th'impostume** the abscess
28 **inward breaks** festers within | **without** externally   32 **inform against**
denounce; take shape against   34 **market of** profit of   36 **discourse** power of
reasoning   37 **Looking before and after** able to review past events and anticipate
the future   39 **fust** grow moldy   40 **oblivion** forgetfulness | **craven** cowardly
41 **precisely** scrupulously | **th'event** the outcome   45 **Sith** since   46 **gross** obvious
47 **charge** expense   48 **delicate and tender** of fine and youthful qualities   50 **Makes
mouths** makes scornful faces | **invisible event** unforeseeable outcome   52 **dare**
could do (to him)

Even for an eggshell. Rightly to be great
Is not to stir without great argument,
But greatly to find quarrel in a straw   55
When honor's at the stake.° How stand I, then,
That have a father killed, a mother stained,
Excitements of my reason and my blood,°
And let all sleep, while to my shame I see
The imminent death of twenty thousand men   60
That for a fantasy° and trick° of fame
Go to their graves like beds, fight for a plot°
Whereon the numbers cannot try the cause,°
Which is not tomb enough and continent°
To hide the slain? Oh, from this time forth   65
My thoughts be bloody or be nothing worth!

                                                          Exit

❖

ACT 4
SCENE 5

Location: The castle

Enter Horatio, [Queen] Gertrude, and a Gentleman

QUEEN I will not speak with her.
GENTLEMAN   She is importunate,
  Indeed distract.° Her mood will needs be pitied.
QUEEN What would she have?
GENTLEMAN She speaks much of her father, says she hears
  There's tricks° i'th' world, and hems,° and beats her heart,°   5
  Spurns enviously at straws,° speaks things in doubt°
  That carry but half sense. Her speech is nothing,
  Yet the unshapèd use° of it doth move

53–56 Rightly . . . stake true greatness is not a matter of being moved to action solely by a great cause; rather, it is to respond greatly to an apparently trivial cause when honor is at the stake **58 blood** (the supposed seat of the passions) **61 fantasy** fanciful caprice, illusion | **trick** trifle, deceit **62 plot** plot of ground **63 Whereon . . . cause** on which there is insufficient room for the soldiers needed to fight for it **64 continent** receptacle, container

2 distract out of her mind **5 tricks** deceptions | **hems** clears her throat, makes "hmm" sounds | **heart** breast **6 Spurns . . . straws** kicks spitefully, takes offense at trifles | **in doubt** of obscure meaning **8 unshapèd use** incoherent manner

The hearers to collection;° they yawn° at it,
And botch° the words up fit to their own thoughts,   10
Which,° as her winks and nods and gestures yield° them,
Indeed would make one think there might be thought,
Though nothing sure, yet much unhappily.°
HORATIO 'Twere good she were spoken with, for she may strew
Dangerous conjectures in ill-breeding° minds.   15
QUEEN Let her come in.   [*Exit Gentleman*]
[*Aside*] To my sick soul, as sin's true nature is,
Each toy° seems prologue to some great amiss.°
So full of artless jealousy is guilt,
It spills itself in fearing to be spilt.°   20

> *Enter Ophelia° [distracted]*

OPHELIA Where is the beauteous majesty of Denmark?
QUEEN How now, Ophelia?
OPHELIA (*she sings*)

> "How should I your true love know
>   From another one?
> By his cockle hat° and staff,   25
>   And his sandal shoon."°

QUEEN Alas, sweet lady, what imports this song?
OPHELIA Say you? Nay, pray you, mark.

> "He is dead and gone, lady,   (*Song*)
>   He is dead and gone;   30
> At his head a grass-green turf,
>   At his heels a stone."

Oho!°

9 **collection** inference, a guess at some sort of meaning | **yawn** gape, wonder; grasp
(the Folio reading, "aim," is possible) 10 **botch** patch 11 **Which** which words |
yield deliver, represent 12–13 **there might . . . unhappily** that a great deal could
be guessed at of a most unfortunate nature, even if one couldn't be at all sure
15 **ill-breeding** prone to suspect the worst and to make mischief 18 **toy** trifle |
amiss calamity 19–20 **So . . . spilt** guilt is so burdened with conscience and
guileless fear of detection that it reveals itself through apprehension of disaster
20.1 s.d. **Enter Ophelia** (in the First Quarto, Ophelia enters, "*playing on a lute, and
her hair down, singing*") 25 **cockle hat** hat with cockleshell stuck in it as a sign
that the wearer had been a pilgrim to the shrine of Saint James of Compostella in
Spain 26 **shoon** shoes 33 **Oho!** (perhaps a sigh)

QUEEN Nay, but Ophelia—
OPHELIA   Pray you, mark.
   [*Sings*] "White his shroud as the mountain snow"—   35

Enter King

QUEEN Alas, look here, my lord.
OPHELIA   "Larded° with sweet flowers;   (*Song*)
     Which bewept to the ground did not go
     With true-love showers."°

KING How do you, pretty lady?   40
OPHELIA Well, God 'ild° you! They say the owl° was a baker's
   daughter. Lord, we know what we are, but know not what
   we may be. God be at your table!
KING Conceit° upon her father.
OPHELIA Pray let's have no words of this; but when they ask 45
   you what it means, say you this:

     "Tomorrow is Saint Valentine's day,   (*Song*)
       All in the morning betime,°
     And I a maid at your window,
       To be your Valentine.   50
     Then up he rose, and donned his clothes,
       And dupped° the chamber door,
     Let in the maid, that out a maid
       Never departed more."

KING Pretty Ophelia—   55
OPHELIA Indeed, la, without an oath, I'll make an end on't:
                            [*Sings*]
     "By Gis° and by Saint Charity,
       Alack, and fie for shame!
     Young men will do't, if they come to't;
       By Cock,° they are to blame.   60

---

37 Larded strewn, bedecked **39 showers** tears **41 God 'ild** God yield or reward |
owl (refers to a legend about a baker's daughter who was turned into an owl for
being ungenerous when Jesus begged a loaf of bread) **44 Conceit** fancy, brooding
48 betime early **52 dupped** did up, opened **57 Gis** Jesus **60 Cock** (a perversion
of "God" in oaths; here also with a quibble on the slang word for penis)

Quoth she, 'Before you tumbled me,
    You promised me to wed.'"

He answers:

  "'So would I ha' done, by yonder sun,
    An° thou hadst not come to my bed.'"   65

KING How long hath she been thus?

OPHELIA I hope all will be well. We must be patient, but I
cannot choose but weep to think they would lay him i'th'
cold ground. My brother shall know of it. And so I thank
you for your good counsel. Come, my coach! Good night, 70
ladies, good night, sweet ladies, good night, good night.
                                                [Exit]

KING *[to Horatio]*
  Follow her close. Give her good watch, I pray you.
                              [Exit Horatio]
  Oh, this is the poison of deep grief; it springs
  All from her father's death—and now behold!
  Oh, Gertrude, Gertrude,   75
  When sorrows come, they come not single spies,°
  But in battalions. First, her father slain;
  Next, your son gone, and he most violent author
  Of his own just remove;° the people muddied,°
  Thick and unwholesome in their thoughts and whispers 80
  For good Polonius' death—and we have done but greenly,°
  In hugger-mugger° to inter him; poor Ophelia
  Divided from herself and her fair judgment,
  Without the which we are pictures or mere beasts;
  Last, and as much containing° as all these,   85
  Her brother is in secret come from France,
  Feeds on this wonder, keeps himself in clouds,°
  And wants° not buzzers° to infect his ear

---

65 An if   **76 spies** scouts sent in advance of the main force   **79 remove** removal |
muddied stirred up, confused   **81 greenly** foolishly   **82 hugger-mugger** secret haste
85 as much containing as full of serious matter   **87 Feeds . . . clouds** feeds his
resentment on this whole shocking turn of events, keeps himself aloof and
mysterious   **88 wants** lacks | **buzzers** gossipers, informers

With pestilent speeches of his father's death,
Wherein necessity,° of matter beggared,°   90
Will nothing stick our person to arraign
In ear and ear.° Oh, my dear Gertrude, this,
Like to a murd'ring piece,° in many places
Gives me superfluous death.°   *A noise within*

QUEEN   Alack, what noise is this?

KING   Attend!°   95
Where is my Switzers?° Let them guard the door.

                          Enter a Messenger

What is the matter?

MESSENGER   Save yourself, my lord!
The ocean, overpeering of his list,°
Eats not the flats° with more impetuous° haste
Than young Laertes, in a riotous head,°   100
O'erbears your officers. The rabble call him lord,
And, as the world were now but to begin,
Antiquity forgot, custom not known,
The ratifiers and props of every word,°
They cry, "Choose we! Laertes shall be king!"   105
Caps,° hands, and tongues applaud it to the clouds,
"Laertes shall be king, Laertes king!"

QUEEN   How cheerfully on the false trail they cry!

                          A noise within

Oh, this is counter,° you false Danish dogs!

                          Enter Laertes with others

KING   The doors are broke.   110

---

90 necessity the need to invent some plausible explanation | **of matter beggared** unprovided with facts   **91–92 Will . . . ear** will not hesitate to accuse my (royal) person in everybody's ears   **93 murd'ring piece** cannon loaded so as to scatter its shot   **94 Gives . . . death** kills me over and over   **95 Attend!** guard me!   **96 Switzers** Swiss guards, mercenaries   **98 overpeering of his list** overflowing its shore, boundary   **99 flats** flatlands near shore | **impetuous** violent (perhaps also with the meaning of *impiteous* ["impitious," Q2], "pitiless")   **100 riotous head** insurrectionary advance   **102–4 And . . . word** and, as if the world were to be started all over afresh, utterly setting aside all ancient traditional customs that should confirm and underprop our every word and promise   **106 Caps** (the caps are thrown in the air)   **109 counter** (a hunting term, meaning to follow the trail in a direction opposite to that which the game has taken)

LAERTES   Where is this King?—Sirs, stand you all without.
ALL   No, let's come in.
LAERTES   I pray you, give me leave.
ALL   We will, we will.
LAERTES   I thank you. Keep the door.   [*Exeunt followers*]
                                 Oh, thou vile king,
   Give me my father!   115
QUEEN [*restraining him*]   Calmly, good Laertes.
LAERTES   That drop of blood that's calm proclaims me bastard,
   Cries cuckold to my father, brands the harlot
   Even here between° the chaste unsmirchèd brow
   Of my true mother.
KING   What is the cause, Laertes,   120
   That thy rebellion looks so giantlike?°
   Let him go, Gertrude. Do not fear our° person.
   There's such divinity doth hedge° a king
   That treason can but peep to what it would,°
   Acts little of his will.° Tell me, Laertes,   125
   Why thou art thus incensed. Let him go, Gertrude.
   Speak, man.
LAERTES   Where is my father?
KING   Dead.
QUEEN   But not by him.
KING   Let him demand his fill.
LAERTES   How came he dead? I'll not be juggled with.°
   To hell, allegiance! Vows, to the blackest devil!   130
   Conscience and grace, to the profoundest pit!
   I dare damnation. To this point I stand,°
   That both the worlds I give to negligence,°
   Let come what comes, only I'll be revenged
   Most throughly° for my father.   135
KING   Who shall stay you?
LAERTES   My will, not all the world's.°

119 between amidst   **121 giantlike** (recalling the rising of the giants of Greek
mythology against Olympus)   **122 fear our** fear for my   **123 hedge** protect, as with
a surrounding barrier   **124 can . . . would** can only peep furtively, as through a
barrier, at what it would intend   **125 Acts . . . will** (but) performs little of what it
intends   **129 juggled with** cheated, deceived   **132 To . . . stand** I am resolved in this
133 both . . . negligence both this world and the next are of no consequence to me
135 throughly thoroughly   **136 My will . . . world's** I'll stop (*stay*) when my will is
accomplished, not for anyone else's

And for° my means, I'll husband them so well
They shall go far with little.
KING   Good Laertes,
If you desire to know the certainty
Of your dear father, is't writ in your revenge   140
That, swoopstake,° you will draw both friend and foe,
Winner and loser?
LAERTES   None but his enemies.
KING   Will you know them, then?
LAERTES   To his good friends thus wide I'll ope my arms,
And like the kind life-rendering pelican°   145
Repast° them with my blood.
KING   Why, now you speak
Like a good child and a true gentleman.
That I am guiltless of your father's death,
And am most sensibly° in grief for it,
It shall as level° to your judgment 'pear   150
As day does to your eye.   *A noise within*
LAERTES   How now, what noise is that?

                              Enter Ophelia

KING   Let her come in.
LAERTES   O heat, dry up my brains! Tears seven times salt
Burn out the sense and virtue° of mine eye!
By heaven, thy madness shall be paid with weight°   155
Till our scale turn the beam.° O rose of May!
Dear maid, kind sister, sweet Ophelia!
O heavens, is't possible a young maid's wits
Should be as mortal as an old man's life?
Nature is fine in love, and where 'tis fine   160
It sends some precious instance of itself
After the thing it loves.°

137 for as for   141 swoopstake indiscriminately (literally, taking all stakes on the gambling table at once; *draw* is also a gambling term, meaning "take from")   145 pelican (refers to the belief that the female pelican fed its young with its own blood)   146 Repast feed   149 sensibly feelingly   150 level plain   154 virtue faculty, power   155 paid with weight repaid, avenged equally or more   156 beam crossbar of a balance   160–62 Nature . . . loves human nature is exquisitely sensitive in matters of love, and in cases of sudden loss it sends some precious part of itself after the lost object of that love (in this case, Ophelia's sanity deserts her out of sorrow for her lost father and perhaps too out of her love for Hamlet)

OPHELIA   "They bore him barefaced on the bier,   (*Song*)
    Hey non nonny, nonny, hey nonny,
  And in his grave rained many a tear—"   165

Fare you well, my dove!

LAERTES   Hadst thou thy wits and didst persuade revenge,
It could not move thus.

OPHELIA   You must sing "A-down a-down," and you "call him
a-down-a."° Oh, how the wheel° becomes it! It is the false   170
steward° that stole his master's daughter.

LAERTES   This nothing's more than matter.°

OPHELIA   There's rosemary,° that's for remembrance; pray you,
love, remember. And there is pansies;° that's for thoughts.

LAERTES   A document° in madness, thoughts and remembrance   175
fitted.

OPHELIA   There's fennel for you, and columbines.° There's rue°
for you, and here's some for me; we may call it herb of grace
o' Sundays. You must wear your rue with a difference.°
There's a daisy.° I would give you some violets,° but they   180
withered all when my father died. They say 'a made a good
end—

[*Sings*] "For bonny sweet Robin is all my joy."

LAERTES   Thought° and affliction, passion,° hell itself,
She turns to favor° and to prettiness.   185

169–70 You . . . a-down-a (Ophelia assigns the singing of refrains, like her own "hey non nonny," to others present)   **170 wheel** spinning wheel as accompaniment to the song, or refrain   **170–71 false steward** (the story is unknown)   **172 This . . . matter** this seeming nonsense is more eloquent than sane utterance   **173 rosemary** (used as a symbol of remembrance both at weddings and at funerals)   **174 pansies** (emblems of love and courtship; perhaps from French *pensées*, "thoughts")   **175 document** instruction, lesson   **177 There's fennel . . . columbines** (*fennel* betokens flattery; *columbines*, unchastity or ingratitude; throughout, Ophelia addresses her various listeners, giving one flower to one and another to another, perhaps with particular symbolic significance in each case) | **rue** (emblem of repentance—a signification that is evident in its popular name, *herb of grace*)   **179 with a difference** (a device used in heraldry to distinguish one family from another on the coat of arms, here suggesting that Ophelia and the others have different causes of sorrow and repentance; perhaps with a play on *rue* in the sense of "ruth," "pity")   **180 daisy** (emblem of love's victims and of faithlessness) | **violets** (emblems of faithfulness)   **184 Thought** melancholy | **passion** suffering   **185 favor** grace, beauty

OPHELIA   "And will 'a not come again?   (*Song*)
      And will 'a not come again?
          No, no, he is dead.
          Go to thy deathbed,
      He never will come again.   190

      "His beard was as white as snow,
      All flaxen was his poll.°
          He is gone, he is gone,
          And we cast away moan.
      God ha' mercy on his soul!"   195

And of all Christian souls, I pray God. God b'wi'you.
           [*Exit, followed by Gertrude*]
LAERTES   Do you see this, O God?
KING   Laertes, I must commune with your grief,
    Or you deny me right. Go but apart,
    Make choice of whom° your wisest friends you will,   200
    And they shall hear and judge twixt you and me.
    If by direct or by collateral hand°
    They find us touched,° we will our kingdom give,
    Our crown, our life, and all that we call ours
    To you in satisfaction; but if not,   205
    Be you content to lend your patience to us,
    And we shall jointly labor with your soul
    To give it due content.
LAERTES   Let this be so.
    His means of death, his obscure funeral—
    No trophy,° sword, nor hatchment° o'er his bones,   210
    No noble rite, nor formal ostentation°—
    Cry to be heard, as 'twere from heaven to earth,
    That° I must call't in question.°
KING   So you shall,
    And where th'offense is, let the great ax fall.
    I pray you, go with me.   215
                    Exeunt

---

192 poll head   **200 whom** whichever of   **202 collateral hand** indirect agency   **203 us touched** me implicated   **210 trophy** memorial | **hatchment** tablet displaying the armorial bearings of a deceased person   **211 ostentation** ceremony   **213 That** so that | **call't in question** demand an explanation

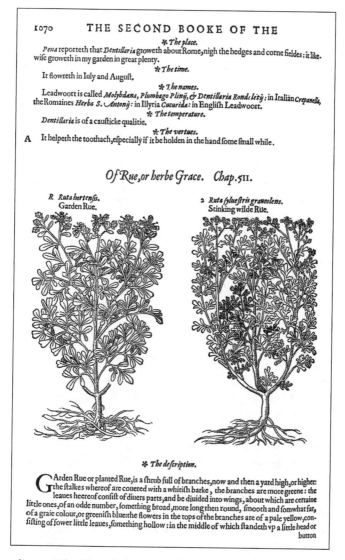

1070   THE SECOND BOOKE OF THE

✽ *The place.*

Pena reporteth that *Dentillaria* groweth about Rome, nigh the hedges and corne fieldes: it like-wise groweth in my garden in great plenty.

✽ *The time.*

It flowreth in Iuly and Auguſt.

✽ *The names.*

Leadwoort is called *Molybdana, Plumbago Plinÿ, & Dentillaria Rondeletÿ*: in Italian *Crepanella,* the Romaines *Herba S. Antonÿ*: in Illyria *Cucurida*: in Engliſh Leadwoort.

✽ *The temperature.*

Dentillaria is of a cauſticke qualitie.

✽ *The vertues.*

A   It helpeth the toothach, eſpecially if it be holden in the hand ſome ſmall while.

Of Rue, or herbe Grace.   Chap. 511.

R   *Ruta hortenſis.*
Garden Rue.

2   *Ruta ſylueſtris graueolens.*
Stinking wilde Rue.

✽ *The deſcription.*

GArden Rue or planted Rue, is a ſhrub full of branches, now and then a yard high, or higher: the ſtalkes whereof are couered with a whitiſh barke, the branches are more greene: the leaues heereof conſiſt of diuers parts, and be diuided into wings, about which are certaine little ones, of an odde number, ſomething broad, more long then round, ſmooth and ſomwhat fat, of a graie colour, or greeniſh blue: the flowers in the tops of the branches are of a pale yellow, con-ſiſting of fower little leaues, ſomething hollow: in the middle of which ſtandeth vp a little head or button

According to John Gerard, the leading herbalist of his day, "Rue, or herbe of Grace," is a medicinal drug that "provoketh urine, bringeth downe the sicknes, expellethe the dead childe and afterbirth, being inwardly taken or the decoction drunke. . . ." It is the only flower that Ophelia not only gives away but also reserves for herself: "There's rue for you, and here's some for me" (4.5.177–78). (John Gerard, *The Herbal or General Historie of Plants* [London, 1597]. By permission of the Folger Shakespeare Library.)

❖

ACT 4
SCENE 6

Location: The castle

Enter Horatio and others

HORATIO What are they that would speak with me?

GENTLEMAN Seafaring men, sir. They say they have letters° for
you.

HORATIO Let them come in.   [*Exit Gentleman*]
I do not know from what part of the world   5
I should be greeted, if not from Lord Hamlet.

Enter Sailors

FIRST SAILOR God bless you, sir.

HORATIO Let him bless thee too.

FIRST SAILOR 'A shall, sir, an't° please him. There's a letter for
you, sir—it came from th'ambassador° that was bound for   10
England—if your name be Horatio, as I am let to know it is.
[*He gives a letter*]

HORATIO [*reads*] "Horatio, when thou shalt have overlooked°
this, give these fellows some means° to the King; they have
letters for him. Ere we were two days old at sea, a pirate of
very warlike appointment° gave us chase. Finding ourselves   15
too slow of sail, we put on a compelled valor, and in the
grapple I boarded them. On the instant they got clear of our
ship, so I alone became their prisoner. They have dealt with
me like thieves of mercy,° but they knew what they did: I am
to do a good turn for them. Let the King have the letters I   20
have sent, and repair° thou to me with as much speed as thou
wouldest fly death. I have words to speak in thine ear will
make thee dumb, yet are they much too light for the bore° of
the matter. These good fellows will bring thee where I am.

---

2 **letters** a letter 9 **an't** if it 10 **th'ambassador** (Hamlet's ostensible role; see
3.3.3–4) 12 **overlooked** looked over 13 **means** means of access 15 **appointment**
equipage 19 **thieves of mercy** merciful thieves 21 **repair** come 23 **bore** caliber,
importance

Rosencrantz and Guildenstern hold their course for England.   25
Of them I have much to tell thee. Farewell.
                He that thou knowest thine, Hamlet."
Come, I will give you way° for these your letters,
And do't the speedier that you may direct me
To him from whom you brought them.   30

                                 Exeunt

❖

ACT 4
SCENE 7

Location: The castle

                           Enter King and Laertes

KING   Now must your conscience my acquittance seal,°
   And you must put me in your heart for friend,
   Sith° you have heard, and with a knowing ear,
   That he which hath your noble father slain
   Pursued my life.
LAERTES   It well appears. But tell me   5
   Why you proceeded not against these feats°
   So crimeful and so capital° in nature,
   As by your safety, greatness, wisdom, all things else,
   You mainly° were stirred up.
KING   Oh, for two special reasons,   10
   Which may to you perhaps seem much unsinewed,°
   But yet to me they're strong. The Queen his mother
   Lives almost by his looks, and for myself—
   My virtue or my plague, be it either which—
   She is so conjunctive° to my life and soul   15
   That, as the star moves not but in his° sphere,°
   I could not but by her. The other motive

---

28 **way** means of access

1 **my acquittance seal** confirm or acknowledge my innocence   3 **Sith** since   6 **feats** acts   7 **capital** punishable by death   9 **mainly** greatly   11 **unsinewed** weak   15 **conjunctive** closely united (an astronomical metaphor)   16 **his** its | **sphere** one of the hollow spheres in which, according to Ptolemaic astronomy, the planets were supposed to move

Why to a public count° I might not go
Is the great love the general gender° bear him,
Who, dipping all his faults in their affection,   20
Work° like the spring° that turneth wood to stone,
Convert his gyves° to graces, so that my arrows,
Too slightly timbered for so loud a wind,°
Would have reverted to my bow again
But not where I had aimed them.   25

LAERTES   And so have I a noble father lost,
A sister driven into desp'rate terms,°
Whose worth, if praises may go back° again,
Stood challenger on mount° of all the age
For her perfections. But my revenge will come.   30

KING   Break not your sleeps for that. You must not think
That we are made of stuff so flat and dull
That we can let our beard be shook with danger
And think it pastime. You shortly shall hear more.
I loved your father, and we love ourself;   35
And that, I hope, will teach you to imagine—

Enter a Messenger with letters

How now? What news?
MESSENGER   Letters, my lord, from Hamlet:
This to Your Majesty, this to the Queen.

[He gives letters]

KING   From Hamlet? Who brought them?
MESSENGER   Sailors, my lord, they say. I saw them not.   40
They were given me by Claudio. He received them
Of him that brought them.
KING   Laertes, you shall hear them.—
Leave us.   *[Exit Messenger]*
[He reads] "High and mighty, you shall know I am set
naked° on your kingdom. Tomorrow shall I beg leave to see   45

---

18 count account, reckoning, indictment   **19 general gender** common people
21 Work operate, act | **spring** a spring with such a concentration of lime that it
coats a piece of wood with limestone, in effect gilding and petrifying it   **22 gyves**
fetters (which, gilded by the people's praise, would look like badges of honor)   **23 Too
. . . wind** with too light a shaft for so powerful a gust (of popular sentiment)
27 terms state, condition   **28 go back** recall what she was   **29 on mount** set up on
high   **45 naked** destitute, unarmed, without following

your kingly eyes, when I shall, first asking your pardon,°
thereunto recount the occasion of my sudden and more
strange return.
Hamlet."
What should this mean? Are all the rest come back?   50
Or is it some abuse,° and no such thing?°

LAERTES Know you the hand?

KING   'Tis Hamlet's character.° "Naked!"
And in a postscript here he says "alone."
Can you devise° me?

LAERTES I am lost in it, my lord. But let him come.   55
It warms the very sickness in my heart
That I shall live and tell him to his teeth,
"Thus didst thou."°

KING   If it be so, Laertes—
As how should it be so? How otherwise?°—
Will you be ruled by me?

LAERTES   Ay, my lord,   60
So° you will not o'errule me to a peace.

KING To thine own peace. If he be now returned,
As checking at° his voyage, and that° he means
No more to undertake it, I will work him
To an exploit, now ripe in my device,°   65
Under the which he shall not choose but fall;
And for his death no wind of blame shall breathe,
But even his mother shall uncharge the practice°
And call it accident.

LAERTES   My lord, I will be ruled,
The rather if you could devise it so   70
That I might be the organ.°

KING   It falls right.
You have been talked of since your travel much,

---

46 pardon (for returning without authorization) **51 abuse** deceit | **no such thing**
not what the letter says **52 character** handwriting **54 devise** explain to **58 Thus
didst thou** here's for what you did to my father **59 As . . . otherwise?** how can this
(Hamlet's return) be true? yet how otherwise than true (since we have the evidence
of his letter)? **61 So** provided that **63 checking at** turning aside from (like a
falcon leaving the quarry to fly at a chance bird) | **that** if **65 device** devising,
invention **68 uncharge the practice** acquit the stratagem of being a plot **71 organ**
agent, instrument

And that in Hamlet's hearing, for a quality
Wherein they say you shine. Your sum of parts°
Did not together pluck such envy from him   75
As did that one, and that, in my regard,
Of the unworthiest siege.°

LAERTES   What part is that, my lord?

KING   A very ribbon in the cap of youth,
   Yet needful too, for youth no less becomes°
   The light and careless livery that it wears   80
   Than settled age his sables and his weeds
   Importing health and graveness.° Two months since
   Here was a gentleman of Normandy.
   I have seen myself, and served against, the French,
   And they can well° on horseback, but this gallant   85
   Had witchcraft in't; he grew unto his seat,
   And to such wondrous doing brought his horse
   As had he been incorpsed and demi-natured
   With the brave beast.° So far he topped° my thought
   That I in forgery° of shapes and tricks   90
   Come short of what he did.

LAERTES   A Norman was't?

KING   A Norman.

LAERTES   Upon my life, Lamord.

KING   The very same.

LAERTES   I know him well. He is the brooch° indeed
   And gem of all the nation.   95

KING   He made confession° of you,
   And gave you such a masterly report
   For art and exercise in your defense,°
   And for your rapier most especial,
   That he cried out 'twould be a sight indeed   100
   If one could match you. Th'escrimers° of their nation,

---

74 **Your . . . parts** all your other virtues   77 **unworthiest siege** least important rank
79 **no less becomes** is no less adorned by   81–82 **his sables . . . graveness** its rich
robes furred with sable and its garments denoting dignified well-being and
seriousness   85 **can well** are skilled   88–89 **As . . . beast** as if, centaurlike, he had
been made into one body with the horse, possessing half its nature   89 **topped**
surpassed   90 **forgery** fabrication   94 **brooch** ornament   96 **confession**
testimonial, admission of superiority   98 **For . . . defense** with respect to your skill
and practice with your weapon   101 **Th'escrimers** the fencers

He swore, had neither motion, guard, nor eye
If you opposed them. Sir, this report of his
Did Hamlet so envenom with his envy
That he could nothing do but wish and beg   105
Your sudden° coming o'er, to play° with you.
Now, out of this—
LAERTES   What out of this, my lord?
KING   Laertes, was your father dear to you?
Or are you like the painting of a sorrow,
A face without a heart?
LAERTES   Why ask you this?   110
KING   Not that I think you did not love your father,
But that I know love is begun by time,°
And that I see, in passages of proof,°
Time qualifies° the spark and fire of it.
There lives within the very flame of love   115
A kind of wick or snuff° that will abate it,
And nothing is at a like goodness still,°
For goodness, growing to a pleurisy,°
Dies in his own too much.° That° we would do,
We should do when we would; for this "would" changes   120
And hath abatements° and delays as many
As there are tongues, are hands, are accidents,°
And then this "should" is like a spendthrift sigh,°
That hurts by easing.° But, to the quick o'th'ulcer:°
Hamlet comes back. What would you undertake   125
To show yourself in deed your father's son
More than in words?
LAERTES   To cut his throat i'th' church.

---

106 **sudden** immediate | **play** fence   **112 begun by time** created by the right circumstance and hence subject to change   **113 passages of proof** actual well-attested instances   **114 qualifies** weakens, moderates   **116 snuff** the charred part of a candlewick   **117 nothing . . . still** nothing remains at a constant level of perfection   **118 pleurisy** excess, plethora (literally, a chest inflammation)   **119 in . . . much** of its own excess | **That** that which   **121 abatements** diminutions   **122 As . . . accidents** as there are tongues to dissuade, hands to prevent, and chance events to intervene   **123 spendthrift sigh** (an allusion to the belief that sighs draw blood from the heart)   **124 hurts by easing** costs the heart blood and wastes precious opportunity even while it affords emotional relief | **quick o'th'ulcer** heart of the matter

KING　No place, indeed, should murder sanctuarize;°
　　Revenge should have no bounds. But good Laertes,
　　Will you do this,° keep close within your chamber.　　130
　　Hamlet returned shall know you are come home.
　　We'll put on those shall° praise your excellence
　　And set a double varnish on the fame
　　The Frenchman gave you, bring you in fine° together,
　　And wager on your heads. He, being remiss,°　　135
　　Most generous,° and free from all contriving,
　　Will not peruse the foils, so that with ease,
　　Or with a little shuffling, you may choose
　　A sword unbated,° and in a pass of practice°
　　Requite him for your father.
LAERTES　　　　　　　　　　I will do't,　　140
　　And for that purpose I'll anoint my sword.
　　I bought an unction° of a mountebank°
　　So mortal that, but dip a knife in it,
　　Where it draws blood no cataplasm° so rare,
　　Collected from all simples° that have virtue°　　145
　　Under the moon,° can save the thing from death
　　That is but scratched withal. I'll touch my point
　　With this contagion, that if I gall° him slightly,
　　It may be death.
KING　　　　　　　Let's further think of this,
　　Weigh what convenience both of time and means　　150
　　May fit us to our shape.° If this should fail,
　　And that our drift look through our bad performance,°
　　'Twere better not assayed. Therefore this project
　　Should have a back or second, that might hold
　　If this did blast in proof.° Soft, let me see.　　155

---

128 sanctuarize protect from punishment (alludes to the right of sanctuary with which certain religious places were invested)　**130 Will you do this** if you wish to do this　**132 put on those shall** arrange for some to　**134 in fine** finally　**135 remiss** negligently unsuspicious　**136 generous** noble-minded　**139 unbated** not blunted, having no button | **pass of practice** treacherous thrust in an arranged bout　**142 unction** ointment | **mountebank** quack doctor　**144 cataplasm** plaster or poultice　**145 simples** herbs | **virtue** potency　**146 Under the moon** anywhere (with reference perhaps to the belief that herbs gathered at night had a special power)　**148 gall** graze, wound　**151 shape** part we propose to act　**152 drift . . . performance** intention should be made visible by our bungling　**155 blast in proof** come to grief when put to the test

We'll make a solemn wager on your cunnings°—
I ha 't!
When in your motion you are hot and dry—
As° make your bouts more violent to that end—
And that he calls for drink, I'll have prepared him   160
A chalice for the nonce,° whereon but sipping,
If he by chance escape your venomed stuck,°
Our purpose may hold there. But stay, what noise?

[*A cry within*]

Enter Queen

QUEEN   One woe doth tread upon another's heel,
So fast they follow. Your sister's drowned, Laertes.   165
LAERTES   Drowned! Oh, where?
QUEEN   There is a willow grows askant° the brook,
That shows his hoar leaves° in the glassy stream;
Therewith fantastic garlands did she make
Of crowflowers, nettles, daisies, and long purples,°   170
That liberal° shepherds give a grosser name,°
But our cold° maids do dead men's fingers call them.
There on the pendent° boughs her crownet° weeds
Clamb'ring to hang, an envious sliver° broke,
When down her weedy° trophies and herself   175
Fell in the weeping brook. Her clothes spread wide,
And mermaidlike awhile they bore her up,
Which time she chanted snatches of old lauds,°
As one incapable of° her own distress,
Or like a creature native and endued°   180
Unto that element. But long it could not be
Till that her garments, heavy with their drink,
Pulled the poor wretch from her melodious lay°

---

156 cunnings respective skills   **159 As** and you should   **161 nonce** occasion
162 stuck thrust (from *stoccado*, a fencing term)   **167 askant** aslant   **168 hoar
leaves** white or gray undersides of the leaves   **170 long purples** early purple orchids
171 liberal free-spoken | **a grosser name** (the testicle-resembling tubers of the orchid,
which also in some cases resemble *dead men's fingers*, have earned various slang
names like "dogstones" and "cullions")   **172 cold** chaste   **173 pendent** overhanging |
crownet made into a chaplet or coronet   **174 envious sliver** malicious branch
175 weedy of plants   **178 lauds** hymns   **179 incapable of** lacking capacity to
apprehend   **180 endued** adapted by nature   **183 lay** ballad, song

To muddy death.

LAERTES   Alas, then she is drowned?

QUEEN   Drowned, drowned.   185

LAERTES   Too much of water hast thou, poor Ophelia,
And therefore I forbid my tears. But yet
It is our trick;° nature her custom holds,
Let shame say what it will. [*He weeps*] When these are gone,
The woman will be out.° Adieu, my lord.   190
I have a speech of fire that fain would blaze,
But that this folly douts° it.   *Exit*

KING   Let's follow, Gertrude.
How much I had to do to calm his rage!
Now fear I this will give it start again;
Therefore let's follow.   195

                                                        Exeunt

❧

ACT 5
SCENE 1

Location: A churchyard

Enter two Clowns° [with spades and mattocks]

FIRST CLOWN   Is she to be buried in Christian burial, when she
willfully seeks her own salvation?°

SECOND CLOWN   I tell thee she is; therefore make her grave
straight.° The crowner° hath sat on her,° and finds it°
Christian burial.   5

FIRST CLOWN   How can that be, unless she drowned herself in
her own defense?

SECOND CLOWN   Why, 'tis found so.°

---

188 It is our trick weeping is our natural way (when sad)   **189–90 When . . . out**
when my tears are all shed, the woman in me will be expended, satisfied   **192 douts**
extinguishes (the Second Quarto reads "drownes")

0.1 s.d. *Clowns* rustics   **2 salvation** (a blunder for "damnation," or perhaps a
suggestion that Ophelia was taking her own shortcut to heaven)   **4 straight**
straightway, immediately (but with a pun on *strait*, "narrow") | **crowner** coroner
| **sat on her** conducted an inquest on her case | **finds it** gives his official verdict
that her means of death was consistent with   **8 found so** determined so in the
coroner's verdict

FIRST CLOWN   It must be *se offendendo*,° it cannot be else. For
here lies the point: if I drown myself wittingly, it argues an   10
act, and an act hath three branches—it is to act, to do, and
to perform. Argal,° she drowned herself wittingly.

SECOND CLOWN   Nay, but hear you, goodman° delve—

FIRST CLOWN   Give me leave. Here lies the water; good. Here
stands the man; good. If the man go to this water and drown   15
himself, it is, will he, nill he,° he goes, mark you that. But if
the water come to him and drown him, he drowns not
himself. Argal, he that is not guilty of his own death
shortens not his own life.

SECOND CLOWN   But is this law?   20

FIRST CLOWN   Ay, marry, is't—crowner's quest° law.

SECOND CLOWN   Will you ha' the truth on't? If this had not
been a gentlewoman, she should have been buried out o'
Christian burial.

FIRST CLOWN   Why, there thou say'st.° And the more pity that   25
great folk should have countenance° in this world to drown
or hang themselves, more than their even-Christian.° Come,
my spade. There is no ancient° gentlemen but gardeners,
ditchers, and grave makers. They hold up° Adam's profession.

SECOND CLOWN   Was he a gentleman?   30

FIRST CLOWN   'A was the first that ever bore arms.°

SECOND CLOWN   Why, he had none.

FIRST CLOWN   What, art a heathen? How dost thou understand
the Scripture? The Scripture says Adam digged. Could he
dig without arms?° I'll put another question to thee. If thou   35
answerest me not to the purpose, confess thyself°—

SECOND CLOWN   Go to.

FIRST CLOWN   What is he that builds stronger than either the
mason, the shipwright, or the carpenter?

---

9 se offendendo (a comic mistake for *se defendendo*, a term used in verdicts of
self-defense)   **12 Argal** (corruption of *ergo*, "therefore")   **13 goodman** (an honorific
title often used with the name of a profession or craft)   **16 will he, nill he** whether
he will or no, willy-nilly   **21 quest** inquest   **25 there thou say'st** that's right
26 countenance privilege   **27 even-Christian** fellow Christians   **28 ancient** going
back to ancient times   **29 hold up** maintain   **31 bore arms** (to be entitled to bear a
coat of arms would make Adam a gentleman, but as one who bore a spade, our
common ancestor was an ordinary delver in the earth)   **35 arms** the arms of the
body   **36 confess thyself** (the saying continues, "and be hanged")

SECOND CLOWN   The gallows maker, for that frame° outlives a   40
thousand tenants.

FIRST CLOWN   I like thy wit well, in good faith. The gallows
does well.° But how does it well? It does well to those that
do ill. Now thou dost ill to say the gallows is built stronger
than the church. Argal, the gallows may do well to thee. To't   45
again, come.

SECOND CLOWN   "Who builds stronger than a mason, a shipwright, or a carpenter?"

FIRST CLOWN   Ay, tell me that, and unyoke.°

SECOND CLOWN   Marry, now I can tell.   50

FIRST CLOWN   To't.

SECOND CLOWN   Mass,° I cannot tell.

Enter Hamlet and Horatio [at a distance]

FIRST CLOWN   Cudgel thy brains no more about it, for your dull
ass will not mend his pace with beating; and when you are
asked this question next, say "a grave maker." The houses   55
he makes lasts till doomsday. Go get thee in and fetch me a
stoup° of liquor.

[Exit Second Clown. First Clown digs]
Song

"In youth, when I did love,° did love,
   Methought it was very sweet,
To contract—oh—the time for—a—my behove,°   60
   Oh, methought there—a—was nothing—a—meet."°

HAMLET   Has this fellow no feeling of his business, 'a° sings in
grave-making?

HORATIO   Custom hath made it in him a property of easiness.°

HAMLET   'Tis e'en so. The hand of little employment hath the   65
daintier sense.°

---

40 frame (1) gallows (2) structure   **43 does well** (1) is an apt answer (2) does a good
turn   **49 unyoke** after this great effort, you may unharness the team of your wits
52 Mass by the mass   **57 stoup** two-quart measure   **58 In . . . love** (this and the
two following stanzas, with nonsensical variations, are from a poem attributed to
Lord Vaux and printed in *Tottel's Miscellany,* 1557; the *oh* and *a* [for "ah"]
seemingly are the grunts of the digger)   **60 To contract . . . behove** to shorten the
time for my own advantage (perhaps he means to *prolong* it)   **61 meet** suitable,
more suitable   **62 'a** that he   **64 property of easiness** something he can do easily
and indifferently   **66 daintier sense** more delicate sense of feeling

FIRST CLOWN   *Song*

> "But age with his stealing steps
>   Hath clawed me in his clutch,
> And hath shipped me into the land,°
>   As if I had never been such."   70

[*He throws up a skull*]

HAMLET   That skull had a tongue in it and could sing once.
How the knave jowls° it to the ground, as if 'twere Cain's
jawbone, that did the first murder! This might be the pate of
a politician,° which this ass now o'erreaches,° one that would
circumvent God, might it not?   75

HORATIO   It might, my lord.

HAMLET   Or of a courtier, which could say, "Good morrow,
sweet lord! How dost thou, sweet lord?" This might be my
Lord Such-a-one, that praised my Lord Such-a-one's horse
when 'a meant to beg it, might it not?   80

HORATIO   Ay, my lord.

HAMLET   Why, e'en so, and now my Lady Worm's, chapless,°
and knocked about the mazard° with a sexton's spade. Here's
fine revolution,° an we had the trick° to see't. Did these
bones cost no more the breeding but to° play at loggets°   85
with them? Mine ache to think on't.

FIRST CLOWN   *Song*

> "A pickax and a spade, a spade,
>   For and° a shrouding sheet;
> Oh, a pit of clay for to be made
>   For such a guest is meet."   90

[*He throws up another skull*]

HAMLET   There's another. Why may not that be the skull of a
lawyer? Where be his quiddities now, his quillities,° his cases,

---

69 into the land toward my grave (?) (but note the lack of rhyme in *steps, land*)
72 jowls dashes (with a pun on *jowl*, "jawbone")   **74 politician** schemer, plotter |
o'erreaches circumvents, gets the better of   **82 chapless** having no lower jaw
83 mazard head (literally, a drinking vessel)   **84 revolution** turn of Fortune's wheel,
change | **trick** knack   **85 cost . . . to** involve so little expense and care in
upbringing that we may | **loggets** a game in which pieces of hard wood shaped like
Indian clubs or bowling pins are thrown to lie as near as possible to a stake   **88 For
and** and moreover   **92 his quiddities . . . quillities** his subtleties, his legal niceties

his tenures,° and his tricks? Why does he suffer this mad knave now to knock him about the sconce° with a dirty shovel, and will not tell him of his action of battery?° Hum, 95 this fellow might be in 's time a great buyer of land, with his statutes,° his recognizances,° his fines,° his double vouchers,° his recoveries.° Is this the fine of his fines and the recovery of his recoveries, to have his fine pate full of fine dirt?° Will his vouchers vouch him no more of his purchases, and double 100 ones too, than the length and breadth of a pair of indentures?° The very conveyances of his lands will scarcely lie in this box,° and must th'inheritor° himself have no more, ha?

HORATIO Not a jot more, my lord.

HAMLET Is not parchment made of sheepskins?   105

HORATIO Ay, my lord, and of calves' skins too.

HAMLET They are sheep and calves which seek out assurance in that.° I will speak to this fellow.—Whose grave's this, sirrah?°

FIRST CLOWN Mine, sir.

[*Sings*] "Oh, pit of clay for to be made   110
  For such a guest is meet."

HAMLET I think it be thine, indeed, for thou liest in't.

FIRST CLOWN You lie out on't, sir, and therefore 'tis not yours. For my part, I do not lie in't, yet it is mine.

HAMLET Thou dost lie in't, to be in't and say it is thine. 'Tis for 115 the dead, not for the quick;° therefore thou liest.

---

93 **tenures** the holding of a piece of property or office, or the conditions or period of such holding 94 **sconce** head 95 **action of battery** lawsuit about physical assault 96–97 **his statutes** his legal documents acknowledging obligation of a debt 97 **recognizances** bonds undertaking to repay debts | **fines** procedures for converting entailed estates into "fee simple" or freehold | **double vouchers** vouchers signed by two signatories guaranteeing the legality of real estate titles 98 **recoveries** suits to obtain the authority of a court judgment for the holding of land 98–99 **Is this . . . dirt?** is this the end of his legal maneuvers and profitable land deals, to have the skull of his elegant head filled full of minutely sifted dirt? (with multiple wordplay on *fine* and *fines*) 99–101 **Will . . . indentures?** will his vouchers, even double ones, guarantee him no more land than is needed to bury him in, being no bigger than the deed of conveyance? (an *indenture* is literally a legal document drawn up in duplicate on a single sheet and then cut apart on a zigzag line so that each pair was uniquely matched) 103 **box** (1) deed box (2) coffin | **th'inheritor** the acquirer, owner 107–8 **assurance in that** safety in legal parchments 108 **sirrah** (a term of address to inferiors) 116 **quick** living

FIRST CLOWN   'Tis a quick lie, sir; 'twill away again from me to
you.

HAMLET   What man dost thou dig it for?

FIRST CLOWN   For no man, sir.   120

HAMLET   What woman, then?

FIRST CLOWN   For none, neither.

HAMLET   Who is to be buried in't?

FIRST CLOWN   One that was a woman, sir, but, rest her soul,
she's dead.   125

HAMLET   How absolute° the knave is! We must speak by the
card,° or equivocation° will undo us. By the Lord, Horatio,
this three years I have took° note of it: the age is grown so
picked that the toe of the peasant comes so near the heel of
the courtier he galls his kibe.°—How long hast thou been   130
grave maker?

FIRST CLOWN   Of all the days i'th' year, I came to't that day that
our last king Hamlet overcame Fortinbras.

HAMLET   How long is that since?

FIRST CLOWN   Cannot you tell that? Every fool can tell that. It   135
was that very day that young Hamlet was born—he that is
mad and sent into England.

HAMLET   Ay, marry, why was he sent into England?

FIRST CLOWN   Why, because 'a was mad. 'A shall recover his
wits there, or if 'a do not, 'tis no great matter there.   140

HAMLET   Why?

FIRST CLOWN   'Twill not be seen in him there. There the men are
as mad as he.

HAMLET   How came he mad?

FIRST CLOWN   Very strangely, they say.   145

HAMLET   How strangely?

FIRST CLOWN   Faith, e'en with losing his wits.

HAMLET   Upon what ground?°

---

126 **absolute** strict, precise   126–27 **by the card** with precision (literally, by the
mariner's compass-card, on which the points of the compass were marked)
127 **equivocation** ambiguity in the use of terms   128 **took** taken   128–30 **the age
. . . kibe** the age has grown so finical and mannered that the lower classes ape their
social betters, chafing at their heels (*kibes* are chilblains on the heels)   148 **ground**
cause (but, in the next line, the gravedigger takes the word in the sense of "land,"
"country")

FIRST CLOWN   Why, here in Denmark. I have been sexton here, man and boy, thirty years. 150

HAMLET   How long will a man lie i'th'earth ere he rot?

FIRST CLOWN   Faith, if 'a be not rotten before 'a die—as we have many pocky° corpses nowadays, that will scarce hold the laying in°—'a will last you° some eight year or nine year. A tanner will last you nine year. 155

HAMLET   Why he more than another?

FIRST CLOWN   Why, sir, his hide is so tanned with his trade that 'a will keep out water a great while, and your water is a sore° decayer of your whoreson° dead body. [*He picks up a skull*] Here's a skull now hath lien you° i'th'earth three-and- 160 twenty years.

HAMLET   Whose was it?

FIRST CLOWN   A whoreson mad fellow's it was. Whose do you think it was?

HAMLET   Nay, I know not. 165

FIRST CLOWN   A pestilence on him for a mad rogue! 'A poured a flagon of Rhenish° on my head once. This same skull, sir, was, sir, Yorick's skull, the King's jester.

HAMLET   This?

FIRST CLOWN   E'en that. 170

HAMLET   Let me see. [*He takes the skull*] Alas, poor Yorick! I knew him, Horatio, a fellow of infinite jest, of most excellent fancy. He hath bore° me on his back a thousand times, and now how abhorred in my imagination it is! My gorge rises° at it. Here hung those lips that I have kissed I 175 know not how oft. Where be your gibes° now? Your gambols, your songs, your flashes of merriment that were wont to set the table on a roar? Not one now, to mock your own grinning? Quite chopfallen?° Now get you to my lady's chamber and tell her, let her paint an inch thick, to this favor° 180

---

153 **pocky** rotten, diseased (literally, with the pox, or syphilis)   153–54 **hold the laying in** hold together long enough to be interred   154 **last you** last (*you* is used colloquially here and in the following lines)   158 **sore** keen, veritable   159 **whoreson** (an expression of contemptuous familiarity)   160 **lien you** lain (see the note at line 153–54)   167 **Rhenish** Rhine wine   173 **bore** borne   174–75 **My gorge rises** I feel nauseated   176 **gibes** taunts   179 **chopfallen** (1) lacking the lower jaw (2) dejected   180 **favor** aspect, appearance

she must come. Make her laugh at that. Prithee, Horatio,
tell me one thing.

HORATIO What's that, my lord?

HAMLET Dost thou think Alexander looked o' this fashion
i'th'earth?   185

HORATIO E'en so.

HAMLET And smelt so? Pah!   [*He throws down the skull*]

HORATIO E'en so, my lord.

HAMLET To what base uses we may return, Horatio! Why may
not imagination trace the noble dust of Alexander till 'a find   190
it stopping a bunghole?°

HORATIO 'Twere to consider too curiously° to consider so.

HAMLET No, faith, not a jot, but to follow him thither with
modesty enough, and likelihood to lead it.° As thus:
Alexander died, Alexander was buried, Alexander returneth   195
to dust, the dust is earth, of earth we make loam,° and why
of that loam whereto he was converted might they not stop
a beer barrel?

Imperious° Caesar, dead and turned to clay,
Might stop a hole to keep the wind away.   200
Oh, that that earth which kept the world in awe
Should patch a wall t'expel the winter's flaw!°

> *Enter King, Queen, Laertes, and the corpse [of
> Ophelia, in procession, with Priest, lords, etc.]*

But soft, but soft° awhile! Here comes the King,
The Queen, the courtiers. Who is this they follow?
And with such maimèd° rites? This doth betoken   205
The corpse they follow did with desperate hand
Fordo° it own life. 'Twas of some estate.°
Couch° we awhile and mark.

> *[He and Horatio conceal themselves;
> Ophelia's body is taken to the grave]*

---

191 bunghole hole for filling or emptying a cask   **192 curiously** minutely
193–94 with . . . lead it with moderation and plausibility   **196 loam** a mixture of
clay, straw, sand, etc. used to mold bricks, or, in this case, bungs for a beer barrel
199 Imperious Imperial   **202 flaw** gust of wind   **203 soft** wait, be careful
205 maimèd mutilated, incomplete   **207 Fordo it** destroy its | **estate** rank
208 Couch we let's hide, lie low

LAERTES   What ceremony else?
HAMLET [*to Horatio*]   That is Laertes, a very noble youth. Mark.
LAERTES   What ceremony else?   210
PRIEST   Her obsequies have been as far enlarged
  As we have warranty.° Her death was doubtful,
  And but that great command o'ersways the order°
  She should in ground unsanctified been lodged°
  Till the last trumpet. For° charitable prayers,   215
  Shards,° flints, and pebbles should be thrown on her.
  Yet here she is allowed her virgin crants,°
  Her maiden strewments,° and the bringing home
  Of bell and burial.°
LAERTES   Must there no more be done?
PRIEST   No more be done.   220
  We should profane the service of the dead
  To sing a requiem and such rest° to her
  As to peace-parted souls.°
LAERTES   Lay her i'th'earth,
  And from her fair and unpolluted flesh
  May violets° spring! I tell thee, churlish priest,   225
  A ministering angel shall my sister be
  When thou liest howling.°
HAMLET [*to Horatio*]   What, the fair Ophelia!
QUEEN [*scattering flowers*]   Sweets to the sweet! Farewell.
  I hoped thou shouldst have been my Hamlet's wife.
  I thought thy bride-bed to have decked, sweet maid,   230
  And not t' have strewed thy grave.
LAERTES   Oh, treble woe
  Fall ten times treble on that cursèd head
  Whose wicked deed thy most ingenious sense°
  Deprived thee of! Hold off the earth awhile,
  Till I have caught her once more in mine arms.   235

---

212 **warranty** ecclesiastical authority 213 **order** (1) prescribed practice (2) religious order of clerics 214 **She should . . . lodged** she should have been buried in unsanctified ground 215 **For** in place of 216 **Shards** broken bits of pottery 217 **crants** garlands betokening maidenhood 218 **strewments** flowers strewn on a coffin 218–19 **bringing . . . burial** laying the body to rest, to the sound of the bell 222 **such rest** to pray for such rest 223 **peace-parted souls** those who have died at peace with God 225 **violets** (see 4.5.180 and note) 227 **howling** in hell 233 **ingenious sense** a mind that is quick, alert, of fine qualities

[*He leaps into the grave and embraces Ophelia*]
Now pile your dust upon the quick and dead,
Till of this flat a mountain you have made
T' o'ertop old Pelion° or the skyish head
Of blue Olympus.
HAMLET [*coming forward*]   What is he whose grief
Bears such an emphasis,° whose phrase of sorrow   240
Conjures the wandering stars° and makes them stand
Like wonder-wounded° hearers? This is I,
Hamlet the Dane.°
LAERTES [*grappling with him*°]   The devil take thy soul!
HAMLET   Thou pray'st not well.   245
I prithee, take thy fingers from my throat,
For though I am not splenitive° and rash,
Yet have I in me something dangerous,
Which let thy wisdom fear. Hold off thy hand.
KING   Pluck them asunder.   250
QUEEN   Hamlet, Hamlet!
ALL   Gentlemen!
HORATIO   Good my lord, be quiet.
                    [*Hamlet and Laertes are parted*]
HAMLET   Why, I will fight with him upon this theme
Until my eyelids will no longer wag.°   255
QUEEN   Oh, my son, what theme?
HAMLET   I loved Ophelia. Forty thousand brothers
Could not with all their quantity of love
Make up my sum. What wilt thou do for her?
KING   Oh, he is mad, Laertes.   260

---

238 Pelion a mountain in northern Thessaly; compare *Olympus* and *Ossa* in lines 239 and 271 (in their rebellion against the Olympian gods, the giants attempted to heap Ossa on Pelion in order to scale Olympus)   **240 emphasis** rhetorical and florid emphasis (*phrase* has a similar rhetorical connotation)   **241 wandering stars** planets   **242 wonder-wounded** struck with amazement   **243 the Dane** (this title normally signifies the King; see 1.1.15 and note)   **244 s.d.** *grappling with him* the testimony of the First Quarto that *"Hamlet leaps in after Laertes"* and of the ballad "Elegy on Burbage," published in *Gentleman's Magazine* in 1825 ("oft have I seen him leap into a grave") seem to indicate one way in which this fight was staged; however, the difficulty of fitting two contenders and Ophelia's body into a confined space (probably the trapdoor) suggests to many editors the alternative, that Laertes jumps out of the grave to attack Hamlet)   **247 splenitive** quick-tempered   **255 wag** move (a fluttering eyelid is a conventional sign that life has not yet gone)

QUEEN   For love of God, forbear him.°

HAMLET   'Swounds,° show me what thou'lt do.
  Woo't° weep? Woo't fight? Woo't fast? Woo't tear thyself?
  Woo't drink up eisel?° Eat a crocodile?°
  I'll do't. Dost come here to whine?   265
  To outface me with leaping in her grave?
  Be buried quick° with her, and so will I.
  And if thou prate of mountains, let them throw
  Millions of acres on us, till our ground,
  Singeing his pate° against the burning zone,°   270
  Make Ossa° like a wart! Nay, an thou'lt mouth,°
  I'll rant as well as thou.

QUEEN   This is mere° madness,
  And thus awhile the fit will work on him;
  Anon, as patient as the female dove
  When that her golden couplets° are disclosed,°   275
  His silence will sit drooping.

HAMLET   Hear you, sir.
  What is the reason that you use me thus?
  I loved you ever. But it is no matter.
  Let Hercules himself do what he may,
  The cat will mew, and dog will have his day.°   280

                              Exit Hamlet

KING   I pray thee, good Horatio, wait upon him.

                              [*Exit*] *Horatio*

[*To Laertes*] Strengthen your patience in° our last night's
  speech;
We'll put the matter to the present push.°—
Good Gertrude, set some watch over your son.—

---

261 **forbear him** leave him alone   262 **'Swounds** by His (Christ's) wounds   263 **Woo't** wilt thou   264 **Woo't . . . eisel?** will you drink up a whole draft of vinegar? (an extremely self-punishing task as a way of expressing grief) | **crocodile** (crocodiles were tough and dangerous, and were supposed to shed crocodile tears)   267 **quick** alive   270 **his pate** its head, top | **burning zone** zone in the celestial sphere containing the sun's orbit, between the tropics of Cancer and Capricorn   271 **Ossa** (see 238n) | **an thou'lt mouth** if you want to rant   272 **mere** utter   275 **golden couplets** two baby pigeons, covered with yellow down | **disclosed** hatched   279–80 **Let . . . day** (1) even Hercules couldn't stop Laertes's theatrical rant (2) I, too, will have my turn; despite any blustering attempts at interference, every person will sooner or later do what he or she must do   282 **in** by recalling   283 **present push** immediate test

This grave shall have a living° monument.   285
An hour of quiet° shortly shall we see;
Till then, in patience our proceeding be.

                                        Exeunt

❖

ACT 5
SCENE 2

Location: The castle

Enter Hamlet and Horatio

HAMLET   So much for this, sir; now shall you see the other.°
You do remember all the circumstance?
HORATIO   Remember it, my lord!
HAMLET   Sir, in my heart there was a kind of fighting
That would not let me sleep. Methought I lay   5
Worse than the mutines° in the bilboes.° Rashly,°
And praised be rashness for it—let us know°
Our indiscretion° sometime serves us well
When our deep plots do pall,° and that should learn° us
There's a divinity that shapes our ends,   10
Rough-hew° them how we will—
HORATIO   That is most certain.
HAMLET   Up from my cabin,
My sea-gown° scarfed° about me, in the dark
Groped I to find out them,° had my desire,
Fingered° their packet, and in fine° withdrew   15
To mine own room again, making so bold,
My fears forgetting manners, to unseal
Their grand commission; where I found, Horatio—

---

285 living lasting (for Laertes' private understanding, Claudius also hints that Hamlet's death will serve as such a monument)   **286 hour of quiet** time free of conflict

1 see the other hear the other news (see 4.6.22–24)   **6 mutines** mutineers | **bilboes** shackles | **Rashly** on impulse (this adverb goes with lines 12 ff)   **7 know** acknowledge   **8 indiscretion** lack of foresight and judgment (not an indiscreet act)   **9 pall** fail, falter, go stale | **learn** teach   **11 Rough-hew** shape roughly   **13 sea-gown** seaman's coat | **scarfed** loosely wrapped   **14 them** Rosencrantz and Guildenstern   **15 Fingered** pilfered, pinched | **in fine** finally, in conclusion

Ah, royal knavery!—an exact command,
Larded° with many several° sorts of reasons   20
Importing° Denmark's health and England's too,
With, ho! such bugs and goblins in my life,°
That on the supervise, no leisure bated,°
No, not to stay° the grinding of the ax,
My head should be struck off.

HORATIO   Is't possible?   25

HAMLET [*giving a document*]
Here's the commission. Read it at more leisure.
But wilt thou hear now how I did proceed?

HORATIO   I beseech you.

HAMLET   Being thus benetted round with villainies—
Ere I could make a prologue to my brains,   30
They had begun the play°—I sat me down,
Devised a new commission, wrote it fair.°
I once did hold it, as our statists° do,
A baseness° to write fair, and labored much
How to forget that learning, but, sir, now   35
It did me yeoman's service. Wilt thou know
Th'effect of what I wrote?

HORATIO   Ay, good my lord.

HAMLET   An earnest conjuration° from the King,
As England was his faithful tributary,
As love between them like the palm° might flourish,   40
As peace should still° her wheaten garland° wear
And stand a comma° 'tween their amities,
And many suchlike "as"es° of great charge,°
That on the view and knowing of these contents,

---

20 Larded garnished | **several** different   **21 Importing** relating to   **22 With . . . life**
with all sorts of warnings of imaginary dangers if I were allowed to continue living
(*bugs* are bugbears, hobgoblins)   **23 That . . . bated** that on the reading of this
commission, no delay being allowed   **24 stay** await   **30–31 Ere . . . play** before I
could consciously turn my brain to the matter, it had started working on a plan
32 fair in a clear hand   **33 statists** politicians, men of public affairs   **34 A baseness**
beneath my dignity   **38 conjuration** entreaty   **40 palm** (an image of health; see
Psalm 92.12)   **41 still** always | **wheaten garland** (symbolic of fruitful agriculture,
of peace and plenty)   **42 comma** (indicating continuity, link)   **43 "as"es** (1) the
"whereases" of a formal document (2) asses | **charge** (1) import (2) burden
(appropriate to asses)

Without debatement further more or less,   45
He should those bearers put to sudden death,
Not shriving time° allowed.

HORATIO   How was this sealed?

HAMLET   Why, even in that was heaven ordinant.°
I had my father's signet° in my purse,
Which was the model° of that Danish seal;   50
Folded the writ° up in the form of th'other,
Subscribed° it, gave't th'impression,° placed it safely,
The changeling° never known. Now, the next day
Was our sea fight, and what to this was sequent°
Thou knowest already.   55

HORATIO   So Guildenstern and Rosencrantz go to't.

HAMLET   Why, man, they did make love to this employment.
They are not near my conscience. Their defeat°
Does by their own insinuation° grow.
'Tis dangerous when the baser° nature comes   60
Between the pass° and fell° incensèd points
Of mighty opposites.°

HORATIO   Why, what a king is this!

HAMLET   Does it not, think thee, stand me now upon°—
He that hath killed my king and whored my mother,
Popped in between th'election° and my hopes,   65
Thrown out his angle° for my proper° life,
And with such coz'nage°—is't not perfect conscience
To quit° him with this arm? And is't not to be damned
To let this canker° of our nature come
In° further evil?   70

HORATIO   It must be shortly known to him from England
What is the issue of the business there.

---

47 shriving time time for confession and absolution **48 ordinant** directing
49 signet small seal **50 model** replica **51 writ** writing **52 Subscribed** signed
(with forged signature) | **impression** with a wax seal **53 changeling** substituted
letter (literally, a fairy child substituted for a human one) **54 was sequent** followed
58 defeat destruction **59 insinuation** intrusive intervention, sticking their noses in
my business **60 baser** of lower social station **61 pass** thrust | **fell** fierce
62 opposites antagonists **63 stand me now upon** become incumbent on me now
65 th'election (the Danish monarch was "elected" by a small number of high-ranking
electors) **66 angle** fishhook | **proper** very **67 coz'nage** trickery **68 quit** requite,
pay back **69 canker** ulcer **69–70 come in** grow into

HAMLET   It will be short. The interim is mine,
And a man's life's no more than to say "one."°
But I am very sorry, good Horatio,   75
That to Laertes I forgot myself,
For by the image of my cause I see
The portraiture of his. I'll court his favors.
But, sure, the bravery° of his grief did put me
Into a tow'ring passion.
HORATIO   Peace, who comes here?   80

Enter a Courtier [Osric]

OSRIC   Your Lordship is right welcome back to Denmark.
HAMLET   I humbly thank you, sir. [*To Horatio*] Dost
know this water fly?
HORATIO   No, my good lord.
HAMLET   Thy state is the more gracious, for 'tis a vice to know   85
him. He hath much land, and fertile. Let a beast be lord of
beasts, and his crib° shall stand at the King's mess.° 'Tis a
chuff,° but, as I say, spacious in the possession of dirt.
OSRIC   Sweet lord, if Your Lordship were at leisure, I should
impart a thing to you from His Majesty.   90
HAMLET   I will receive it, sir, with all diligence of spirit. Put
your bonnet° to his° right use; 'tis for the head.
OSRIC   I thank Your Lordship, it is very hot.
HAMLET   No, believe me, 'tis very cold. The wind is northerly.
OSRIC   It is indifferent° cold, my lord, indeed.   95
HAMLET   But yet methinks it is very sultry and hot for my
complexion.°
OSRIC   Exceedingly, my lord. It is very sultry, as 'twere—I can-
not tell how. My lord, His Majesty bade me signify to you
that 'a has laid a great wager on your head. Sir, this is the   100
matter—

---

74 a man's . . . "one" one's whole life occupies such a short time, only as long as it
takes to count to 1   **79 bravery** bravado   **86–87 Let . . . mess** if a man, no matter
how beastlike, is as rich in livestock and possessions as Osric, he may eat at the
King's table   **87 crib** manger   **88 chuff** boor, churl (the Second Quarto spelling,
"chough," is a variant spelling that also suggests the meaning here of "chattering
jackdaw")   **92 bonnet** any kind of cap or hat | **his** its   **95 indifferent** somewhat
97 complexion constitution

HAMLET I beseech you, remember.

[*Hamlet moves him to put on his hat*]

OSRIC Nay, good my lord; for my ease,° in good faith. Sir, here
is newly come to court Laertes—believe me, an absolute°
gentleman, full of most excellent differences,° of very soft   105
society° and great showing.° Indeed, to speak feelingly° of
him, he is the card or calendar of gentry,° for you shall find
in him the continent of what part a gentleman would see.°

HAMLET Sir, his definement suffers no perdition in you, though
I know to divide him inventorially would dozy th'arithmetic   110
of memory, and yet but yaw neither in respect of his quick
sail.° But, in the verity of extolment, I take him to be a soul
of great article, and his infusion of such dearth and rareness
as, to make true diction of him, his semblable is his mirror
and who else would trace him his umbrage, nothing more.°   115

OSRIC Your Lordship speaks most infallibly of him.

HAMLET The concernancy,° sir? Why do we wrap the gentleman in our more rawer breath?°

OSRIC Sir?

HORATIO Is't not possible to understand in another tongue?°   120
You will do't,° sir, really.

HAMLET What imports the nomination° of this gentleman?

---

103 **for my ease** (a conventional reply declining the invitation to put the hat back
on) 104 **absolute** perfect 105 **differences** special qualities 105–6 **soft society**
agreeable manners 106 **great showing** distinguished appearance | **feelingly** with
just perception 107 **the card . . . gentry** the model or paradigm (literally, a chart or
directory) of good breeding 108 **the continent . . . see** one who contains in himself
all the qualities a gentleman would like to see (a *continent* is that which contains)
109–12 **his definement . . . sail** the task of defining Laertes's excellences suffers no
diminution in your description of him, though I know that to enumerate all his
graces would stupify one's powers of memory, and even so could do no more than
veer unsteadily off course in a vain attempt to keep up with his rapid forward
motion; (Hamlet mocks Osric by parodying his jargon-filled speeches) 112–15 **But
. . . more** but, in true praise of him, I take him to be a person of remarkable value,
and his essence of such rarity and excellence as, to speak truly of him, none can
compare with him other than his own mirror; anyone following in his footsteps can
only hope to be the shadow to his substance, nothing more 117 **concernancy**
import, relevance 118 **rawer breath** unrefined speech that can only come short in
praising him 120 **Is't . . . tongue?** is it not possible for you, Osric, to understand
and communicate in any other tongue than the overblown rhetoric you have used?
(alternatively, Horatio could be asking Hamlet to speak more plainly) 121 **You
will do't** you can if you try, or, you may well have to try (to speak plainly)
122 **nomination** naming

OSRIC   Of Laertes?

HORATIO [*to Hamlet*]   His purse is empty already; all 's golden
words are spent.   125

HAMLET   Of him, sir.

OSRIC   I know you are not ignorant—

HAMLET   I would you did, sir. Yet in faith if you did, it would
not much approve me.° Well, sir?

OSRIC   You are not ignorant of what excellence Laertes is—   130

HAMLET   I dare not confess that, lest I should compare with
him in excellence. But to know a man well were to know
himself.°

OSRIC   I mean, sir, for his weapon; but in the imputation laid
on him by them, in his meed he's unfellowed.°   135

HAMLET   What's his weapon?

OSRIC   Rapier and dagger.

HAMLET   That's two of his weapons—but well.°

OSRIC   The King, sir, hath wagered with him six Barbary
horses, against the which he° has impawned,° as I take it, six   140
French rapiers and poniards,° with their assigns,° as girdle,
hangers,° and so.° Three of the carriages, in faith, are very
dear to fancy, very responsive to the hilts, most delicate
carriages, and of very liberal conceit.°

HAMLET   What call you° the carriages?   145

HORATIO [*to Hamlet*]   I knew you must be edified by the
margent° ere you had done.

128–29 I would . . . approve me (responding to Osric's incompleted sentence as
though it were a complete statement, Hamlet says, with mock politeness, "I wish
you did know me to be not ignorant [to be knowledgeable] about matters," and
then turns this into an insult: "but if you did, your recommendation of me would be
of little value in any case")   **131–33 I dare . . . himself** I dare not boast of knowing
Laertes's excellence lest I seem to imply a comparable excellence in myself; certainly,
to know another person well, one must know oneself   **134–35 I mean . . .
unfellowed** I mean his excellence with his rapier, not his general excellence; in the
reputation he enjoys for use of his weapons, his merit is unequaled   **138 but well**
but never mind   **140 he** Laertes | **impawned** staked, wagered   **141 poniards**
daggers | **assigns** appurtenances   **142 hangers** straps on the sword belt (*girdle*),
from which the sword hung | **and so** and so on   **142–44 Three . . . conceit** three
of the hangers, truly, are very pleasing to the fancy, decoratively matched with the
hilts, delicate in workmanship, and made with elaborate ingenuity   **145 What call
you** what do you refer to when you say   **147 margent** margin of a book, place for
explanatory notes

OSRIC   The carriages, sir, are the hangers.

HAMLET   The phrase would be more germane to the matter if
we could carry a cannon by our sides; I would it might be   150
hangers till then. But, on: six Barbary horses against six
French swords, their assigns, and three liberal-conceited
carriages; that's the French bet against the Danish. Why is
this impawned, as you call it?

OSRIC   The King, sir, hath laid,° sir, that in a dozen passes°   155
between yourself and him, he shall not exceed you three
hits. He hath laid on twelve for nine, and it would come to
immediate trial, if Your Lordship would vouchsafe the
answer.°

HAMLET   How if I answer no?   160

OSRIC   I mean, my lord, the opposition of your person in trial.

HAMLET   Sir, I will walk here in the hall. If it please His
Majesty, it is the breathing time° of day with me. Let° the
foils be brought, the gentleman willing, and the King hold
his purpose, I will win for him an I can; if not, I will gain   165
nothing but my shame and the odd hits.

OSRIC   Shall I deliver you° so?

HAMLET   To this effect, sir—after what flourish your nature
will.

OSRIC   I commend° my duty to Your Lordship.   170

HAMLET   Yours, yours.   [*Exit Osric*]
'A does well to commend it himself; there are no tongues
else for 's turn.°

HORATIO   This lapwing° runs away with the shell on his head.

---

155 laid wagered | **passes** bouts (the odds of the betting are hard to explain;
possibly the King bets that Hamlet will win at least five out of twelve, at which
point Laertes raises the odds against himself by betting he will win nine)
158–59 vouchsafe the answer be so good as to accept the challenge (Hamlet
deliberately takes the phrase in its literal sense of replying)   **163 breathing time**
exercise period | **Let** if   **167 deliver you** report what you say   **170 commend**
commit to your favor (a conventional salutation, but Hamlet wryly uses a more
literal meaning, "recommend," "praise," in line 172)   **173 for 's turn** for his
purposes, to do it for him   **174 lapwing** (a proverbial type of youthful
forwardness; also, a bird that draws intruders away from its nest and was thought
to run about with its head in the shell when newly hatched; a seeming reference to
Osric's hat)

HAMLET   'A did comply with his dug° before 'a sucked it. Thus   175
has he—and many more of the same breed that I know the
drossy age dotes on—only got the tune of the time, and, out
of an habit of encounter, a kind of yeasty collection, which
carries them through and through the most fanned and
winnowed opinions; and do but blow them to their trial, the   180
bubbles are out.°

Enter a Lord

LORD   My lord, His Majesty commended him to you by young
Osric, who brings back to him that you attend him in the
hall. He sends to know if your pleasure hold to play° with
Laertes, or that° you will take longer time.   185

HAMLET   I am constant to my purposes; they follow the King's
pleasure. If his fitness speaks, mine is ready;° now or whensoever, provided I be so able as now.

LORD   The King and Queen and all are coming down.

HAMLET   In happy time.°   190

LORD   The Queen desires you to use some gentle entertainment°
to Laertes before you fall to play.

HAMLET   She well instructs me.   [*Exit Lord*]

HORATIO   You will lose, my lord.

HAMLET   I do not think so. Since he went into France, I have   195
been in continual practice; I shall win at the odds. But thou
wouldst not think how ill all's here about my heart; but it is
no matter.

HORATIO   Nay, good my lord—

HAMLET   It is but foolery, but it is such a kind of gaingiving° as   200
would perhaps trouble a woman.

HORATIO   If your mind dislike anything, obey it. I will forestall
their repair° hither and say you are not fit.

---

175 comply . . . dug observe ceremonious formality toward his nurse's or mother's
teat   **175–81 Thus . . . are out** thus has he—and many like him of the sort our
frivolous age dotes on—acquired the trendy manner of speech of the time, and, out
of habitual conversation with courtiers of their own kind, have collected together a
kind of frothy medley of current phrases, which enables such gallants to hold their
own among persons of the most select and well-sifted views; and yet do but test
them by merely blowing on them, and their bubbles burst   **184 play** fence
185 that if   **187 If . . . ready** if he declares his readiness, my convenience waits on
his   **190 In happy time** (a phrase of courtesy indicating that the time is convenient)
191 entertainment greeting   **200 gaingiving** misgiving   **203 repair** coming

HAMLET Not a whit, we defy augury.° There is special
providence in the fall of a sparrow. If it be now, 'tis not to   205
come; if it be not to come, it will be now; if it be not now;
yet it will come. The readiness is all. Since no man of aught
he leaves knows, what is't to leave betimes? Let be.°

> *A table prepared.* [*Enter*] *trumpets, drums,*° *and officers*
> *with cushions; King, Queen,* [*Osric,*] *and all the state;*°
> *foils, daggers,* [*and wine borne in;*] *and Laertes*

KING Come, Hamlet, come and take this hand from me.
                    [*The King puts Laertes's hand into Hamlet's*]
HAMLET [*to Laertes*]
  Give me your pardon, sir. I have done you wrong,   210
  But pardon't as you are a gentleman.
  This presence° knows,
  And you must needs have heard, how I am punished°
  With a sore distraction. What I have done
  That might your nature, honor, and exception°   215
  Roughly awake, I here proclaim was madness.
  Was't Hamlet wronged Laertes? Never Hamlet.
  If Hamlet from himself be ta'en away,
  And when he's not himself does wrong Laertes,
  Then Hamlet does it not, Hamlet denies it.   220
  Who does it, then? His madness. If't be so,
  Hamlet is of the faction° that is wronged;
  His madness is poor Hamlet's enemy.
  Sir, in this audience
  Let my disclaiming from a purposed evil   225
  Free me so far in your most generous thoughts
  That I have shot my arrow o'er the house
  And hurt my brother.
LAERTES   I am satisfied in nature,°
  Whose motive° in this case should stir me most
  To my revenge. But in my terms of honor   230

---

204 augury the attempt to read signs of future events in order to avoid predicted
trouble   **207–8 Since . . . Let be** since no one has knowledge of what he is leaving
behind, what does an early death matter after all? enough; forbear   **208.1 s.d.**
trumpets, drums trumpeters, drummers   **208.2 s.d.** *all the state* the entire court
212 presence royal assembly   **213 punished** afflicted   **215 exception** disapproval
222 faction party   **228 in nature** as to my personal feelings   **229 motive** prompting

I stand aloof, and will no reconcilement
Till by some elder masters of known honor
I have a voice° and precedent of peace°
To keep my name ungored.° But till that time
I do receive your offered love like love,   235
And will not wrong it.

HAMLET   I embrace it freely,
And will this brothers' wager frankly° play.—
Give us the foils. Come on.

LAERTES   Come, one for me.

HAMLET   I'll be your foil,° Laertes. In mine ignorance
Your skill shall, like a star i'th' darkest night,   240
Stick fiery off° indeed.

LAERTES   You mock me, sir.

HAMLET   No, by this hand.

KING   Give them the foils, young Osric. Cousin Hamlet,
You know the wager?

HAMLET   Very well, my lord.
Your Grace has laid the odds o'th' weaker side.°   245

KING   I do not fear it; I have seen you both.
But since he is bettered,° we have therefore odds.

LAERTES   This is too heavy. Let me see another.

            [*He exchanges his foil for another*]

HAMLET   This likes° me well. These foils have all a length?

            [*They prepare to fence*]

OSRIC   Ay, my good lord.   250

KING   Set me the stoups of wine upon that table.
If Hamlet give the first or second hit,
Or quit in answer of the third exchange,°
Let all the battlements their ordnance fire.
The King shall drink to Hamlet's better breath,°   255
And in the cup an union° shall he throw

---

233 voice authoritative pronouncement | **of peace** for reconciliation   **234 name ungored** reputation unwounded   **237 frankly** without ill feeling or the burden of rancor   **239 foil** thin metal background which sets a jewel off (with pun on the blunted rapier for fencing)   **241 Stick fiery off** stand out brilliantly   **245 laid . . . side** backed the weaker side   **247 is bettered** is the odds-on favorite (Laertes's handicap is the "three hits" specified in line 156–57)   **249 likes** pleases   **253 Or . . . exchange** or draws even with Laertes by winning the third exchange   **255 better breath** improved vigor   **256 union** pearl (so called, according to Pliny's *Natural History*, 9, because pearls are *unique*, never identical)

Vincentio Sauiolo his Practiſe.

THE THYRDE DAYES
Diſcourſe, of Rapier *and*
Dagger.

Luk:.

I Know not certainly, whether it hath been my earneſt deſire to encounter you, that raiſde me earlier this morning than my accuſtomed houre, or to be aſſertained of ſome doubtfull queſtions, which yeſter-night were propoſed by ſome gentlemen and my ſelfe, in diſcourſe

Vincentio Saviolo, *His practise* (1595). Hamlet supposes that he and Laertes duel with "foils," rapiers (or long swords) whose pointed ends have been blunted by placing a knob or button over them. He wants to know that these weapons are matched and give neither player an advantage. He asks: "These foils have all a length?" (5.2.249). Duels were sometimes fought with a second weapon, a dagger (or short sword), as in this illustration. (By permission of the Folger Shakespeare Library.)

Richer than that which four successive kings
In Denmark's crown have worn. Give me the cups,
And let the kettle° to the trumpet speak,
The trumpet to the cannoneer without,   260
The cannons to the heavens, the heaven to earth,
"Now the King drinks to Hamlet." Come, begin.

                            Trumpets the while

And you, the judges, bear a wary eye.

HAMLET   Come on, sir.

LAERTES   Come, my lord. [*They fence. Hamlet scores a hit.*]

HAMLET   One.

LAERTES   No.

HAMLET   Judgment.   265

OSRIC   A hit, a very palpable hit.

    Drum, trumpets, and shot. Flourish. A piece° goes off

LAERTES   Well, again.

KING   Stay, give me drink. Hamlet, this pearl is thine.

    [*He drinks, and throws a pearl in Hamlet's cup*]

Here's to thy health. Give him the cup.

HAMLET   I'll play this bout first. Set it by awhile.   270

Come. [*They fence*] Another hit; what say you?

LAERTES   A touch, a touch, I do confess't.

KING   Our son shall win.

QUEEN   He's fat° and scant of breath.

Here, Hamlet, take my napkin,° rub thy brows.

The Queen carouses° to thy fortune, Hamlet.   275

HAMLET   Good madam!

KING   Gertrude, do not drink.

QUEEN   I will, my lord, I pray you pardon me.   [*She drinks*]

KING [*aside*]   It is the poisoned cup. It is too late.

HAMLET   I dare not drink yet, madam; by and by.   280

QUEEN   Come, let me wipe thy face.

LAERTES [*aside to the King*]

My lord, I'll hit him now.

KING   I do not think't.

LAERTES [*aside*]   And yet it is almost against my conscience.

---

259 kettle kettledrum   **266.1 s.d.** *A piece* a cannon   **273 fat** not physically fit, out of training   **274 napkin** handkerchief   **275 carouses** drinks a toast

HAMLET   Come, for the third, Laertes. You do but dally.
   I pray you, pass° with your best violence;   285
   I am afeard you make a wanton of me.°
LAERTES   Say you so? Come on.   [*They fence*]
OSRIC   Nothing neither way.
LAERTES   Have at you now!
              [*Laertes wounds Hamlet; then, in scuffling,*
              they change rapiers,° and Hamlet wounds Laertes]
KING   Part them! They are incensed.
HAMLET   Nay, come, again.   [*The Queen falls*]
OSRIC   Look to the Queen there, ho!
HORATIO   They bleed on both sides. How is it, my lord?   290
OSRIC   How is't, Laertes?
LAERTES   Why, as a woodcock° to mine own springe,° Osric;
   I am justly killed with mine own treachery.
HAMLET   How does the Queen?
KING   She swoons to see them bleed.
QUEEN   No, no, the drink, the drink—Oh, my dear Hamlet—   295
   The drink, the drink! I am poisoned.   [*She dies*]
HAMLET   Oh, villainy! Ho, let the door be locked!
   Treachery! Seek it out.   [*Laertes falls. Exit Osric*]
LAERTES   It is here, Hamlet. Hamlet, thou art slain.
   No med'cine in the world can do thee good;   300
   In thee there is not half an hour's life.
   The treacherous instrument is in thy hand,
   Unbated° and envenomed. The foul practice°
   Hath turned itself on me. Lo, here I lie,
   Never to rise again. Thy mother's poisoned.   305
   I can no more. The King, the King's to blame.
HAMLET   The point envenomed too? Then, venom, to thy work.
                 [*He stabs the King*]
ALL   Treason! Treason!

---

285 pass thrust   **286 make . . . me** treat me like a spoiled child, trifle with me
288.1–2 s.d. in scuffling, they change rapiers (this stage direction occurs in the
Folio; according to a widespread stage tradition, Hamlet receives a scratch, realizes
that Laertes's sword is unbated, and accordingly forces an exchange)
292 woodcock a bird, a type of stupidity or as a decoy | **springe** trap, snare
303 Unbated not blunted with a button | **practice** plot

KING   Oh, yet defend me, friends! I am but hurt.

HAMLET [*forcing the King to drink*]

    Here, thou incestuous, murderous, damnèd Dane,   310

    Drink off this potion. Is thy union° here?

    Follow my mother.   [*The King dies*]

LAERTES   He is justly served.

    It is a poison tempered° by himself.

    Exchange forgiveness with me, noble Hamlet.

    Mine and my father's death come not upon thee,   315

    Nor thine on me!   [*He dies*]

HAMLET   Heaven make thee free of it! I follow thee.

    I am dead, Horatio. Wretched Queen, adieu!

    You that look pale and tremble at this chance,°

    That are but mutes° or audience to this act,   320

    Had I but time—as this fell sergeant,° Death,

    Is strict° in his arrest°—oh, I could tell you—

    But let it be. Horatio, I am dead;

    Thou livest. Report me and my cause aright

    To the unsatisfied.

HORATIO   Never believe it.   325

    I am more an antique Roman° than a Dane.

    Here's yet some liquor left.

          [*He attempts to drink from the poisoned cup;*

                Hamlet prevents him]

HAMLET   As thou'rt a man,

    Give me the cup! Let go! By heaven, I'll ha 't.

    Oh, God, Horatio, what a wounded name,

    Things standing thus unknown, shall I leave behind me!   330

    If thou didst ever hold me in thy heart,

    Absent thee from felicity awhile,

    And in this harsh world draw thy breath in pain

    To tell my story.   *A march afar off* [*and a volley within*]

        What warlike noise is this?

                    Enter Osric

---

311 union pearl (see line 268; with grim puns on the word's other meanings: marriage, shared death) **313 tempered** mixed **319 chance** mischance **320 mutes** silent observers (literally, actors with nonspeaking parts) **321 fell sergeant** remorseless arresting officer **322 strict** (1) severely just (2) unavoidable | **arrest** (1) taking into custody (2) stopping my speech **326 Roman** (suicide was an honorable choice for many Romans as an alternative to a dishonorable life)

OSRIC   Young Fortinbras, with conquest come from Poland,   335
   To th'ambassadors of England gives
   This warlike volley.
HAMLET   Oh, I die, Horatio!
   The potent poison quite o'ercrows° my spirit.
   I cannot live to hear the news from England,
   But I do prophesy th'election lights   340
   On Fortinbras. He has my dying voice.°
   So tell him, with th'occurrents° more and less
   Which have solicited.° The rest is silence.   [He dies]
HORATIO   Now cracks a noble heart. Good night, sweet prince,
   And flights of angels sing thee to thy rest!   345

                          [March within]

   Why does the drum come hither?

       Enter Fortinbras, with the [English] Ambassadors
            [with drum, colors, and attendants]

FORTINBRAS   Where is this sight?
HORATIO   What is it you would see?
   If aught of woe or wonder, cease your search.
FORTINBRAS   This quarry cries on havoc.° O proud Death,
   What feast° is toward° in thine eternal cell,   350
   That thou so many princes at a shot
   So bloodily hast struck?
FIRST AMBASSADOR   The sight is dismal,
   And our affairs from England come too late.
   The ears are senseless that should give us hearing,
   To tell him his° commandment is fulfilled,   355
   That Rosencrantz and Guildenstern are dead.
   Where should we have our thanks?
HORATIO   Not from his mouth,
   Had it th'ability of life to thank you.
   He never gave commandment for their death.

---

338 **o'ercrows** triumphs over (like the winner in a cockfight)   341 **voice** vote
342 **th'occurrents** the events, incidents   343 **solicited** moved, urged (Hamlet
doesn't finish saying what the events have prompted—presumably, his acts of
vengeance, or his reporting of those events to Fortinbras)   349 **This . . . havoc** this
heap of dead bodies loudly proclaims a general slaughter   350 **feast** death feasting
on those who have fallen | **toward** in preparation   355 **his** Claudius's

But since, so jump upon this bloody question,°   360
You from the Polack wars and you from England
Are here arrived, give order that these bodies
High on a stage° be placèd to the view,
And let me speak to th' yet unknowing world
How these things came about. So shall you hear   365
Of carnal, bloody, and unnatural acts,
Of accidental judgments,° casual° slaughters,
Of deaths put on° by cunning and forced cause,°
And, in this upshot, purposes mistook
Fall'n on th'inventors' heads. All this can I   370
Truly deliver.

FORTINBRAS   Let us haste to hear it,
And call the noblest to the audience.
For me, with sorrow I embrace my fortune.
I have some rights of memory° in this kingdom,
Which now to claim my vantage° doth invite me.   375

HORATIO   Of that I shall have also cause to speak,
And from his mouth whose voice will draw on more.°
But let this same be presently° performed,
Even while men's minds are wild, lest more mischance
On° plots and errors happen.

FORTINBRAS   Let four captains   380
Bear Hamlet, like a soldier, to the stage,
For he was likely, had he been put on,°
To have proved most royal; and for his passage,°
The soldiers' music and the rite of war
Speak° loudly for him.   385
Take up the bodies. Such a sight as this
Becomes the field,° but here shows much amiss.
Go bid the soldiers shoot.
                    [*marching, bearing off the dead
                    bodies; a peal of ordnance is shot off*]
                                                    Exeunt

---

360 **so jump . . . question** so hard on the heels of this bloody business   363 **stage** platform   367 **judgments** retributions | **casual** occurring by chance   368 **put on** instigated | **forced cause** contrivance   374 **of memory** traditional, remembered, unforgotten   375 **vantage** favorable opportunity   377 **voice . . . more** vote will influence still others   378 **presently** immediately   380 **On** on top of   382 **put on** invested in royal office and so put to the test   383 **for his passage** to mark his passing   385 **Speak** (let them) speak   387 **Becomes the field** suits the field of battle

Notes

Copy text: the Second Quarto of 1604–1605 [Q2]. The First Folio text also represents an independently authoritative text; although seemingly not the correct choice for copy text, the Folio text is considerably less marred by typographical errors than is Q2. The adopted readings in these notes are from F unless otherwise indicated; [eds.] means that the adopted reading was first proposed by some editor since the time of F. Some readings are also supplied from the First Quarto of 1603 [Q1]. Act and scene divisions are missing in Quartos 1–2; the Folio provides such markings only through 1.3 and at Act 2.

Abbreviations:

F	The First Folio	s.d.	stage direction
Q	Quarto	s.p.	speech prefix

1.1 1 Who's Whose   **17 soldier** [F, Q1] souldiers   **40 off** [Q1] of   **44 harrows** horrowes   **63 sledded Polacks** [eds.] sleaded pollax   **73 why** [F, Q1] with   **cast** cost   **87 heraldry** [F, Q1] heraldy   **88 those** [F, Q1] these   **91 returned** returne   **93 cov'nant** comart   **94 designed** [eds.] desseigne   **108 e'en so** [eds.] enso   **112 mote** [eds.] moth   **115 tenantless** tennatlesse   **121 feared** [eds.] feare   **138 you** [F, Q1] your   **140 at it** it   **175 conveniently** [F, Q1] conuenient

1.2. 0.2 [and elsewhere] *Gertrude* Gertrad   **1 KING** *Claud.*   **67 so** so much   **77 good** coold   **82 shapes** [Q3] chapes   **83 denote** deuote   **96 a** or   **105 corpse** [eds.] course   **112 you. For** you for   **114 retrograde** retrogard   **129 sullied** [eds.] sallied [Q2] solid [F]   **132 self** seale   **133 weary** wary   **137 to this** thus   **140 satyr** [F4] satire   **143 would** [F, Q1] should   **149 even she** [F; not in Q2]   **174 to drink deep** [F, Q1] for to drinke   **177 to see** [F, Q1] to   **197 waste** [F2] wast [Q2, F]   **204 jelly with . . . fear,** gelly, with . . . feare   **208 Where, as** [Q5] Whereas   **223 Indeed, indeed** [F, Q1] Indeede   **236 Very like, very like** [F, Q1] Very like   **237 hundred** hundreth   **238 MARCELLUS, BERNARDO** [eds.] *Both*   **241 tonight** to nigh   **250 fare** farre   **251 eleven** a leauen   **253.1** *Exeunt* [at line 253 in Q2]   **256 Foul** [F, Q1] fonde

1.3. 3 convoy is conuay, in   **12 bulk** bulkes   **18** [F; not in Q2]   **29 weigh** way   **49 like a** a   **74 Are** Or   **75 be** boy   **76 loan** loue   **109 Running** [eds.] Wrong [Q2] Roaming [F]   **115 springes** springs   **125 tether** tider   **129 implorators** imploratotors   **130 bawds** [eds.] bonds   **131 beguile** beguide

1.4. 2 is a is **6.1 go off** [eds.] *goes of* **17 revel** [Q3] reueale **19 clepe** clip **36 evil** [eds.] eale [Q2] ease [Q3] **37 often dout** [eds.] of a doubt **49 inurned** interr'd [Q2, Q1] **61, 79 wafts** waues **80 off** of **82 artery** arture **86.1 *Exeunt Exit* 87 imagination** [F, Q1] imagion

1.5. 1 Whither [eds.] Whether **18 on** [eds.] an **19 fretful porcupine** [F, Q1] fearfull Porpentine **41 wit** [eds.] wits **45 what a** what **53 lust** [F, Q1] but angel Angel **54 sate** [F] sort **56 scent** [eds.] sent **65 alleys** [eds.] allies **66 posset** possesse **93 stiffly** swiftly **114 bird** and **120 HORATIO, MARCELLUS** *Booth* [also at line 143] heaven, my lord heauen **130 Look you,** I'll I will **147 s.d. *cries** Ghost cries* **166 some'er** so mere **172 Well** well, well [Q1, Q2]

2.1. 0.1 *man* [eds.] *man or two* **3 marvelous** meruiles **28 Faith, no** Fayth **39 warrant** wit **40 sullies** sallies **41 wi'th'** with **58 o'ertook** or tooke **62 takes** take **73 s.d. *Exit Reynaldo. Enter Ophelia*** [after line 72 in Q2] **104 passion** passions **111 quoted** [eds.] coted

2.2. 0.1 [and elsewhere] *Rosencrantz Rosencraus* **57 o'erhasty** hastie **73 three** [F, Q1] threescore **90 since brevity** breuitie **125 This** [Q2 has a speech prefix: Pol.] This] **126 above** about **137 winking** working **143 his** her **148 watch** wath **149 to a** to **151 'tis** [F, Q1; not in Q2] **170.1. *Exeunt*** [eds.] *Exit* **208 sanity** sanctity **209–10 and suddenly . . . him** [F; not in Q2] **211 honorable lord** Lord **211 most humbly take** take **212 cannot, sir** cannot **213 more** not more **221 excellent** extent **224 overhappy. / On** [at line 169 in Q2] euer happy on **225 cap** lap **234–63 Let . . . attended** [F; not in Q2] **259 ROSENCRANTZ, GUILDENSTERN** *Both* [F] **265 even** euer **279 could** can **283 off** of **294 What a** What **296–97 admirable, in action how . . . angel, in** [F, subst.] admirable in action, how . . . Angell in **299 no, nor** nor **303 you** yee **310 of** on **312–13 the clown . . . sear** [F; not in Q2] **tickle** [eds.] tickled [F] **314 blank** black **325–48 How . . . too** [F; not in Q2] **329 berattle** [eds.] beratled [F] **336–37 most like** [eds.] like most [F] **357 lest my** let me **366 too** to **383–84 tragical-historical, tragical-comical-historical-pastoral** [F; not in Q2] **385–86 light . . . these** [eds.] light for the lawe of writ, and the liberty: these **408 By'r** by **412–13 e'en to 't** ento't **French falconers** friendly Fankners **416** [and elsewhere] **FIRST PLAYER** *Player* **419 caviare** cauiary **425 affectation** affection **428 tale** [F, Q1] talke **437 heraldry** [F, Q1] heraldy **dismal. Head** dismall head **455 Then senseless Ilium** [F; not in Q2] **462 And, like** Like **476 fellies** [F4] follies [Q2] Fallies [F] **484 "Moblèd queen" is good** [F; not in Q2; F reads "Inobled'] **486 bisson** Bison **494 husband's** [F, Q1] husband **499 whe'er** where **518 a** [F; not in Q2] **519 or** [F, Q1] lines, or **523 s.d. *Exeunt players*** [see textual note at line 526] **524 till** tell **526.1 *Exeunt*** [F; Q2 has *"Exeunt Pol. and Players"* after line 525] **532 his** the **534 and** an **537 to Hecuba** [F, Q1] to her **539 the cue** that **560 O, vengeance** [F; not in Q2]

562 **father** [Q1, Q3, Q4; not in Q2, F]   566 **scullion** [F] stallyon [Q2]
scalion [Q1]   578 **the devil** a deale the devil the deale
3.1. 1 **And** An   28 **too** two   32 **lawful espials** [F; not in Q2]   33 **Will**
Wee'le   46 **loneliness** lowliness to too   55 **Let's withdraw** with-draw
55.2 *Enter Hamlet* [after line 55 in Q2]   64 **wished. To** wisht to
72 **disprized** despiz'd   83 **of us all** [F, Q1; not in Q2]   85 **sicklied**
sickled   92 **well, well, well** well   100 **the** these   105 **your honesty**
you   116 **inoculate** euocutat   119 **to a** a   126 **knaves all** knaues
140 **paintings too** [Q1] paintings   142 **jig, you amble** gig & amble
142 **lips** list   143 **your ignorance** [F, Q1] ignorance   150 **Th'expectancy**
Th'expectation   154 **music** musickt   155 **that** what   156 **tune** time
157 **feature** stature   159 [Q2 has *"Exit"* at the end of this line]
186 **unwatched** vnmatcht
3.2. 9 **tatters** totters split [F, Q1] spleet   24–25 **of the** of   27 **praise** praysd
34 **sir** [F; not in Q2]   41.1 *Enter . . . Rosencrantz* [after line 42 in Q2]
83 **detecting** detected   90 **now. My lord,** now my Lord.   100 [and
elsewhere] QUEEN *Ger.*   101 **metal** mettle   105–6 [F; not in Q2]
119 **devil** deule [Q2] Diuel [F]   125.1 *sound* [eds.] *sounds*   125.6 s.d.
Anon Comes anon come   127 **miching** [F, Q1] munching   130 **keep**
counsel [F, Q1] keepe   140 [and throughout scene] PLAYER KING
King   141 **orbèd** orb'd the   146 [and throughout scene] PLAYER
QUEEN *Quee.*   149 **your** our   151 [Q2 follows here with an
extraneous unrhymed line: "For women feare too much, euen as they
loue"]   152 **For** And   153 **In** Eyther none, in   154 **love** Lord
166 **Wormwood, wormwood** That's wormwood   167 PLAYER
QUEEN [not in Q2]   175 **like the** 184 **joys** joy   204 **An** And
208 **a widow** [F, Q1] I be a widow be [F] be a   213.1 *Exit* [F, Q1]
Exeunt   226 **wince** [Q1] winch [Q2, F]   226.1 [after line 227 in Q2]
238 **Confederate** [F, Q1] Considerat   240 **infected** [F, Q1, Q4]
inuected   242 **usurp** vsurps   248 [F; not in Q2]   256 **with two** with
269.1 [F; after line 273 in Q2]   285 **start** stare   293 **of my** of
318.1 [after line 316 in Q2]   332 **thumb** the vmber   340 **to the top**
of to   344 **can fret me** [F] fret me not [Q2] can fret me, yet [Q1]
345.1 [after line 346 in Q2]   358 POLONIUS [F; not in Q2]   359
Leave me, friends [so F; Q2 places before "I will say so," and assigns
both to Hamlet]   361 **breathes** breakes   363 **bitter . . . day** business
as the bitter day   368 **daggers** [F, Q1] dagger
3.3. 19 **huge** hough   22 **ruin** raine   23 **but** with but   35.1 *Exit* [after
"I know" in F]   50 **pardoned** pardon   58 **Offense's** [eds.] Offences
shove showe   73 **pat . . . a-praying** but now a is a praying   75
revenged reuendge   79 **hire and salary** base and silly   81 **With all**
Withall
3.4. 5–6 **with him . . . Mother, Mother, Mother** [F; not in Q2]   7 **warrant**
wait   8.2 *Enter Hamlet* [at line 5 in Q2]   21 **inmost** most   23 **Help,**
ho! Helps how   42 **off** of   50 **tristful** heated   52 [assigned in Q2 to

Hamlet] **59 heaven-kissing** heaue, a kissing **88 panders** pardons
89 mine . . . soul my very eyes into my soule **90 grainèd** greeued
91 not leave leaue there **98 tithe** kyth **141 Ecstasy** [F; not in Q2]
145 I the the **160 live** leaue **167 Refrain tonight** to refraine night
188 ravel rouell **200 to breathe** [eds] to breath **217 a** [F, Q1] a
most **219.1** *Exeunt* [eds.] *Exit*

4.1. 32.1 [at 31 in Q2]

4.2. 0.1 [Q2: *"Enter Hamlet, Rosencraus, and others."*] **2–3** [F; not in
Q2; the s.p. in F is *"Gentlemen"*] **3 HAMLET** [not in Q2] **4.1** [F;
not in Q2] **6 Compounded** Compound **17 an ape** [not in Q2]
29 Hide . . . after [F; not in Q2]

4.3. 42 With fiery quickness [F; not in Q2] **51 and so** so **66 were** will
begun begin

4.4. 19 name. To name To

4.5. 16 Let . . . in [assigned in Q2 to Horatio] **20.1** [after line 16 in Q2]
39 with all with **51 clothes** close **56 Indeed, la** Indeede **60 to** too
80 in their in **94** [F; not in Q2] **96.1** [below line 95 in Q2]
99 impetuous [Q3, F2] impitious [Q2] impittious [F] **105 They** The
141 swoopstake [eds.] soopstake [Q1 reads "Swoop-stakelike"]
152 Let her come in [assigned in Q2 to Laertes and placed before
"How now, what noyse is that?"] s.d. *Enter Ophelia* [after line 151 in
Q2] **156 Till** Tell **159 an old** [F, Q1] a poore **160–62, 164** [F; not
in Q2] **179 must** [F, Q1] may **184 affliction** [F, Q1] afflictions
192 All flaxen Flaxen **196 Christian** [F] Christians **souls, I pray God**
[F, Q1] soules **197 you see** you **210 trophy, sword** trophe sword

4.6. 7, 9 FIRST SAILOR *Say.* **9 an't** and **20 good turn** turne **23 bore**
bord **27 He** So **28 will give** will

4.7. 6 proceeded proceede **7 crimeful** criminall **15 conjunctive** concliue
22 gyves Giues **23 loud a wind** loued Arm'd **25 had** haue **37 How
. . . Hamlet** [F; not in Q2] **38 This** These **46 your pardon** you
pardon **47–48 and more strange** [F; not in Q2] **49 Hamlet** [F; not in
Q2] **57 shall live** [F, Q1] live **63 checking** the King **78 ribbon** [eds.]
ribaud **89 my** me **101 escrimers** [eds.] Scrimures **116 wick** [eds.]
weeke **123 spendthrift** [Q5] spend thirfts **135 on** ore **139 pass** pace
141 for that for **151 shape. If** shape if **157 ha't** hate **160 prepared**
prefard **168 hoar** horry **172 cold** cullcold **192 douts** [F "doubts"]
drownes

5.1. 1 [and throughout] **FIRST CLOWN** *Clowne* **3** [and throughout]
SECOND CLOWN *Other* **9 se offendendo** so offended **11–12 and
to** to **Argal** or all **32–35 SECOND CLOWN: Why . . . arms?** [F; not
in Q2] **40 that frame** that **52.1** [before line 63 in Q2] **57 stoup**
soope **66 daintier** dintier **80 meant** [F, Q1, Q3] went **83 mazard**
massene **98–99 Is . . . recoveries** [F; not in Q2] **99 Will his** will
100–1 double ones too doubles **110 Oh** or **111** [F; not in Q2]
131 Of all Of **153 nowadays** [F; not in Q2] **171 Let me see** [F; not

in Q] **180 chamber** [F, Q1] table **194 As thus** [F; not in Q2]
202 winter's waters **211, 220 PRIEST** *Doct.* **216 Shards, flints** Flints
231 t'have haue **231 trebel** double **247 and rash** rash **273 thus** this
281.1 *[Exit] Horatio and Horatio* **286 shortly** thereby **287 Till** Tell
5.2. 5 Methought my thought **6 bilboes** bilbo **9 pall** fall **17 unseal**
vnfold **19 Ah,** [eds.] A **29 villainies** villaines **30 Ere** Or **43 "as"** es
as sir **52 Subscribed** Subscribe **57, 68–80** [F; not in Q2] **73 interim**
is [eds.] *interim's* [F] **78 court** [eds.] count [F] **81 [and throughout]**
OSRIC *Cour.* **82 humbly** humble **91–92 Put your** your **96 sultry**
sully **for** or **105 gentleman** [eds.] gentlemen **106 feelingly** [Q4]
fellingly **110 dozy** [eds.] dazzie yaw [eds.] raw **134 his** [eds.] this
135 him by them, him, by them **142 hangers** hanger **148 carriages**
carriage **150 might be** be might **154 impawned, as** [eds.] all [Q2]
impon'd, as [F] **165 purpose, I** purpose; I **171 Yours, yours.** 'A does
Yours doo's **175 comply** so sir **178 yeasty** histy **179 fanned** [eds.]
prophane [Q2] fond [F] **180 winnowed** trennowed **196 But thou**
thou **205 be now** be **207 will come** well come **224** [F; not in Q2]
234 To keep To till all **238 foils. Come on** foiles. **241 off** of
247 bettered better **256 union** Vnice ["Onixe" in some copies]
272 A touch, a touch, I I **286 afeard** sure **299 Hamlet.** Hamlet
Hamlet **302 thy** [F, Q1] my **310 murderous** [F; not in Q2] **311 off**
of **thy union** [F, Q1] the Onixe **328 ha't** [eds.] hate [Q2] have't [F]
349 proud prou'd **353 FIRST AMBASSADOR** *Embas.* **364 th'** yet
yet **368 forced** for no **377 on** no

Passages contained only in F and omitted from Q2 are noted in the
textual notes above. Listed here are the more important instances
in which Q2 contains words, lines, and passages omitted in F.

1.1. 108–25 BERNARDO I think . . . countrymen
1.2. 58–60 wrung . . . consent
1.3. 9 perfume and
1.4 17–38 This heavy-headed . . . scandal **75–78** The very . . . beneath
2.1. 119 Come
2.2. 17 Whether . . . thus **213** except my life **349** very **352** 'Sblood
(and some other profanity passim) **356** then **426–27** as wholesome . . .
fine **501** of this **567** Hum
3.2. 156–57 Where . . . there **203–204** To . . . scope
3.4. 71–76 Sense . . . difference **78–81** Eyes . . . mope **163–67** That
monster . . . put on **169–72** the next . . . potency **182** One word . . .
lady **204–12** There's . . . meet
4.1. 4 Bestow . . . while **41–44** Whose . . . air
4.2. 3 But soft
4.3. 26–28 KING Alas . . . worm

4.4. 8.1–66 Enter Hamlet. . . worth
4.5. 33 Oho
4.7. 69–82 LAERTES My lord . . . graveness **101–3** Th' escrimers . . .
them **115–24** There . . . ulcer
5.1. 142 There
5.2. 103–35 here is . . . unfellowed (replaced in F by "you are not
ignorant of what excellence Laertes is at his weapon") **146–47**
HORATIO [to Hamlet] I knew . . . done **181.1–194** Enter a Lord . . .
lose, my lord (replaced in F by "You will lose this wager, my lord")
208 Let be

CONTEXTS

Spiritual and Mental Life

Shakespeare and his contemporaries were used to entertaining the possibility that they were surrounded by a spirit world, one that for the most part was unseen and unheard but that could exert an influence on their lives. Such influence could be delightful and comforting; it could also provoke terrible torments. When Caliban reports "The isle is full of noises, sounds, and sweet airs that give delight and hurt not" (*Tempest*, 3.2.137–38), he represents the best of such experiences. The worst appear in the terror of the guards on the ramparts of Elsinore, and the deep confusion of Hamlet on hearing the ghost of his father exhort him to avenge his "foul and most unnatural murder" (1.5.24). Hamlet fears for his own salvation: "The spirit that I have seen / May be the devil . . . [who] Abuses me to damn me" (2.2.577–82). To believe in a spirit world did not mean that it was possible to determine the nature and extent of its effect on human behavior.

In Shakespeare's day, commentary on this subject ranges from Timothy Bright's hardheaded refutation of the claim that spirits cause "melancholy," a disease he attributes to an abundance of humors in the brain, to Joseph Hall's defense of the idea that human beings are immersed in a contest between the spiritual forces of good and evil. Between the opinions of the rational Bright and the sensitive Hall were various others, all of which attempted to make sense of extraordinary or seemingly inexplicable emotional states. George Gifford sought explanation in the Scriptural account of Lucifer's fall from heaven, which he sees as describing a division in creation, which led to a war between the infernal and the heavenly angels for the souls of the living. Joseph Hall offered a more encompassing and less dreadful view; spirits of good and evil are everywhere and faith protects us who are in their midst. Ludwig Lavater (his first name was "Englished" as Lewes) addressed the meaning of ghostly appearances without determining their agency. On the one hand, they may be emanations of a sick brain; on the other, they may be emissaries from purgatory returned to earth to seek the help of the living in reducing the term of punishment. Hamlet's encounter with the ghost allows for both possibilities. Samuel Harsnett regards evidence of diabolical "possession" and "exorcism" as merely the stuff of good theater. Timothy Bright sees hyperemotional states as the consequence of physiological disorder or psychological maladjustment.

The most comprehensive and searching psychological approach, with particular relevance to Hamlet's famous epithet, "the Melancholy Dane," is Robert Burton's monumental study of human emotions, *The Anatomy of Melancholy*. Burton takes a sympathetic view of "melancholy," reading a range of affective disorders in its symptoms. Designating a spiritual or mental state, "melancholy" can refer simply to a slight, transient disability brought about by some unusual circumstance, but if it persists, it becomes a "habit," marked by exaggerated and erratic moods in which fits of terror and grief alternate with outbursts of jesting or dismal wit.

Joseph Hall (1574–1656)

A prolific writer of satire, Bishop Hall is remembered chiefly for his critique of the Catholic Church, Mundus Alter et Idem, *translated as* The Discovery of a New World *(1608). Of his many treatises on the principles of Protestant practice and theology, those on the unseen spirit world are especially useful in understanding the uncertainty with which Shakespeare's contemporaries faced life's challenges.* Meditations and Vows *assumes the ubiquity of such a spirit world, while* The Invisible World *worries about the deceptiveness of its manifestations. In both, Hall shows a keen regard for what we might call the conflict between immaterial forces of good and evil. He describes a spirit world that is manifest in intensely emotional moments, whether fearful or joyful; he assumes that diabolical or angelic entities affect human behavior. While he is confident that angels are in charge of all of human history, he also conveys the terror provoked by the possibility that one of the faithful might meet with their malevolent counterparts.*

from *Meditations and Vows*[1]

[Our existence is permeated with the life of spirits]

There is no man, nor place, free from spirits, although they testify their presence by visible effects but in few. Every man is a host to entertain angels, though not in visible shapes, as Abraham, and Lot.[2] The evil ones do nothing but provoke us to sin and plot mischiefs against us by casting into our way dangerous objects, by suggesting sinful motions to our minds, by stirring up enemies against us amongst men, by frighting us with terrors in ourselves, by accusing us to God. On the contrary, the good angels are ever removing our hindrances from good and our occasions of evil, mitigating our temptations, helping us against our enemies, delivering us from dangers, comforting us in sorrows, furthering our good purposes, and, at last, carrying up our souls to heaven. It would affright a weak Christian that knows the power and malice of wicked spirits to consider their presence and number; but when, with the eyes of Elisha's servant,[3] he sees those on his side at present, as diligent, more powerful, he cannot but take heart again; especially if he consider, that neither of them is without God; limiting the one, the bounds of their temptation; directing the other,[4] in the safeguard of his children. Whereupon it is come to pass, that, though there be many legions of devils, and every one more strong than many legions of men and more malicious than strong, yet the little flock of God's church liveth and prospereth. I have everwith me invisible friends and enemies. The consideration of mine enemies shall keep me from security, and make me fearful of

[1]Joseph Hall, *Meditations and Vows* and *The Invisible World* in *Works*, 12 vols., London, 1837; vol. 8, pp. 88, 409.

[2]Abraham, the patriarch of the tribes of Israel, was addressed by God on numerous occasions. See Genesis 15–18. Lot was visited by angels. See Genesis 19.1, 2.

[3]Gehazi, the servant of Elisha who sees his master's spiritual power, although he himself has none; see 2 Kings 4.

[4]The evil spirit and the good spirit.

doing ought to advantage them. The consideration of my spiritual friends shall comfort me against the terror of the other, shall remedy my solitariness, shall make me wary of doing ought indecently, grieving me rather that I have ever heretofore made them turn away their eyes for shame of that whereof I have not been ashamed, that I have no more enjoyed their society, that I have been no more affected with their presence. What though I see them not? I believe them. I were no Christian, if my faith were not as sure as my sense.

from *The Invisible World*

[Spirits can take what form they like—a fear Hamlet expresses]

How vain is the observation of those authors who make this the difference between the apparitions of good angels and evil: That the good make choice of the shapes, either of beautiful persons or of those creatures which are clean and hurt less . . . ; whereas the evil put themselves into the forms of deformed men or of harmful and filthy beasts, as of a goat to the assembly of witches, . . . when we see that the very glory of angels escapes not their counterfeisance.

Ludwig Lavater (1527–1586)

A Swiss Protestant theologian, Ludwig Lavater composed a number of works in Latin which were later translated into English and published in London. Testifying to the vital interest of his contemporaries in a spirit world, his treatise on ghosts, De spectris, *translated as* Of Ghosts and Spirits Walking by Night, *rehearses various opinions on their provenance, the evidence for their appearance, and the likelihood that they are no more than phantasms produced by melancholy. Even so, Lavater is intrigued by the possibility that ghosts may be the souls of the dead who, although sentenced to a term in purgatory, are allowed to wander for a time on earth—precisely the situation the ghost of Hamlet's father describes. Lavater supposes that the reason such souls return to earth is to thank those living men and women who have made restitution for their sins. This is certainly not the reason the vengeful ghost seeks out his son, Hamlet. Lavater concludes by repudiating the doctrine of purgatory as inconsistent with a godly reading of Scripture, but his lengthy account of this intermediate station between hell and heaven suggests how fascinating its imaginative and emotional appeal might have been even to those who were compelled to reject it on theological grounds.*

from *Of Ghosts and Spirits Walking by Night*[1]

[How people speak of strange sights]

There have been very many in all ages which have utterly denied that there be any spirits or strange sights. The philosophers of Epicurus's[2] sect did jest and laugh at all those things which were reported of them, and counted them as feigned and counterfeit, by the which only children and fools, and plain simple men were made afraid. When Cassius, who was an Epicurian, understood by Brutus that he had seen a certain vision, he (as Plutarch doth testify) endeavored to attribute the matter to natural causes.[3] We read in the twenty-third chapter of the Acts of the Apostles that the Sadduceys[4] did not believe there should be any resurrection of the dead, and that they denied there were any spirits of angels. Yea, and at this day, many good and godly men believe those things to be but tales, which are talked of to and fro concerning those imagined visions, partly because in all their life, they never saw any such and partly or rather especially, because in time past men have been so often deceived with apparitions, visions and false miracles done by monks and priests, that now they take things that are true to be as utterly false. Whatsoever the cause is, it may be proved, by witness of many writers and by daily experience also, that spirits and strange sights do sometime appear, and that in very deed many strange and marvelous things do happen. True it is, that many men

---

[1]Ludwig Lavater, *Of Ghosts and Spirits Walking by Night*, trans. R.H., London, 1572; pp. 9, 10, 71, 72, 102–104, 109, 114.

[2]Epicurus (341–270 BCE) relied only on evidence from the senses and rejected the idea of a supernatural world.

[3]Gaius Cassius, one of the assassins of Julius Caesar, committed suicide after losing the battle of Philippi (42 BCE). Marcus Junius Brutus, another of Caesar's assassins, also committed suicide after Philippi. The biographies of the Greek historian Plutarch (d. 120), known as *Parallel Lives*, provided Shakespeare with source material for his Greek and Roman plays. On Brutus's dream, see Shakespeare's *Julius Caesar*, 4.2.326–337.

[4]Sadduceys (or Sadducees) were members of a sect of Jews that flourished c. 200 BCE. They followed only the written law and disputed oral tradition, the existence of demons, and the concept of the Messiah. See Acts 23.6–9.

do falsely persuade themselves that they see or hear ghosts: for that
which they imagine they see or hear proceedeth either of melancholy, madness, weakness of the senses, fear, or of some other perturbation; or else when they see or hear beasts, vapors, or some
other natural things, then they vainly suppose they have seen sights
I wote[5] not what. [. . .] There is no doubt but that almost all those
things which the common people judge to be wonderful sights are
nothing less than so. But in the mean season[6] it cannot be denied
but that strange sights and many other such like things are sometimes heard and also seen.

[How spirits affect people]

[N]o man can deny but that [there are] many honest and credible
persons of both kinds, as well men as women of whom some are living and some already departed, which have and do affirm that they
have sometimes in the day and sometimes in the night seen and
heard spirits. Some man walketh alone in his house and behold a
spirit appeareth in his sight, yea and sometimes the dogs also perceive them, and fall down at their master's feet, and will by no means
depart from them, for they are sore afraid themselves too. Some man
goeth to bed, and layeth him down to rest, and by and by there is
something pinching him, or pulling off the clothes; sometimes it sit-
teth on him or lieth down in the bed with him, and many times it
walketh up and down in the chamber. . . . Many times in the night
season there have been certain spirits heard softly going or spitting
or groaning, who, being asked what they were have made answer
that they were the souls of this or that man, and that they now
endure extreme torments. If by chance any man did ask of them by
what means they might be delivered out of those tortures, they have
answered that in case a certain number of masses were sung for
them, or pilgrimages vowed to some saints, or some other such like
deed done for their sake, that then surely they should be delivered.
Afterward appearing in great light and glory, they have said that
they were delivered and have therefore rendered great thanks to
their good benefactors and have in like manner promised that they

[5]Know.
[6]The poor season, a time of dearth and desperation.

will make intercession to God and our Lady for them.[7] And thereby it may be well proved that they were not always priests or other bold and wicked men which have feigned themselves to be souls of men deceased, as I have before said, in so much that even in those men's chambers when they have been shut, there have appeared such things, [even] when they have with a candle diligently searched before, whether anything have lurked in some corner or no.

[Spirits from purgatory]

The papists in former times have publicly both taught and written that those spirits which men sometime see and hear be either good or bad angels or else the souls of those which either live in everlasting bliss, or in purgatory, or in the place of damned persons. And that divers of them are those souls that crave aid and deliverance of men. [. . .]

Of this place, to wit, purgatory, popish writers teach marvelous things. Some of them say that purgatory is also under the earth as hell is. Some say that hell and purgatory are both one place, albeit the pains be divers according to the deserts of souls. Furthermore they say, that under the earth there are more places of punishment in which the souls of the dead may be purged. For they say that this or that soul hath been seen in this or that mountain, flood, or valley, in which it hath committed offence, and that these are particular purgatories, assigned unto them for some special cause before the day of Judgment, after which time all manner of purgatories as well general as particular shall cease. Some of them say that the pain of purgatory is all one with the punishment of hell and that they differ only in this, that the one hath an end the other no end; and that it is far more easy to endure all the pains of this world which all men since Adam's time have sustained, even unto the day of the last Judgment than to bear one day's space of the least of those two punishments.

Hereunto they add that the spirits as well of the good as the ill do come and are sent unto men living from hell. And that by the common law of justice, all men at the day of Judgment shall come to their trial from hell; and that none before that time can come from thence. Farther they teach, that by God's license and dispensation certain, yea before the day of judgment, are permitted to come

[7]The benefactors.

out of hell and that not for ever but only for a season, for the instructing and terrifying of the living. Moreover that God doth license souls to return from those two places, partly for the comfort and warning of the living and partly to pray aid of them.

Now touching the suffrages or ways of succor whereby souls are dispatched out of purgatory, popish doctors appoint four means: That is, the healthful offering of the sacrifice in the sacrament of the altar, almsgiving, prayer, fasting. And under these members, they comprise all other, as vowed pilgrimages, visiting of churches, helping of the poor, and the furthering of God's worship and glory, etc. But above all, they extol their mass as a thing of greatest force to redeem souls out of misery, of whose wonderful effect, and of the rest even now recited by us, they allege many strange examples.

Neither only in their writings, but in open pulpit also they have taught, how excellent and noble an act it is for men touched with compassion with these aforesaid works to rid the soul that appeareth unto them and craveth their help out of the pains of purgatory. Or if they cannot so do, yet to ease and assuage their torture. For say they, the souls after their deliverance, cease not in most earnest manner to pray for their benefactors and helpers. On the other side, they teach that it is an horrible and heinous offence if a man give no succor to such as seek it at his hands, especially if it be the soul of his parents, brethren and sisters. For except by them they might conveniently be released of so manifold miseries they would not so earnestly crave their help. Wherefore say they, no man should be so void of natural affection, so cruel and outrageous, that he should at any time deny to bestow some small wealth to benefit those by whom he hath before by divers and sundry ways been pleasured.

If they were not the souls of the dead which crave help and succor but devilish spirits, they would not will them to pray, fast, or give alms for their sakes, for that the devils do hate those as also all other good works.

[Why purgatory is not to be believed in]

Now that the souls neither of the faithful nor of infidels do wander any longer on the earth when they be once severed from the bodies, I will make it plain and evident unto you by these reasons following. First certain it is, that such as depart hence, either die in faith or in unbelief. Touching those that go hence in a right belief, their souls are by and by in possession of life everlasting and they that depart in unbelief do straightway become partakers of eternal damnation. The souls do not vanish away and die with the body, as the Epicures' opinion is, neither yet be in every place, as some do imagine. Touching this matter I will allege pithy and manifold testimonies out of the holy Scripture, out of which alone this question may and ought to be tried and discussed.

George Gifford (d. 1620)

Minister of St. Peter's in Maldon, Essex, and author of various tracts endorsing a radical and nonconforming Protestantism, Gifford lost his post in 1584 for refusing to subscribe to the articles of the established English church. He was allowed to remain a lecturer, however, and in this office continued to write on religious and ecclesiastical matters. A Discourse . . . of Devils *draws on the ancient story of Lucifer's fall from heaven to explain the presence of devils in our world. Gifford recalls the prophet's account of the angels' rebellion: "How art thou fallen from Heaven, O Lucifer, son of the morning . . . Yet thou saidest in thine heart, I will ascend into heaven . . . I will be like the most High" (Isaiah 14.12–14). Condemned by arrogant disobedience, Lucifer became the archdevil Satan, and his allies in sin became devils. Lacking bodily form, Gifford proposes, devils assume a human appearance in order to mislead and corrupt the faithful. The faithful, however, may call on good angels for help: "Angels and ministers of grace defend us!" cries Hamlet when he first sees his father's ghost (1.4.39). Yet his faith notwithstanding, Hamlet's psychology is also, in Gifford's view, the perfect target, for the devils work most effectively on a person of "subtle mind" and of "a melancholic constitution."*

from *A Discourse of . . . Devils*[1]

[The origin of devils]

The devils being the principal agents and chief practitioners in witchcrafts and sorceries, it is much to the purpose to describe

---

[1]George Gifford, *A Discourse of the Subtle Practices of Devils by Witches and Sorcerers*, London, 1587; sigs. C4 verso, D, E, I2 verso–I3 verso.

and set[2] them, for whereby we shall be the better instructed to see what he[3] is able to do, in what manner, and to what end and purpose. At the beginning (as God's word doth teach us) they were created holy Angels, full of power, and glory. They sinned, they were cast down from heaven, they were utterly deprived of glory, and preserved for judgment.[4] This therefore and this change of theirs did not destroy nor take away their former faculties, but utterly corrupt, pervert, and deprave the same: the essence of spirits remained, and not only, but also power and understanding, such as in angels. . . .

The infernal angels are for their strength called principalities and powers. Those blessed ones apply all their might to set up and advance the glory of God, to defend and succor his children; the devils bend all their force against God, against his glory, his truth and his people. And this is done with such fierceness, rage, and cruelty, that the Holy Ghost painteth them out under the figure of a great red or fiery dragon, and roaring lion, in very deed anything comparable to them. He[5] hath such power and authority indeed, that he is called the God of the world. His kingdom is bound and enclosed within certain limits, for he is the prince but of darkness; but yet within his said dominion (which is in ignorance of God), he exerciseth a mighty tyranny.

There be great multitudes of infernal spirits, as the holy scriptures do everywhere show, but yet they do so join together in one that they be called the devil in the singular number. . . . The holy angels are ministering spirits, sent forth for their sakes, which shall inherit the promise.[6] They have no bodily shape of themselves, but to set forth their speediness, the Scripture applieth itself unto our rude capacity,[7] and painteth them out with wings. When they are to rescue and succor the servants of God, they can straight way from the high heavens, which are thousands of thousands of miles distant

---

[2]Identify.

[3]The devil.

[4]"For . . . God spared not the angels that had sinned, but cast them down into hell, and delivered them into chains of darkness, to be kept unto damnation" (2 Peter 2.4).

[5]The devil.

[6]Of heaven, eternal life.

[7]Ignorance.

from the earth, be present with them. Such quickness is also in the devils, for their nature being spiritual and not laden with any heavy matter as our bodies are, but afford unto them such a nimbleness as we cannot conceive. By this they fly through the world over sea and land, and espy out all advantages and occasions to do evil. . . .

[The nature of devils]

Our Savior Christ saith that a spirit hath neither flesh nor bones. A spirit hath a substance, but yet such as is invisible, whereupon it must needs be granted, that devils in their own nature have no bodily shape, nor visible form; moreover it is against the truth and against piety to believe that devils can create or make bodies, or change one body into another for those things are proper[8] to God. It followeth therefore that whensoever they appear in a visible form, it is no more but an apparition and counterfeit show of a body, unless a body be at any time lent them. And when as they make one body to bear the likeness of another, it is but a color.[9]

[Persons who are susceptible to attacks by devils]

[The devil] doth observe time and place, with all other circumstances, and . . . he seeketh convenient persons as matter to work upon; he chooseth out fit instruments to work withal when he raiseth up some heresy to destroy the true faith, which[10] is with subtle show to be defended. [H]e suggesteth not the same into the mind of a blunt learned fool which is able to say little; but if it be possible, he espieth out a subtle mind, which is also proud, vainglorious, and stiff[11] to maintain any purpose. . . . If there be above all these a melancholic constitution of body, his[12] impressions print the deeper in the mind. If they be fell[13] and given to anger, and ready to revenge, they be so much the fitter. . . .

[8]Belong.

[9]An illusion; as Horatio identifies the ghost (1.1.127).

[10]The heresy.

[11]Fortified.

[12]The devil's.

[13]Cruel.

[How to defeat devils]

The sum of the whole is that by faith in the gospel of Jesus Christ we are armed with power of grace, with true knowledge and light, with sincere integrity of heart, and with a godly life, with zeal, with patience, and with all other heavenly virtues, so that the fiery darts of the devil, neither in tempting unto filthy sins, nor yet in damnable heresies and opinions can fasten upon us. If we want the true faith, we want grace; we be not in Christ, we have not his spirit. This faith is grounded upon the word of God; for the word is sent to be preached, that men may hear and believe. If men be ignorant in the word of God, they cannot have power to resist the devil; they have no sword to fight with him. Christ our great captain hath left unto us an example, which we ought to follow, when he resisted the devil. For at every temptation, he draweth forth this same spiritual sword,[14] and saith it is written, and so woundeth Satan therewith. . . .

Samuel Harsnett (1561–1631)

Educated at Pembroke Hall, Cambridge, where he received his A.B. in 1580 and took orders in 1583, Harsnett went on to a distinguished career as a teacher, clergyman, and administrator, becoming Vice-Chancellor of Cambridge University in 1614 and Archbishop of York in 1629. Having served on the commission investigating the exorcist John Darrel, he wrote A Discovery of the Fraudulent Practices of John Darrel, *1599, an even-handed critique of exorcism as practiced by both Protestants and Catholic sympathizers. He followed with* A Declaration of Egregious Popish Impostures . . . under the Pretence of Casting Out Devils *(1603), Shakespeare's source for Edgar's spirit-names in* King Lear *(3.4.114, 139, 141, 142). Harsnett's satiric account of Darrel's theatrics of possession and exorcism suggests how the skeptics in Shakespeare's audience could have interpreted Hamlet's fits as skillful deceptions, even as the more credulous took them as the devil's work.*

---

[14]St. Paul advises his readers to take up "the sword of the Spirit, which is the word of God" (Ephesians 6.17).

from *A Discovery of the Fraudulent Practices of John Darrel*[1]

[What really happened when Somers was "exorcised"]

But to insist no longer upon these vanities and foolish surmises[2]: The true occasion that moved her Majesty's said Commissioners to intermeddle with this impostor (wherewith his confederates and companions are so much grieved), and to proceed therein as they have done, was as followeth.

William Somers having counterfeited himself to be possessed, dispossessed, and repossessed, and held[3] on that course successively for the space of about three months, he did at the last, being got out of Mr. Darrel's hands, confess and avow that all he had done that while was but dissembled, showing to the Mayor and Aldermen of Nottingham how he had acted all his former fits. Herewith Mr. Darrel and his friends were greatly moved, especially when they perceived the boy's said confession to be so generally believed, as that there began a heartburning amongst the neighbors, some holding with Mr. Darrel, and some against him. To meet therefore with this mischief, and hearing (as it is supposed) that the Archdeacon of Darby had written to the Lord Archbishop of Canterbury touching that matter, it was thought good to use some prevention, and to procure a Commission from the Archbishop of York[4] for the examination of such witnesses, as should be produced in the behalf of Mr. Darrel, to prove that Somers had not dissembled. The said Commission obtained,[5] exceptions were taken against it, because all the Commissioners were addicted to[6] Mr. Darrel. Thereupon it was renewed,[7] and upon one Mr. Ewington's motion, some were made Commissioners to join with the rest that were known to have dislike of Mr. Darrel's proceedings. When the time came that this

---

[1]Samuel Harsnett, *A Discovery of the Fraudulent Practices of John Darrel, Bachelor of Arts, in his Proceedings Concerning the Pretended Possession and Dispossession of William Somers at Nottingham*, London, 1599, pp. 6–9, 61–63.

[2]Darrel's claims.

[3]Having continued.

[4]To request the Archbishop of York to establish a Commission.

[5]Appointed.

[6]Biased in favor of.

[7]Reconstituted.

second Commission was to be executed[8] (certain persons having been examined), Somers was brought before the Commissioners, who shortly after his coming, fell to the acting of some of his fits in their presence upon a former compact and agreement made bewixt him and others before he came thither.

Herewith, all that favored Mr. Darrel began to rejoice, and to run abroad into the town telling their friends with great joy that Somers was now found to have been no dissembler; but the rest that had held a contrary opinion, they were greatly rated[9] and checked, insomuch as when some of them came out of the house where the Commissioners sat, they were not only rated at exceedingly, but to one of them by the throwing of a stone some violence was offered. Thus Mr. Darrel and his friends triumphed for nine or ten days, having by the direction of the said Commissioners Somers amongst them again, who, playing his old tricks, denied that he had dissembled. But this their joy ended when the said days were expired. [F]or Somers, by the direction of the Lord Chief Justice of the Common Pleas, was no sooner gotten again out of the hands of Mr. Darrel and his friends, but of himself he confessed (as before) the whole course of his dissimulation, and why he had affirmed to the said Commissioners that the fits acted before them were not counterfeited. With his alteration Mr. Darrel and his adherents were greatly troubled. [T]he parts taking on both sides began to be more violent, and the town became to be extraordinarily divided, one railing upon another at their meeting in the streets, as they were affected in that cause. The pulpits also rang of nothing but devils and witches; wherewith men, women, and children were so affrighted, as many of them durst not stir in the night nor so much as a servant almost go into his master's cellar about his business without company. Few grew to be sick or evil at ease, but straightway they were deemed to be possessed. Briefly, such were the stirs in Nottingham about this matter, as it was feared the people would grow (if they were not prevented) to further quarrels and mutinies or to some greater inconvenience.

Hereof the Lord Archbishop of Canterbury being advertised by the said Lord Chief Justice and others, did think it in his wisdom

[8]Arrive at a judgment.
[9]Berated.

very necessary to call for Mr. Darrel by virtue of her Majesty's Commission for Causes Ecclesiastical, who, being accordingly sent for, appeared before him and others at Lambeth; from whence he was committed to prison by reason of his absurd and untrue (but yet very confident) assertions, giving thereby just occasion to suspect that he was but a counterfeiter, and order was taken for the further examination of that cause, according to the usual course by the laws of the realm in such cases provided.[10]

[Exorcism as theater]

[Exorcists] are driven to their shifts and sleights. . . . Sometimes they make choice of some such boys or wenches as they think are fit for their purpose, whom they procure by many promises and allurements to keep their counsel and to be (as they term it) advised by them. And these are commonly of the poorer sort, either the children or servants of such persons as the exorcists do well know to be of their own stamp and well affected towards them. It falleth out now and then that they have some scholars[11] of their own, whom they mean to prefer, the popish sort[12] to some seminaries and others as they may. And there are none to these[13] they are so apt to work upon: howbeit they can soon frame the other[14] to their bent by their cunning. When they have any of these[15] in hand, they do instruct them so perfectly as when they come to exorcise them, they are in a manner secure, their scholars knowing as well what to do as their false masters themselves. These are not dealt with but there must be a great assembly gathered together in one corner or another, all of them such persons as they know to be their friends or at the least such as their said friends do bring with them and are thought fit to be perverted. The company met, the exorcists do tell them, what a work of God they have in hand, and after a long discourse, how Satan doth afflict the parties, and what strange things they shall see;

---

[10]Darrel, a priest, was eventually tried, convicted of fraud, defrocked and imprisoned.

[11]Apprentices.

[12]Sympathetic to Catholicism.

[13]Their apprentices, "scholars."

[14]Darrel and his "scholars" can persuade others to learn exorcism.

[15]Subjects of persuasion.

the said parties are brought forth, as it were a bear to the stake, and being either bound in a chair or otherwise held fast, they fall to their fits, and play their pranks point by point exactly according as they have been instructed. And if they be of the new cut:[16] they cry, they wallow, they foam, and show signs of possession mentioned in the Scriptures, with some others. But if they be of the old instructions:[17] then there are notable tragedies. Out cometh the priest in massing attire; the hallowed candles are lightened; their relics with their *Agnus Dei* are brought forth; the holy water flieth about the chamber; their hallowed frankincense perfumeth the place, and so forth. Whereupon all that are present (having worshipped the said holy mysteries) no sooner cast their eyes towards the parties pretended to be possessed, but there is starting, struggling, and striving; they screech, they rail, they spit, they cry, they rage and fare as not being able in any wise without danger of present death to endure the presence of the Catholic priests and of their holy complements.

Timothy Bright (1551–1615)

Timothy Bright, a physician by training, was an early exponent of a rational approach to claims for the existence of a spirit world. Best known as the inventor of shorthand (his Characterie: An Art of Short Swift and Secret Writing by Characters *[1588] was his first publication), Bright produced two books on the health of the human body (one recommending ways to preserve health, the other to cure disease) before writing his incisive work on melancholy. Bright subscribes to the Galenic theory of medicine, which posited that just as a sound body depended on a salutary balance among the four principal humors— blood, phlegm, bile, and lymph—so a diseased body was brought about by humoral imbalances. He attributes melancholy to the collection of a "gross humor" in the brain which causes fantastic apparitions. The resulting delusions bode permanent mental damage: fantastic apparitions could remain in the memory and distort every aspect of a worldview. By contrast, Bright insists, profound feelings of guilt and unworthiness are not symptomatic of true melancholy, although they*

[16]Protestants.
[17]Catholics.

can result in moods that resemble those created by the disease. Rather, they are the perfectly understandable reactions of a sinner who is struggling with his past. For Bright's contemporaries, this important distinction between melancholy as a mental disease and spiritual anxiety as a condition of the soul discouraged belief in a spirit world. For Bright, the person who believed he saw spirits was either suffering from the effects of a humoral imbalance or speaking figuratively about his fear of God's wrath.

from *A Treatise of Melancholy*[1]

[The emotions created by melancholy]

Now let us consider what passions they are that melancholy driveth us unto, and how it doth so diversely distract those that are oppressed therewith. The perturbations of melancholy are for the most part sad and fearful and [also] such as rise of them: as distrust, doubt, diffidence, or despair, sometimes furious, and sometimes merry in appearance, through a kind of Sardonian[2] and false laughter, as the humor is disposed that procureth these diversities. Those which are sad and pensive rise of the melancholic humor which is the grossest part of the blood. [. . .] This for the most part is settled in the spleen and with his vapors annoyeth the heart; and, passing up to the brain, counterfeiteth terrible objects to the fantasy; and, polluting both the substance and spirits of the brain, causeth it without external occasion to forge monstrous fictions and terrible to the conceit, which the judgment taking as they are presented by the disordered instrument, deliver over to the heart, which hath no judgment of discretion in itself, but giving credit to the mistaken report of the brain, breaketh out into that inordinate passion, against reason.

This cometh to pass because the instrument of discretion is depraved by these melancholic spirits, and a darkness and clouds of melancholy vapors, rising from that puddle of the spleen, obscure the clearness which our spirits are endued with and is requisite to the due discretion of outward objects. This at the first is not so extreme, neither doth it shew so apparently, as in process of time,

---

[1]Timothy Bright, *A Treatise of Melancholy*, London, 1586; sigs. Giii–Giiii verso; Mviii verso.

[2]Sardonic, sarcastic.

when the substance of the brain hath plentifully drunk of that splenetic fog,[3] whereby his nature is become of the same quality, and the pure and bright spirits so defiled and eclipsed, that their indifferency alike to all sensible things is now drawn to a partiality and inclination, as by melancholy they are enforced. For where that natural and internal light is darkened, their fancies arise vain, false and void of ground, even as in the external sensible darkness a false illusion will appear unto our imagination, which, the light being brought in, is discerned to be an abuse of fancy.

Now the internal darkness, affecting more nigh by our nature[4] than the outward, is cause of greater fears and more molesteth us with terror than that which taketh from us the sight of sensible things especially,[5] arising not of absence of light only but by a presence of a substantial obscurity, which is possessed with an actual power of operation.[6] This, taking hold of the brain by process of time, giveth it an habit of depraved conceit, whereby it fancieth not according to truth but as the nature of that humor leadeth it, altogether ghastly and fearful. This causeth not only fantastical apparitions wrought by apprehension only of common sense[7]; but [also] fantasy, another part of internal sense, compoundeth and forgeth disguised shapes,[8] which give great terror unto the heart, and cause it with the lively spirit[9] to hide itself as well as it can, by contraction in all parts, from those counterfeit goblins, which the brain dispossessed of right discerning, feigneth unto the heart.

Neither only is common sense and fantasy thus overtaken with delusion [sic], but memory also receiveth a wound therewith, which disableth it both to keep in memory and to record those things whereof it took some custody before this passion, and after therewith are defaced. For as the common sense and fantasy, which do offer [things] unto the memory to lay up, deliver but fables instead of true report—and those tragical that dismay all the

[3]Of the spleen, bitter.

[4]Affecting us more.

[5]The night; physical blindness.

[6]The inner darkness or "substantial obscurity" actually affects what we think we see.

[7]The interpretation of ordinary sense perceptions.

[8]Fantastic images.

[9]The heart and its internal spirit.

sensible frame of our bodies—so either is the memory wholly distracted by importunity of those doubts and fears that it neglecteth the custody of other store[10]; or else it recordeth and apprehendeth only such as by this importunity is thrust thereupon, [that is], nothing but darkness, peril, doubt, frights, and whatsoever the heart of man doth abhor.

[Melancholy as a misery of the soul]

Of all kinds of miseries that befall unto man, none is so miserable as that which riseth of the sense of God's wrath and revenging hand against the guilty soul of a sinner. Other calamities affect the body and one part only of our nature; this the soul, which carrieth the whole[11] into society of the same misery. Such as are of the body, although they approach nigher the quick[12] than poverty or want of necessaries for maintenance of this life, yet they fail in degree of misery and come short of that which this[13] forceth upon the soul. The other touch those parts where the soul commandeth: poverty, nakedness, sickness and other of that kind are mitigated with a mind resolute in patience or endued with wisdom to ease that [which] grieveth by supply of remedy. [T]his seizeth upon the seat of wisdom itself, and chargeth upon all the excellency of understanding, and grindeth into powder all that standeth firm, and melteth like the dew before the sun whatsoever we reckon of as support of our defects, and subdueth that wherewith all things else are of us subdued. [T]he cause, the guilt, the punishment, the revenge, the ministers of the wrath, all [are] concurring together in more forcible sort (and that against the universal state of our nature, not for a time, but for ever) than in any other kind of calamity whatsoever.

Here the cause is not either wound or surfeit, shipwreck or spoil, infamy or disgrace, but all kinds of misery joined together with a troubled spirit, feeling the beginnings and expecting with desperate fear the eternal consummation of the indignation and fierce wrath of God's vengeance against the violation of his holy

[10]Memory.

[11]The whole person.

[12]What is alive, vital.

[13]Guilt.

commandments; which, although in this life it taketh not away the use of outward benefits, yet doth the internal anguish bereave us of all delight of them and that pleasant relish they are endued with to our comforts; so that manifold better were it [that] the use of them were quite taken away than for us in such sort to enjoy them. Neither is here the guiltiness[14] of breach of human laws (whose punishment extendeth no farther then this present life, which even of itself is full of calamities not much inferior to the pain adjoined unto the transgression of civil laws) but of the law divine and the censure executed with the hand of God, whose fierce wrath prosecuteth the punishment eternally as his displeasure is like to himself, and followeth us into our graves, and receiveth no satisfaction with any punishment, either in regard of continuance or of extremity.[15]

Robert Burton (1577–1640)

Robert Burton's popular treatise The Anatomy of Melancholy *examines all aspects of a disease we would be hard put to identify. But in the seventeenth century, it was a familiar if protean condition: Melancholy could manifest itself as a kind of discouragement with the exigencies of life or (at the opposite extreme) as a radical rejection of all affective relations. Burton's treatise appeared in eight successively more elaborate editions throughout the century. It was widely read well into the nineteenth century.*

Melancholy, as Burton theorized it, was not a simple condition of the body induced by a humoral imbalance; rather, it was a complex illness implicating mind and body in various ways and degrees. This kind of symptomology would be variously named in later epochs as "demonic possession," "hysteria," or "shell shock." Burton also saw that its manifestations among different persons might be quite variable: While the common sense of one person might be able to withstand the effects of a fairly severe trauma, the emotional disposition of another less capable of moral fortitude could cause him to collapse completely.

[14]Owing to.
[15]Here Bright explicitly repudiates the doctrine of purgatory.

Especially evocative for Hamlet is Burton's idea that melancholy can begin as a kind of moodiness and become progressively more debilitating—even a permanent disorder. Such a sense of the range of melancholy behavior allows us to speculate on how Hamlet's mental state may be changing during the course of the play. In Act 1, we see that he suffers from deep grief over the death of his father; by Act 3, we sense that he has become obsessively crazed by the news he has heard from the Ghost. Burton also identifies a melancholy peculiar to women, which he attributes to a lack of work and discipline. Its chief victims are "nice gentlewomen [. . .] that fare well in great houses"—a situation like that of Ophelia. Finally, Burton's emphasis on sexual abstinence as a cause of melancholy suggests that Hamlet and Ophelia may share a disability; we can read Hamlet's rejection of Ophelia as a would-be "breeder of sinners" (3.1.120) as an index of his own frustration.

from *The Anatomy of Melancholy*[1]

[A melancholy disposition]

Melancholy, the subject of our present discourse, is either in disposition or habit. In disposition[2] is that transitory melancholy which goes and comes upon every small occasion of sorrow, need, sickness, trouble, fear, grief, passion, or perturbation of the mind, any manner of care, discontent, or thought, which causeth anguish, dullness, heaviness and vexation of spirit, any ways opposite to pleasure, mirth, joy, delight, causing frowardness in us, or a dislike. In which equivocal and improper sense, we call him melancholy that is dull, sad, sour, lumpish, ill-disposed, solitary, any way moved or displeased. And from these melancholy dispositions no man living is free, no Stoic,[3] none so wise, none so happy, none so patient, so generous, so godly, so divine that can vindicate himself, so well-composed, but more or less, some time or other, he feels the smart of it. Melancholy in this sense is the character of mortality.

---

[1]Robert Burton, *The Anatomy of Melancholy*, ed. A. R. Shilleto, 3 vols., London, 1896; vol. 1, pp. 164–166, 471–472, 479–480.

[2]By nature.

[3]Stoic philosophy, initiated by Zeno in the 4th c. BCE, promoted a stringent moral discipline that required indifference to the emotions.

[Melancholy as a habitual frame of mind]

But forasmuch as so few can embrace this good counsel of his (*St. Paul, 2 Tim. 2.3*[4]), or use it aright, but rather—as so many brute beasts give a way to their passion—voluntarily subject and precipitate themselves into a labyrinth of cares, woes, miseries, and suffer their souls to be overcome by them, [and] cannot arm themselves with that patience as they ought to do, it falleth out oftentimes that these dispositions become habits, and [that] many affects contemned (as Seneca notes *Epist. 96. lib. 10*[5]) make a disease. Even as one distillation not yet grown to custom makes a cough but [one] continual and inveterate causeth a consumption of the lungs, so do these our melancholy provocations; and according as the humor itself is intended or remitted in men, as their temperature of body or rational soul is better able to make resistance, so are they more or less affected. For that which is but a flea-biting to one, causeth insufferable torment to another; and [that] which one by his singular moderation and well-composed carriage can happily overcome, a second is not [one] whit able to sustain. But upon every small occasion of misconceived abuse, injury, grief, disgrace, loss, cross, rumor, etc. (if solitary or idle), [he] yields so far to passion that his complexion is altered, his digestion hindered, his sleep gone, his spirits obscured, and his heart heavy, his hypochondries misaffected.[6] Wind, crudity on a sudden overtake him, and he himself [is] overcome with melancholy. [. . .] This melancholy of which we are to treat is an habit [. . .] a chronic or continual disease, a settled humor, as Aurelianus[7] and others call it, not errant, but fixed; and as it was long increasing, so, now being (pleasant or painful) grown to an habit, it will hardly be removed.

[Symptoms of melancholy]

The symptoms of the mind are superfluous and continual cogitations; for, when the head is heated, it scorcheth the blood, and from

[4]"Thou therefore suffer affliction as a good soldier of Jesus Christ."

[5]Roman philosopher Seneca (4 BCE–65) wrote primarily in the field of ethics; his *Epistles* (letters) promote a prudent way of life.

[6]His upper abdomen disturbed.

[7]Physician of Sicca in Numidia (fl. 5th c.) who translated works on the passions by Soranus of Ephesus, a physician under the emperors Hadrian and Trajan, 98–137. Soranus's almost twenty books of medicine were widely translated and distributed throughout the late classical period.

thence proceed melancholy fumes, which trouble the mind, *Avicenna*.[8] They are very choleric, and soon hot, solitary, sad, often silent, watchful, discontent, *Montaltus, cap. 24*.[9] If anything trouble them, they cannot sleep, but fret themselves still, till another object mitigate or time wear it out. They have grievous passions and immoderate perturbations of the mind—fear, sorrow, &c.—yet not so continual but that they are sometimes merry, apt to profuse laughter, which is more to be wondered at. . . . [I]f they be ruddy,[10] they are delighted in jests and oftentimes scoffers themselves, conceited and merry, witty, of a pleasant disposition, and yet grievously melancholy anon after.

[Women's melancholy]

[T]he best and surest remedy of all is to see them well placed and married to good husbands in due time; [. . .] this [is] the ready cure, to give them content to their desires. I write not this to patronize any wanton, idle flirt, lascivious or light housewives, which are too forward many times, unruly, and apt to cast away themselves on him that comes next, without all care, counsel, circumspection, and judgment. If religion, good discipline, honest education, wholesome exhortation, fair promises, fame, and loss of good name, cannot inhibit and deter such (which to chaste and sober maids cannot choose but avail much), labor and exercise, strict diet, rigor and threats, may more opportunely be used, and are able of themselves to qualify and divert an ill-disposed temperament. For seldom shall you see a hired servant, a poor handmaid, although ancient, that is kept hard to her work and bodily labor, [or] a coarse country wench troubled in this kind. But rather noble virgins, nice gentlewomen, such as are solitary and idle, live at ease, lead a life out of action and employment, that fare well in great houses and jovial companies, ill-disposed peradventure of themselves, and not willing to make any resistance, discontented otherwise, of weak judgment, able bodies and subject to passions [. . .] , such for the most part are misaffected and prone to this dis-

[8]An 11th c. Arabian philosopher who wrote over 100 treatises on the natural sciences. His medicine was based on Galenic principles.

[9]Portuguese physician Filotea Eliao Montalto (d. 1616) wrote a work on optics.

[10]Of a sanguine humor, cheerful and optimistic.

ease. I do not so much pity them that may otherwise be eased. But [in] those alone that out of a strong temperament [and an] innate constitution are violently carried away with this torrent of inward humors [. . .] yet cannot make resistance—these grievances will appear, this malady will take place, and now manifestly show itself, and may not otherwise be helped.

[The dangers of celibacy]

How odious and abominable are those superstitious and rash vows of popish monasteries to bind and enforce men and women to vow virginity, to lead a single life against the laws of nature, opposite to religion, policy, and humanity, so to starve, to offer violence, to suppress the vigor of youth by rigorous statutes, severe laws, vain persuasions, to debar them of that to which by their innate temperature they are so furiously inclined, urgently carried, and sometimes precipitated, even irresistibly led, to the prejudice of their soul's health and good estate of body and mind! [. . .] Better marry than burn, saith the Apostle,[11] but they are otherwise persuaded. They will by all means quench their neighbor's house if it be on fire, but that fire of lust, which breaks out into such lamentable flames, they will not take notice of; their own bowels oftentimes, flesh and blood, shall so rage and burn, and they will not see it.

[11]St. Paul. See 1 Corinthians 7.9: "But if they cannot abstain, let them marry, for it is better to marry than to burn." By "burn" St. Paul means either to suffer sexual frustration or indulge in sex out of wedlock and thus burn in sin.

Purgatory

The Christian doctrine of purgatory is at least as old as the church itself and may even derive from the ancient Jewish belief in prayers for the dead as noted in the Apocrypha: Judas asks his host to pray for their comrades killed in battle and sends money to Jerusalem to compensate for their sins (2 Maccabees 12.42–44). A rationale for the doctrine is suggested by one of the early doctors, Clement of Alexandria (150–216?), who, having asked himself what can be expected of those who die without having fulfilled the requirement of penance, answers:

> [T]he believer through discipline divests himself of his passions and passes to the mansion which is better than the former one, passes to the greatest torment, taking with him the characteristic of repentance for the faults he may have committed after baptism. He is tortured then still more, not yet attaining what he sees others have acquired. The greatest torments are assigned unto the believer, for God's righteousness is good, and His goodness righteous . . . those punishments cease in the course of expiation and purification.

The idea that a soul undergoing purgation in this "mansion" can be helped by the prayers of his fellows is expressed by Ambrose of Alexandria (d. 250) in his funeral oration for the emperor Theodosius: "I loved him, therefore . . . I will not leave him till by my prayers and lamentations he shall be admitted unto the holy mount of the Lord to which his deserts call him." These concepts—of a place of purgation preparatory to entering heaven and the possibility of a loving communion of the living with those in purgatory—remain definitive for Roman Catholics, involving a belief in salvation through charitable works and in the church as a mystical body transcending the limits of real time and place. The doctrine of purgatory, which allowed for the satisfaction of or retribution for venial (though not mortal) sin, was established as a feature of Catholic theology by the councils of Lyons (1274) and Florence (1439); bishops were required to teach it to the faithful by the council of Trent (1545–1563).

Protestants rejected the doctrine of purgatory for the very reasons Catholics affirmed it. Denying the necessity of charitable works for salvation and insisting on faith alone, Protestants followed Martin Luther in regarding purgatory as a deception. Not only did this notion demean the significance of Christ's sacrifice, but its social effects were also scandalous. The sale of pardons and indulgences by the clergy used up the charity that should have gone to relieve the poor and needy. The abuse of pardons and indulgences was protested by Simon Fish, probably a Lollard sympathizer, in *A Supplication for the Beggars* (1529); scriptural objections were detailed by Luther and Calvin, principal exponents of the Protestant reformation, and by their English followers, including the Huguenot John Véron. John Foxe's *Ecclesiastical History, containing Acts and Monuments* (1563), a comprehensive history of Protestants who rejected and indeed ridiculed Catholic doctrine, documents this pervasive resistance. Even so, the doctrine of purgatory continued to be widely known and represented, with such plays as *The Last Judgment* dramatizing purgatorial punishment. As one who will be saved by his suffering says:

> As hard pains, I dare well say,
> In purgatory are night and day,
> As are in hell, save by one way:
> That one shall have an end.

English Catholics continued to promote belief in purgatory both to strengthen bonds among the faithful and to encourage penance for sin. Cardinal William Allen's *Defense and Declaration of the Catholic Church's Doctrine Touching Purgatory* (1577) stressed the fellowship of Catholics in life as well as in death and through the fires of purgatory, seeing it as an expression of the "natural compassion of the church [that] passeth through every member thereof." For a Catholic, moral behavior in this life was a factor in gaining eternal salvation, and purgatory provided the way to atone for venial sins. For a Protestant, however, Christ's sacrifice was entirely sufficient; to say that a Christian might earn salvation by moral action was to misread Scripture.

Purgatory looms in *Hamlet* when the Ghost of the old king, Hamlet's father, refers to his "prison-house," where for "a certain term" he is "confined to fast in fires, / Till the foul crimes done in my days of nature / Are burnt and purged away" (1.5.9–12). His request to his son is not, however, for prayers or the purchase of indulgences but for revenge on his murderer, the new king Claudius. As murder in another name, this kind of revenge was not a request that Catholic doctrine could condone, particularly from a sinful soul in purgatory. Not only Christian precept but also natural law, English law, and custom forbad individual acts of revenge; a wrongdoer was to be punished only by the institutions of law and according to its provisions. Even so, a vast and rich tradition of fictions, from Greek tragedy to Jacobean drama, was devoted to representing acts of vengeance and retribution, often validated on the grounds of personal honor. It is this tradition that encourages Laertes to avenge his father's murder "in my terms of honor," even though he is "satisfied in nature" that Hamlet acted in all innocence (5.2.228–30). The extraordinary nature of the Ghost's request explains some of Hamlet's hesitation throughout the play. Even assuming the Ghost is "honest," Hamlet risks damnation if he commits murder, a mortal sin. In light of Christian doctrine, the Ghost is suspect; if he is not a "goblin damned," he is also not "a spirit of health" (1.4.40).

Simon Fish (d. 1531)

Simon Fish was clearly interested in the new theology proposed by reformers on the continent. Committed to the study of God's word, he sold William Tyndale's translation of the New Testament to persons interested in the reformation of the church in England. On hearing Fish's attack on the doctrine of purgatory and the practice of granting indulgences in his Supplication for the Beggars *(1529), Henry VIII is said to have responded, "If a man should pull down an old stone wall and begin at the lower part, the upper part thereof might chance to fall upon his head"—an image that warns against challenging clerical practice before the crown acquires supreme control of the church, as it did in 1537.*

from A Supplication for the Beggars[1]

[Clerical greed and the doctrine of purgatory]

Neither have they any other color[2] to gather these yearly exactions[3] into their hands, but that they say they pray for us to God to deliver our souls out of the pains of purgatory, without whose prayer, they say, or at least without the Pope's pardon, we could never be delivered thence; which if it be true, then is it good reason that we give them all these things, although were it a hundred times as much. But there be many men of great literature and judgment that—for the love they have unto the truth and unto the commonwealth—have not feared to put themselves into the greatest infamy that may be in abjection of[4] all the world, ye, in peril of death, to declare their opinion in this matter; which is that there is no purgatory, but that it is a thing invented by the covetousness of the spirituality,[5] only to translate all kingdoms from other princes unto them, and that there is not one word spoken of it in all Holy Scripture. They say also that if there were a purgatory, and also that if the pope with his pardons for money may deliver one soul thence, he may deliver him as well without money; if he may deliver one, he may deliver a thousand; if he may deliver a thousand, he may deliver them all, and so destroy purgatory. And then is he a cruel tyrant without all charity if he keep them there in prison and in pain till men will give him money. Likewise, say they—of all the whole sort of the spirituality—that if they will not pray for no man but for them that give them money, they are

[1]Simon Fish, *A Supplication for the Beggars*, ed. Frederick J. Furnivall, London, 1871; pp. 10–11.

[2]Justification.

[3]Tithes were collected annually (an indulgence was granted occasionally for a consideration).

[4]In abasement before.

[5]Clergy.

tyrants and lack charity, and suffer those souls to be punished and pained uncharitably for lack of their prayers. These sort of folks they call heretics, these they burn, these they rage against, put to open shame, and make them bear faggots. But whether they be heretics or not, well I wote that this purgatory and the Pope's pardons is [sic] all the cause of translation of your kingdom so fast into their hands,[6] wherefore it is manifest it cannot be of Christ, for he gave more to the temporal kingdom, he himself paid tribute to Caesar, he took nothing from him but taught that the high powers should be always obeyed; ye, he himself (although he were most free lord of all and innocent) was obedient unto the high powers unto death.

Martin Luther (1483–1540)

In 1517, Martin Luther, a young Augustinian monk, challenged centuries of Catholic teaching by repudiating a principal article of its faith: salvation by works. In ninety-five theses nailed to the doors of the cathedral at Wittenburg, Luther insisted that Christians were to be saved by grace alone and not by any action, however generous it might be. He especially rejected the idea that the saints in heaven had bequeathed a treasury of merits or good works known as "indulgences," which the living could purchase for the remission of their sins and relief from purgatorial punishment. The living could also purchase indulgences to help those already in purgatory.

Luther devoted the rest of his life to opposing the doctrine of salvation by works and what he regarded as other papal abuses. In 1520, he wrote two controversial treatises: An Address to the Christian Nobility, *stating that the church should be merely a spiritual institution; and the* Babylonian Captivity, *identifying only baptism and the Eucharist as sacraments. He was excommunicated in 1521. In* The Chief and Principal Articles of the Christian Faith *(1548), first published in German in 1543, Luther dismisses the idea of purgatory altogether: unknown to the "old Church and the Apostles," it is a "diabolical illusion."*

---

[6]Fish claims that the commonwealth or the property of the people is being transferred to the church by those seeking remission from time in purgatory.

from *The Chief and Principal Articles of the Christian Faith*[1]

[On justification by faith alone]

Here is the first and chief article: That Jesus Christ our God and
Lord suffered death for our sins and rose again for our justification.
And that he only is the lamb of God, which beareth the sins of the
world. And that God hath laid all our sins upon him. They[2] are all
sinners and are justified freely without deserving by his grace
through the redemption of Jesus Christ in his blood. Forasmuch
now, as this must be believed and otherwise cannot be obtained or
comprehended by no work, law, nor deserving, so is it clear, evident
and sure that only such faith maketh us righteous. . . . I believe [in]
the resurrection of the dead at the last day, both of the good and the
bad, that ever there every man may receive in his body according to
his deserving, and that the good shall live perpetually with Christ,
and the wicked die everlastingly with the devil and his angels, for I
hold not with them that teach that the devils also shall at the last
come to salvation.

[On kinds of idolatry]

First Purgatory: There have men handled and made market with
soul masses, dirges, sevenths, trentals, month's minds and year's
minds, and at the last with the common week's minds and All
Souls' Day, and beadrolls,[3] insomuch that the mass almost is used
only for the dead. Notwithstanding that Christ did institute the
Sacrament only for the living. Therefore is purgatory with all the
pomp of God's service and purchase of the same to be counted for
a mere diabolical illusion. For it is also against the chief and princi-

---

[1]Martin Luther, *The Chief and Principal Articles of the Christian Faith, to Hold
Against the Pope and all Papists, and the Gates of Hell*, London, 1548; sigs. A7, A7
verso, B2 verso, B3, H8, H8 verso.

[2]All Christians.

[3]Luther rehearses the schedules of requiem masses for the souls of the dead in purgatory: sevenths and trentals refer to two series of requiem masses, celebrated each day
for seven or thirty days, respectively. Month's, year's, and week's minds are individual requiem masses, celebrated a month, year, or week after the death of a person. All
Soul's Day, a day of prayer for the dead, follows Halloween, usually on November 2.
Beadrolls are rosaries.

pal article that only Christ, and not man's works must help the souls. Besides that, also we have no charge or commandment given unto us concerning the dead. Wherefore it may well be left and omitted, although it were neither heresy, error, nor idolatry. . . . There are yet many more of those new knacks,[4] as purgatory, relics, hallowing of churches, and of such swarmings,[5] [together with] the whole decrees and decretals[6] with other innumerable books full of clean new inventions, whereof the old Church and the Apostles never knew.

John Calvin (1509–1564)

John Calvin provided the Protestant reformation with its most articulate apologist. Trained in theology and law, he conveyed a vision of human affairs in relation to divine action that comprehended the course of human history from its beginnings in the Fall from Paradise to the Last Judgment and the end of time. Educated to be a Catholic priest, Calvin was given the curacy of the parish of St. Martin de Marteville in 1527 at the age of eighteen. Electing to study law, he then settled in Bourges, where he worked with the great Italian jurist Andrea Alciati. He went on to learn Greek and Hebrew, immersing himself in Scripture, and in 1534, after experiencing a sudden conversion to reformist thinking, he resigned his Catholic offices and began his life's work, The Institution of Christian Religion, *a work that went into many editions. This profoundly analytical exposition of Christian doctrine covers its essential elements: law, faith, prayer, sacraments, false sacraments, and Christian liberty. The following excerpts are taken from its chapters on prayer.*

Calvin reads Scripture with an unfailing commitment to discovering its divine reasonableness: he argues that because God is omnipotent, the shaper of human history, man can have no other part in its drama than as God's instrument. Human nature, determined by its derivation from the fallen Adam and Eve, is inherently sinful, yet it can be inspired by the Holy Spirit. God may impute the

[4]Tricks, devices.

[5]Celebrations.

[6]The collection of papal decrees on doctrine, a part of canon law.

righteousness of Christ to the penitent, although the divine choice is inscrutable. Calvin's sharp distinction between divine power and human weakness is the basis of his repudiation of the doctrine of purgatory. Man is not to be saved by works, acts that he may have experienced as willed or chosen; he has to rely on God's saving grace, the scriptural promise of Christ's perfect atonement for human sin. At the time of its publication, Calvin's theology effectively undermined the grand moral and spiritual economy that had sustained the Catholic Church since its beginning.

In danger of arrest by French authorities, Calvin lived for a time in Basel and eventually settled in Geneva, where he continued his scholarly and ecclesiastical work by amplifying The Institution, *writing* A Commentary on the Epistle to Romans *and other works of theology, and establishing that city as a Protestant theocracy. He died in Geneva in 1564.*

from *The Institution of Christian Religion*[1]

[The Catholic practice of granting pardons and indulgences]

Out of this doctrine of satisfactions do flow indulgences or pardons. For they say that that which our power wanteth to make satisfaction is supplied by these pardons. And they run so far forth into madness that they define them to be the distribution of the merits of Christ and of the martyrs, which the Pope dealeth abroad by his bulls.[2] But although they have more need of *helleborus*[3] to purge their frantic brain than arguments to answer them, so that it is not much worthy the travail to stand upon confuting such trifling errors, which are already shaken with many battlerams and of themselves grow into decayed age and bend toward falling, yet because a short confutation of them shall be profitable for some that be ignorant, I will not altogether omit it. As for this: that pardons have so long stood safe and have so long been unpunished, having been used with so outrageous and furious licentiousness . . . may serve to teach us in how dark a night of

---

[1] John Calvin, *The Institution of Christian Religion*, trans. Thomas Norton, London, 1587; pp. 218, 219 verso, 220, 220 verso.

[2] An edict, order, or official document from the Pope could grant a formal pardon for sins.

[3] Plant thought to have healing power.

errors men in certain ages past have been drowned. They saw themselves to be openly and uncoloredly scorned of the Pope and his Bullbearers; [they saw themselves as] gainful markets to be made of the salvation of their souls, the price of salvation to be valued at a few pence and nothing set out to be freely given; [they saw] that by this color they be wiped of offerings to be filthily spent upon brothels, bawds and bankerings,[4] that the greatest blowers abroad of pardons are the greatest despisers of them, that this monster doth daily more and more with greater licentiousness overrun the world and grow into outrage, and that there is no end, new lead daily brought and new money gotten. Yet with high reverence they received, they worshipped and bought pardons, and such as among the rest saw somewhat farther, yet thought them to be godly deceits whereby men might be beguiled with some profit. At the length, since the world suffered itself to be somewhat wise, pardons wax cold[5] and by little and little become frozen till they utterly vanish away.

[Why the practice of granting pardons and
indulgences denies the words of the gospel]

Now [. . .] who taught the Pope to enclose in lead and parchment the grace of Jesus Christ, which the Lord willed to be distributed by the word of the Gospel? Truly either the gospel of God must be false, or their pardons false. For, that Christ is offered us in the gospel, with all abundance of heavenly benefits, with all his merits, with all his righteousness, wisdom and grace, without any exception, Paul witnesseth where he saith that the word of reconciliation was delivered to the ministers, whereby they might use this form of message, as it were Christ giving exhortation by them: "we beseech you, be ye so reconciled to God."[6] He hath made him that knew no sin to be made sin for us, that we might be made the righteousness of God in him. And the faithful know of what value is that common partaking of Christ, which (as the same Apostle witnesseth) is offered us to be enjoyed in the Gospel. Contrariwise the pardons do

---

[4] By this device, their offerings would be taken to pay for the luxuries bought by clergy. Bankerings are feasts.

[5] Become unpopular.

[6] Paul asks that ministers preach salvation by faith alone.

bring out [of] the storehouse of the Pope a certain pittance of grace and fasten it to lead parchment, yea and to a certain place,[7] and sever it from the word of God. If a man should ask whence this abuse took beginning: it seemeth to have proceeded hereof, that when in time past penitents were charged with more rigorous satisfactions than all could bear, they which felt themselves above measure oppressed with penance enjoined them, required of the church a release. The mitigation that was granted to such was called an indulgence or pardon. But when they turned satisfactions from the church to God, and said that they were recompenses whereby men may redeem themselves from the judgment of God, then they therewithal did also draw these indulgences or pardons to be propitiatory remedies to deliver us from deserved punishments. As for these blasphemers that we have recited, they forged them so shamelessly that they can have no color at all.

[Purgatory is a device of Satan]

Now let them no more trouble us with their purgation, because it is with this axe already broken, hewed down, and overthrown from the very foundations. For I do not agree to [sic] some men that think best to dissemble in this point and make no mention at all of purgatory, whereupon (as they say) great contentions do arise, but small edification is gotten. Truly I myself would also think such trifles worthy to be negligently passed over, if they did not account them earnest matters. But forasmuch as purgatory is built of many blasphemies, and is daily upheld with new blasphemies, and raiseth up many and grievous offenses, truly it is not to be winked at. This peradventure might after a sort have been dissembled for a time, that it was invented by curious and bold rashness without the word of God; that men believed of it by I wot[8] not what revelations, feigned by the craft of Satan; that for the confirmation of it certain places of Scripture were fondly wrested. Albeit the Lord giveth not leave to man's presumptuousness so to break into the secret places of his judgments, and hath severely forbidden men to enquire for truth at dead men, neglect-

---

[7]Where the indulgence was issued.
[8]Know.

ing his word, and permitteth not his word to be so unreverently defiled. But let us grant, that all those things might for a while have been borne with as things of no great importance. But when the cleansing of sins is sought elsewhere than in the blood of Christ, when satisfaction is given away to any other thing, then it is most perilous not to speak of it. Therefore we must cry out not only with vehement stretching of our voice, but also of our throat and sides[9]: that purgatory is the damnable device of Satan, that it maketh void the cross of Christ, that it layeth an intolerable slander upon the mercy of God, that it feebleth and overthroweth our faith. For what else is purgatory among them but the satisfaction that the souls of men departed to pay after their death? So that overthrowing the opinion of satisfaction, purgatory is immediately overthrown by the very roots. But if in our former discourse it is more than evident that the blood of Christ is the only satisfaction, propitiatory sacrifice, and cleansing for the sins of the faithful, what remaineth but that purgatory is a mere and horrible blasphemy against Christ? I pass over the robberies of God wherewith it is daily defended, the offenses that it breedeth in religion, and other things innumerable, which we see to have come out of the same spring of ungodliness.

John Véron (d. 1563)

After studying theology in Orleans, John Véron, a Huguenot clergyman, settled in England in 1536. He was ordained under Edward VI in 1551, was deprived of his benefice under Mary in 1554, and became vicar of St. Sepulchre under Elizabeth in 1560. A staunch supporter of continental reformers, he followed their lead by writing treatises on free will, against justification by works, and on clerical marriage. The Hunting of Purgatory to Death *follows Calvin's reasons for repudiating the doctrine of purgatory and emphasizes forms of charity particularly enjoined of Protestants: helping the living and serving their "brethren," neighbors, and fellow citizens.*

[9]Lungs.

from *The Hunting of Purgatory to Death*[1]

[The greed of the clergy promotes belief in purgatory]

The causes that did move me to write this present book are so manifest and known of all men that I need not in a manner but to open them. First and foremost, we see that if this feigned purgatory and vain opinion of praying for the dead, which be only grounded upon the foolish imaginations and dreams of a sort of superstitious and covetous persons, were once taken away, their abominable and most blasphemous sacrifice of the mass—wherewith they do altogether blaspheme and tread under feet the whole merits of the earth,[2] passion and bloodshedding of our savior Jesus Christ—could never take place again, what alteration or change soever for our ingratitude and unthankfulness ensue and follow. For take away the lucre and gains that the popish priests have had by saying of masses for the dead, and then few or none will they say, so that this popish merchant being once driven away from among Christian men, Mistress Missa[3] hath lost the chiefest stay and best friend that she hath in all the world and is never like to recover.

Secondly, by this abominable doctrine of purgatory, the true purgatory of the Christians, which is the most precious blood of the only begotten son of God, our savior Jesus Christ that doth truly purge and cleans us from all our sins, when by the hearing of God's word our hearts are through faith sprinkled with it, is altogether abolished. Yea, Christ himself is made an imperfect and as it were half a savior and of less authority and power than their holy father the pope is. For where as they do attribute unto their Antichrist[4] authority and power to absolve men, *a paena et culpa*,[5] that is to say from the offence and the punishment that is due unto it, they be not ashamed to say that Christ doth only by his death deliver us from the offence, and that we must suffer the pain or punishment that is due unto our sins in the fire of purgatory and there make sat-

---

[1]John Véron, *The Hunting of Purgatory to Death*, London, 1561; sigs. Aiiii–Avii.

[2]The body.

[3]The mass.

[4]"Antichrist" was a Protestant term for the erroneous Christ they claimed was worshipped by the Roman Catholics.

[5]From punishment to blame.

isfaction[6] for them; and that if any do escape without going through this roasting fire of theirs, it is because they have done their penance and made full satisfaction for their sins in this life. Who could hear our savior Jesus Christ, the merits of his death and passion, and the efficacy and virtue of his bloodshedding thus horribly to be blasphemed and hold his peace?

[How to live godly[7] in this world]

Moreover as long as men's minds be possessed with such vain opinion that they can make satisfaction for their sins in the fire of purgatory, and that they may be delivered from thence for a piece of money, who will care to live godly in this world or to make restitution of the goods that he hath wrongfully gotten, sith[8] the paying a little tribute and as it were part of the booty unto the priests, he may be assoiled and acquitted of all his robberies and immediately be delivered from those intolerable pains and torments, or not come into them at all, if he will in his lifetime with a sum of money purchase a general pardon of all his sins, that is to say from the pain and offence at the bishop of Rome's hand? Whereas on the contrary, if men were thoroughly persuaded that there is none other purgatory but the blood of our savior Jesus Christ, taken hold upon through a lively faith working through charity, and that there is no hope of pardon and forgiveness to be obtained at God's hands except we do to the uttermost of our power endeavor ourselves to be reconciled unto our brethren, and to make amends and restitution unto them that we have done wrong and injury unto, and not to a sort of gaping ravens which we never offended, then would they live otherwise than they do, and take better heed how they get their goods. And if they have taken wrongfully away any man's goods, they would seek all manner of means for to agree with their adversary, that is to say, with their neighbor and brother, whom they have offended and wronged, while they be yet in the way and in this present life. They would not tarry to make restitution and to be at unity and peace, both with God and their neighbor.

---

[6]Atone.

[7]For Protestants, "godly" described the behavior and practices of a devout Christian, faithful to the Calvinist principles of predestination and salvation by faith alone.

[8]Since.

John Foxe (1516–1587)

John Foxe's vivid account of England's Protestant martyrs, The Ecclesiastical History, Containing Acts and Monuments, *known as* The
Book of Martyrs, *shows how deeply reformation theology affected
popular religious belief. These martyrs are ordinary persons who
rejected all sacraments except baptism (including the Eucharist,
regarded as a memorial action only) and refused to worship saints or
follow penitential practices.*

*Having refused to take orders, in part because he rejected the idea
of a celibate clergy, Foxe moved to the Protestant city of Strasburg in
1554 and then to Basle, where he worked for the Protestant printer
Johann Herbst. During this period he wrote a draft of what would
later become the first part of* Acts and Monuments, *a Latin history of
the martyrs John Wycliffe and Jan Huss. Returning to England after
the death of Mary Tudor in 1558, he was ordained a priest by Edmund
Grindal, Bishop of London, and in 1661 began his long association
with the printer John Day, who published the first English edition of*
Acts and Monuments *in 1563. Three other editions followed in Foxe's
lifetime, and five more were posthumously published. Their accounts
have generally been regarded as based on testimonies by the martyrs
themselves or by their friends, transmitted to Foxe or persons associated with him. Protestant rejection of Catholic doctrine was not
restricted to persons who were educated. The illiterate or "silly"
woman from Exeter, who is identified only as the wife of a man called
Prest, was burned at the stake for dismissing the doctrine of purgatory,
a position she supported by citing Scripture.*

from *The Ecclesiastical History,*
Containing Acts and Monuments[1]

[Ms. Prest exemplifies popular criticism of purgatory]

The trouble and Martyrdom of a godly poor woman which suffered
at Exeter. Anno 1558.

I cannot pass over a certain poor woman and a silly creature, burned
under the said queen's reign in the City of Exeter . . . who, dwelling
sometime about Cornwall, having a husband and children there
much addicted to the superstitious sect of popery, was many times

---

[1]John Foxe, *The Ecclesiastical History, Containing Acts and Monuments*, 2 vols.,
London, 1583; vol. 2, pp. 2050–2051.

rebuked of them and driven to go to the church, to their idols and ceremonies, to shrift,[2] to follow the Cross in procession, to give thanks to God for restoring Antichrist again into this realm, etc., which when her spirit could not abide to do she made her prayer unto God, calling for help and mercy, and so at length lying in her bed about midnight, she thought there came to her a certain motion and feeling of singular comfort. Whereupon in short space she began to grow in contempt of her husband and children, and so taking nothing from them but even as she went departed from them, seeking her living by labor and spinning as well as she could, here and there for a time. . . .

[Ms. Prest is questioned by the clergy and Bishop of Exeter]

"O Lord God," said she, "what profit riseth by you that teach nothing but lies for truth? How save you souls when you preach nothing but damnable lies and destroy souls?"

"How provest you that"? said they.

"Do you not damn souls," said she, "when you teach the people to worship idols, stocks and stones, the work of men's hands?[3] And to worship a false God of your own making of a piece of bread and teach that the Pope is God's Vicar, and hath power to forgive sins? And that there is a purgatory when God's son hath by his passion purged all? And say you make God and sacrifice him when Christ's body was a sacrifice once for all? Do you not teach the people to number their sins in your ears and say they be damned if they confess not all, when God's word saith: 'who can number his sins?'[4] Do you not promise them trentals[5] and dirges and masses for souls, and sell your prayers and trust to such foolish inventions of your own imaginations? Do you not altogether against God? Do you not teach us to pray upon beads and to pray unto saints and say they can pray for us? Do you not make holy water and holy bread to fray[6] devils? Do you not a thousand more abominations? And yet

---

[2]Confession.

[3]Cf. Exodus 20.3–4: "Thou shalt have none other gods before me. Thou shalt make thee no graven image, neither any similitude of things that are in heaven above, neither that are in the earth beneath, nor that are in the water under the earth."

[4]Cf. Psalms 40.12: "My sins have taken such hold upon me . . . they are more in number than the hairs of mine head."

[5]Requiem masses every day for thirty days.

[6]Frighten.

you say you come for my profit and to save my soul. No, no one hath saved me. Farewell you with your salvation."

[The Bishop of Exeter allows Ms. Prest to go free]

In the mean time, during this her month's liberty granted to her by the Bishop . . . it happened that she, entering Saint Peter's church beheld there a cunning Dutchman, how he made new noses to certain fine images which were disfigured in King Edward's time. "What a mad man art thou," said she, "to make them new noses, which within a few days shall all lose their heads." The Dutchman accused her and laid it hard to her charge.[7] And she said unto him, "Thou art accursed and so are thy images." He called her whore. "Nay," said she, "thy images are whores and thou are a whore hunter, for doth not God say: 'you go a-whoring after strange gods,[8] figures of your own making and thou are one of them.'" Then was she sent for and clapped fast[9] and from that time had no more liberty.

[Her testimony in prison]

[T]here resorted to her a certain worthy gentlewoman, the wife of one Walter Rauley, a woman of noble wit. She said her creed to the gentlewoman and when she came to the article: *He ascended*,[10] there she stayed and bade the gentlewoman to seek his blessed body in heaven not earth and told her plainly that God dwelleth not in temples made with hands and that sacrament to be nothing else but a remembrance of his blessed passion, and yet, said she, as they now use it is but an idol and far wide from any remembrance of Christ's body, which, said she, will not long continue, and so take it

---

[7]Charged her severely.

[8]Cf. Exodus 34.14–16: "[F]or thou shalt bow down to none other god: because the Lord, whose name is Jealous, is a jealous God. Lest thou make a compact with the inhabitants of the land when they got a whoring after their gods and do sacrifice unto their gods, some man call thee and thou eat of his sacrifice. . . . And thou take of their daughters unto thy sons and their daughters go a whoring after their gods, and make thy sons go a whoring after their gods."

[9]Sent to prison.

[10]"And the third day he rose again according to the Scriptures: And ascended into heaven"; from the Nicene Creed.

good masters.[11] So that as soon as she came home to her husband, she declared to him that in her life she never heard a woman of such simplicity to see to talk so godly,[12] so perfectly, so sincerely, and so earnestly; insomuch that if God were not with her, she could not speak such things. "To the which I am not able to answer her," said she, "who can read and she can not."

[Her testimony is discredited]

Albeit she was of such simplicity and without learning, yet you could declare no place of Scripture but she would tell you the chapter, yea, she would recite to you the names of all the books of the Bible. For the which cause one Gregory Basset, a rank papist, said she was out of her wit and talked of the Scripture as a dog rangeth far off from his master when he walketh in the fields, or, as a stolen sheep out of his master's hands, she wist no whereat,[13] as all heretics do, with many other such taunts which she utterly defied. Whereby as almighty God is highly to be praised, working so mightily in such a weak vessel, so men of stronger and stouter nature have also to take example how to stand in like case when as we see this poor woman, how manfully she went though with such constancy and patience.

Cardinal William Allen (1532–1594)

The written work of William Allen illustrates how strongly the recusant movement in England (comprising its Roman Catholic subjects) could register its beliefs during the last decades of the sixteenth century. Refusing the Oath of Supremacy, which established that the monarch, Queen Elizabeth, was the head of the English church, Allen left England in 1565, visiting thereafter only on short trips. He founded a college for training English priests at Douai in northern France in 1568, where he and his colleagues began the translation into

---

[11]Learned divines foresee that the doctrine supporting the sacrament of the Mass will not prevail for long.

[12]Devoutly; also a term used to describe professed Puritans.

[13]She didn't know where she was or to whom she belonged.

Latin of a Bible designed especially for Catholics. Having known of Spanish plans for invading England in 1587, he was in no position to continue his influence in England after the defeat of the Armada in 1588. He died in poverty in Rome in 1594.

His treatise in defense of the doctrine of purgatory, published in 1577, stresses the responsibility of Catholics to make restitution for their sins within the setting of the mystical church in which "every good work of any one member wonderfully redoundeth to all the rest." On Allen's account, purgatory not only provides a term and a place for the restitution of venial sin after death but also offers the living a way to maintain contact with the dead through acts of charity. Allen envisages a Catholic Church held together in a "unity of love" that has existed from the moment of its foundation. To assert anything else, he states, is to take refuge in a "cloaked paganism."

from *A Defense and Declaration of the Catholic Church's Doctrine, Touching Purgatory*[1]

[One finds salvation within the body of the church]

As it is most true, and the very ground of all Christian comfort, that Christ's death hath paid duly and sufficiently for the sins of all the world, by that abundant price of redemption paid upon the cross, so it is of like credit to all faithful that no man was ever partaker of this singular benefit but in the knot and unity of his body mystical which is the church, to the members whereof the streams of his holy blood and beams of his grace for the remission of sin and sanctification be orderly, through the blessed sacraments as conduits of God's mercy, conveyed. For as in baptism, where man is perfectly renewed, it was seemly to set the offender at this first entrance on clear ground, and make him free for all things done abroad, so it exceedingly setteth forth God's justice and nothing impaireth his mercy to use (as in all commonwealths by nature and God's prescription if practiced) with grace, discipline; with justice, clemency; with favor, correction; and with love, due chastisement of such sins as have by the household children been committed. Now therefore, if after thy free admission to this family of Christ, thou do grievously offend, remission may then be had again, but not commonly without sharp discipline, see-

---

[1]Cardinal William Allen, *A Defense and Declaration of the Catholic Church's Doctrine, Touching Purgatory,* London, 1577; pp. 31–33, 90, 197, 202, 252–253.

ing the father of this our holy household punisheth where he loveth and chastiseth every child whom he receiveth. Whose justice in punishment of sin not only the wicked but also the good must fear.

[Purgatory]

After the sins of man be pardoned, God oftentimes punisheth the offender, the church punisheth him, and man punisheth himself, ergo there is some pain due after sin be remitted. Secondly, this pain cannot always be discharged in this world, either for lack of space after the remission, as it happeth in repentance at the hour of death, or else when the party liveth in perpetual wealth without care or cogitation of any satisfaction; therefore it must be answered in another place. Thirdly, the common infirmities and the daily trespasses which abase and defile the works even of the virtuous, of their proper condition do deserve pain for a time, as the mortal offence deserveth perpetual. Therefore as the mortal sin, being not here pardoned, must of justice have the reward of everlasting punishment, so it must needs follow that the venial fault, not here forgiven, should have the reward which of nature it requireth: that is to say, temporal pain.

And therefore not only the wicked but the very just also must travail to have their daily infirmities and frailty of their corrupt natures forgiven: crying without ceasing "forgive us our debts." [. . .] For no man alive shall be able to stand before the face of God in his own justice or righteousness, and if these light sins should never be imputed, then it were needless to cry for mercy or confess debt, as every man doth, be he never so passing holy. To be brief, this debt of pain for sin, by any way remaining at the departure hence, must of justice be answered: Which, [as this] cannot be without punishment in the next life, then there must a place of judgment for temporal and transitory pains in the other world.

[The communion of the faithful with the dead]

But now what means may be found to ease our brethren departed of their pain? Or what ways can be acceptable in the sight of God to procure mercy and grace, where the sufferers themselves, being out of the state of deserving and place of well working, cannot help themselves, nor by any motion of mind attain more mercy than their life past did deserve? Where shall we then find ease for them? Surely nowhere else but in the unity and knot of that holy fellowship, in which the benefit of the head pertaineth to all the members and every good work of any one member wonderfully redoundeth to all the rest. This society is called in our creed the communion of saints, that is to say, a blessed brotherhood under Christ the head, by love and religion so wrought and wrapped together that what any one member of this fast body hath, the other lacketh it not; what one wanteth the other supplieth; when one smarteth all feeleth in a manner the life sorrow; when one joyeth, the other rejoyseth withall. [. . .] The souls and saints in heaven, the faithful people on earth, the chosen children that suffer chastisement in purgatory, are, by the perfect bond of this unity, as one aboundeth, ready to serve the other; as one lacketh, to crave of the other. The souls happily promoted to the joy of Christ's blessed kingdom in this unity and knot of love, perpetually pray for the doubtful state of their own fellows beneath: the careful condition of the members below, continually crieth for help at their hands in heaven above. [. . .]

[T]his natural compassion of the church, passeth through every member thereof, and ought to move every man by the law of nature to procure as much help as he may. And so much the more do we owe this natural duty unto them, because they now cannot help themselves, being out of the state of deserving and place of well working, only abiding God's mercy in the sore sufferance of pains intolerable. They themselves, as yet your brethren and a portion of your body, require to be partakers of your benefits. They feel ease of every prayer; your alms quensheth their heat, your fasting releaseth their pain, your sacrifice wipeth their sins and sores; so strong is the communion of saints, that, whatsoever you do that is acceptable, it issueth abundantly down to them.

[How those in purgatory benefit from the prayers of the living]

The benefit bestowed upon the poor is a sovereign ground of God's rewarding. And in thy oblations[2] for the departed, have always the same intent and scope that a father hath practising for the recovery of his sick child, being young and tender, who, for

[2]Prayers.

his sick son, bringeth into the church of our Lord God, wax, oil, incense, and with devotion and faith lighteth them in the boy's behalf. For that the child himself, being wholly unskillful of the ordinances of our Christianity, would never go about any such thing, even so must a man think of the deceased person's case, that he may and doth offer (as in another man's person) wax, oil and such like, as commonly for redemption are offered. [. . .] The reader as he list, may perchance with more leisure, or at least with less injury to other, weigh the wonderful waste that sin and heresy hath wrought in our days of darkness. And when he considereth these things, that be now of most men counted mere madness, to have been liked, allowed, preached, avouched, sent out in solemn works and writings—to the view of the world and the sight of all posterity—from the very heart and spring of the Christian church, [. . .] shall he not wonder with all wise men at our downfall so deep? Shall he not marvel [that] under one name of Christianity, that goeth yet common to our days with those happy times past, [there is] such diversity of case and conditions that the one under so glorious a name must be nothing else but a cloaked paganism? But yet I would not he should occupy overmuch his mind in this consideration, till he see the whole rank of God's holy host and all the blessed band of martyrs and saints stand with us for the full defense of truth and the common church, their mother and ours.

Revenge

To explore the workings of justice in a Christian society, Shakespeare drew on themes and motifs traditionally associated with revenge tragedy, a system of retribution in ancient pre-Christian societies. Unlike the popular revenge tragedies of the late Elizabethan and early Stuart theater—Marlowe's *Jew of Malta* (1592), Kyd's *The Spanish Tragedy* (1592), Shakespeare's own *Titus Andronicus* (1594), and Middleton's *The Revenger's Tragedy* (1607)—*Hamlet* is strongly inflected by Christian theology: even as it lays out the motives and impulse to revenge, it also gestures toward the prohibition of revenge in divine and positive law. And while the protagonists of traditional revenge tragedy tend not to invoke providence, Hamlet believes that a providential order inheres in human affairs. Hamlet's political justification for killing Claudius, whom Hamlet's father has identified as his murderer, is also problematic. At the time of Shakespeare's play, English political thought was divided as to rights of resistance against lawfully instituted authority (Claudius was elected to the throne and only Hamlet suspects regicide); most opinion declared that a wronged subject had no recourse against tyranny but prayer. Shakespeare's audiences, moreover, saw dramatizations of revenge in light of familiar common law procedures guaranteeing that persons accused of a crime would get a fair trial. American law today, following many of these procedures, preserves the rights they instituted: to be presumed innocent until proven guilty, against self-incrimination, and to call witnesses in a trial by a jury whose verdict is final.

But Shakespeare provides a complex scenario in *Hamlet*. Hamlet is not just a wronged subject with a case to prosecute; he is also a prince. Does Claudius's crime (and therefore his illicit rule) put Hamlet in a privileged position? Ought we to see that Hamlet is acting for his father and therefore as de facto king of Denmark, one who, by rightfully punishing his uncle, is performing not an act of revenge but rather of exemplary justice? Such is the implication of the Ghost's request to Hamlet to avenge his murder. But would a soul in purgatory make such a request? The action of the play raises these questions without answering them.

The Bible

In Shakespeare's day, English men and women believed that Scripture was the Word of God and the equivalent of divine law. Like natural law, comprised in the unwritten primal codes of conduct shared by all people, divine law was thought to provide positive law, decided by the courts and made by statute in Parliament, with its immutable foundations. Cain's mark and God's words on vengeance announced in both Old and New Testaments (Leviticus, Deuteronomy, Hebrews, and Romans) not only illustrated a universal prohibition against vengeful murder but also implied the law administered by the state and sanctioned by God. Persons harmed by particular injuries had to seek satisfaction in courts of justice. Claudius identifies himself as "Cain" when he speaks of his "offence" as one that has "the primal eldest curse upon't" (3.3.37) and so calls into question any right to revenge that Hamlet, a Christian, might claim. When urged to revenge by his beloved father, Hamlet confronts a hideous dilemma: either he fails to honor his father or he damns himself with the sin of murder.

from Genesis 4.9–15[1]

Then the Lord said unto Cain, Where is Abel thy brother? Who answered, I cannot tell. Am I my brother's keeper? Again he said, What hast thou done? the voice of thy brother's blood crieth unto me from the ground. Now therefore thou art cursed from the earth which hath opened her mouth to receive thy brother's blood from thine hand. When thou shalt till the ground, it shall not henceforth yield unto thee her strength: a vagabond and a

---

[1] The Bible, translated according to the Hebrew and Greek, London, 1595. Known as the Geneva Bible, this text remained the standard text for English Protestants until the publication of The Authorized Version in 1611.

renegade shalt thou be in the earth. Then Cain said to the Lord, My punishment is greater than I can bear. Behold, thou hast cast me out this day from the earth, and from thy face shall I be hid, and shall be a vagabond and a renegade in the earth, and whosoever findeth me shall slay me. Then the Lord said unto him, Doubtless whosoever slayeth Cain, he shall be punished sevenfold. And the Lord set a mark upon Cain lest any man finding him should kill him.

from Romans 12.19

Dearly beloved, avenge not yourselves, but give place unto wrath: for it is written, Vengeance is mine: I will repay, saith the Lord.

William Dickinson (b. 1585)

Endorsing divine right theory, William Dickinson asserts the absolute right of kings to assume judicial power and to assign it to their magistrates as required. Stressing positive law's derivation from the Word of God, Dickinson declares that it prohibits an individual person from taking vengeful action on his own and insists that the monarch's subjects adhere to prescribed legal procedures.

from *The King's Right*[1]

[The subject's place; the sovereign's power]

[L]et every one, whether he be a vessel of honor or dishonor, content himself with his place and submit his will to the obedience of those laws which his maker hath set down to be observed. And of all creatures men have most cause to yield their obedience unto God as the judge, not only because *Quia fecit*, he made them, *Sed donavit* too, he hath bestowed on them those honors and privileges which may justly challenge this acknowledgement from them, that he is the judge. [. . .] [I]t hath pleased God even from the beginning to rule and judge by men. Some power he hath put

---

[1]William Dickinson, *The King's Right*, London, 1619; sigs. B4 verso, C verso, C2, D2.

over and deputed to such amongst us as he knoweth fittest for so high a calling. [. . .]

[N]ot only our goods and bodies but our lives also ought to be subject to secular princes in that they may lawfully require. To whom then God said *Dii estis*: ye are gods, they are kings, princes, law-givers, and the judges of earth [. . .] . And again, they who are kings, and law-givers, and judges are gods, as it is in Exodus 22 [8]: Thou shalt not revile the gods, nor curse the ruler of the people. But some will say, all kings and judges do not behave themselves in their places as gods; some are usurpers, others tyrants, many are profane and wicked persons, neither fearing god, nor regarding man: But to cut these men off from their conclusion, they must understand that notwithstanding the person and power of the king, [he] is always sacred and inviolable.[2] It is not for those whom God hath appointed to obey to examine titles and pedigrees, or how kings came to their power and to be rulers over them. It sufficeth that being under we must obey, not only for fear but for conscience sake, lest through our disobedience, our conscience accuse us for resisting the ordinance of God, for the powers that be are ordained of God.[3]

[But] all men are not willing to hear of this doctrine. When passion leads the line, we may observe every particular man almost to take upon him to be a god, and the judge, and a revenger to execute wrath upon him that doth evil. Who is reviled, that back-biteth not again? Who is threatened, that threatneth not? Who is in any sort offended and crossed, that seeketh not revenge? [. . .] All of us, I know not by what ill spirit set on, being desperately prone both to give and execute sentence upon our own wrongs (if happily[4] wrongs) by dint of sword and bloody death. Beloved, what high presumption is it and boldness, that for every sleight affront and idle word the king must have a subject, or two, or more ravished from him? [. . .] Amongst other reasons why God appointed and set up kings and princes to rule over the Sons of men, I think this was not the least, that in so quarrelling a generation, and so prone to blood and violence, every man might not be the judge and revenger of his

---

[2]A king is beyond the power of positive law.

[3]"Let every soul be subject unto the higher powers. For there is no power but of God; the powers that be are ordained of God." Romans 13.1.

[4]Haply, by chance.

own grief, and that wrath and passion might not take the place of law. Leave a passage for this insolence, let every man have the freedom of his own sword, suffer them to abuse their own bodies and lives unto the satisfying of the bloody purpose of their own or other mean desperate and malicious disposition, there will soon be an end of all civil society, and good order amongst the affairs of men.

Thomas Beard (d. 1632)

Thomas Beard, the Puritan schoolmaster of Oliver Cromwell, is known for his treatise on the severe and immutable justice of God, superior in its providential outcomes to any that could be devised by a human judge. Beard illustrates why Christians who left vengeance to God could hope for justice in this world even under corrupt and tyrannical kings. Unlike Shakespeare's Richard III, Beard's account of Richard's reign does not mention the decisive role of Henry Richmond, afterward Henry VII, in opposing Richard's tyranny. Rather, he stresses what he regards as divinely authorized: Richard's spiritual torment when alive and the physical degradation of his body when dead.

from *The Theater of God's Judgments*[1]

[The fate of those who murder their rulers]

Among this rank of murderers of kings we may fitly place also Richard the third, usurper of the crown of England, and divers others which he used as instruments to bring his detestable purpose to effect: as namely, Sir James Tirrell knight, a man for nature's gifts worthy to have served a much better prince then this Richard if he had well served God, and been endued with as much truth and honesty as he had strength and wit; also Miles Forest and John Dighton, two villains fleshed in murders. But to come to the fact. It was on this sort: when Richard the usurper had enjoined Robert Brackenbury to this piece of service of murdering the young king Edward the fifth, his nephew, in the tower, with his brother the

---

[1]Thomas Beard, *The Theater of God's Judgments*, London, 1597; pp. 225, 229.

duke of York, and saw it refused by him [Brackenbury], he committed the charge of the murder to Sir James Tirrell. [He], hastening to the tower by the king's commission, received the keys into his own hands, and by the help of those two butchers, Dighton and Forest, smothered the two princes in their bed and buried them at the stair's feet; which being done, Sir James rode back to king Richard, who gave him great thanks and as some say, made him knight for his labor. All which things on every part well pondered, it appeareth that God never gave the world a notabler example, both of the inconstancy of worldly weal, and also of the wretched end which ensueth such despiteful cruelty. [F]or first to begin with the ministers: Miles Forest rotted away piecemeal at St Martin's; Sir James Tirrell died at the tower hill beheaded for treason; king Richard himself (as it is declared elsewhere) was slain in the field, hacked and hewed of his enemies, carried on horseback dead, his hair in despite torn and tugged like a dog. [B]esides the inward torments of his guilty conscience were more than all the rest, for it is most certainly reported that after this abominable deed done, he never had quiet in his mind. [W]hen he went abroad his eye whirled about, his body was privily fenced, his hand ever upon his dagger, his countenance and manner like one always ready to strike, his sleep short and unquiet, full of fearful dreams, insomuch that he would often suddenly start up and leap out of his bed, and run about the chamber, his restless conscience was so continually tossed and tumbled with the tedious impression of that abominable murder.

Francis Bacon (1561–1626)

Deeply informed by the history and philosophy of the classical past, the literary works of Francis Bacon represent the final flowering of English humanist thought. His Essays, *written over a twenty-five-year period and published in successive editions, address topics that are central to understanding how Shakespeare's audiences responded to* Hamlet. *"Of Revenge" represents the benefits that come to an injured party who renounces revenge; it also rather daringly approves of revenge for a wrong for "which there is no law to remedy," provided that the avenger is himself free from having to give an account of his actions to the law.*

"Of Delays" considers the importance of fortune and its timing in a manner that recalls the decisiveness of Brutus in Julius Caesar *("There is a tide in the affairs of men / Which taken at the flood, leads on to fortune" [4.3.218–219]) and, by contrast, Hamlet's belief that it is useless to plan ahead. What happens, Hamlet argues at the end of the play, is mandated by providence: "The readiness is all" (5.2.207). "Of Suspicion" is a virtual lesson in court politics: Bacon counsels caution and circumspection, especially when confronting "men of base natures." Consider your suspicions to be true, he warns, but act so that your suspect does not hurt you. Hamlet is tormented by suspicion, not only of his uncle but also of his mother, of Ophelia, and of the lackeys Rosencrantz and Guildenstern. He dissembles to protect himself, not always successfully.*

from Essays[1]

Of Revenge.

Revenge is a kind of wild justice; which the more man's nature runs to, the more ought law to weed it out. For as for the first wrong, it doth but offend the law; but the revenge of that wrong putteth the law out of office. Certainly, in taking revenge, a man is but even with his enemy; but in passing it over, he is superior; for it is a prince's part to pardon. And Salomon, I am sure, saith, *It is the glory of a man to pass by an offence.* That which is past is gone, and irrevocable; and wise men have enough to do with things present and to come; therefore they do but trifle with themselves, that labor in past matters. There is no man doth a wrong for the wrong's sake; but thereby to purchase himself profit, or pleasure, or honor, or the like. Therefore why should I be angry with a man for loving himself better than me? And if any man should do wrong merely out of ill-nature, why, yet it is but like the thorn or briar, which prick and scratch, because they can do no other. The most tolerable sort of revenge is for those wrongs which there is no law to remedy; but then let a man take heed the revenge be such as there is no law to punish; else a man's enemy is still beforehand, and it is two for one.[2] Some, when they take revenge, are desirous the party should know

[1]Francis Bacon, *The Works of Francis Bacon*, eds. James Spedding, Robert Leslie Ellis, and Douglas Denon Heath, 15 vols., London, 1858; vol. 6, pp. 384–385, 427–428, 454–455. (The *Essays* were first published in 1597 and thereafter, in various editions, to 1625.)

[2]A revenger puts himself in jeopardy by exposing himself to punishment.

whence it cometh. This the more generous.[3] For the delight seemeth to be not so much in doing the hurt as in making the party repent. But base and crafty cowards are like the arrow that flieth in the dark. Cosmus, duke of Florence,[4] had a desperate saying against perfidious or neglecting friends, as if those wrongs were unpardonable; *You shall read* (saith he) *that we are commanded to forgive our enemies; but you never read that we are commanded to forgive our friends.* But yet the spirit of Job was in a better tune: *Shall we* (saith he) *take good at God's hands, and not be content to take evil also?* And so of friends in a proportion. This is certain, that a man that studieth revenge keeps his own wounds green, which otherwise would heal and do well. Public revenges are for the most part fortunate; as that for the death of Caesar; for the death of Pertinax; for the death of Henry the Third of France; and many more.[5] But in private revenges it is not so. Nay rather, vindictive persons live the life of witches, who, as they are mischievous, so end they infortunate.[6]

Of Delays.

Fortune is like the market; where many times, if you can stay a little, the price will fall. And again, it is sometimes like Sibylla's offer[7]; which at first offereth the commodity at full, then consumeth part and part, and still holdeth up the price. For occasion (as it is in the common verse) *turneth a bald noddle, after she hath presented her locks in front, and no hold taken;* or at least turneth the handle of the bottle first to be received, and after the belly, which is hard to clasp.[8] There is surely no greater wisdom than well to time the beginnings and onsets of things. Dangers are no more light, if they

[3]Noble.

[4]Cosimo de Medici, 1519–1574, Duke of Florence and eventually Archduke of Tuscany.

[5]"Fortunate" because beneficial to society. Julius Caesar was assassinated in 44 BCE by Brutus and other Roman senators who worried for the safety of the republic under Caesar's ambitions. Pertinax (d. 193) was Emperor of Rome for three months, then murdered for instituting governmental reforms. Although Henri III of France (1551–1589) defended the Catholic Church, he sought to accommodate the thought and practices of the Protestant Huguenots; this provoked Jacques Clément, a Dominican monk, to murder him.

[6]Unfortunate.

[7]The Sibyls were Roman goddesses of prophecy.

[8]Opportunities prove more difficult to grasp after the first moment.

once seem light; and more dangers have deceived men than forced them. Nay, it were better to meet some dangers halfway, though they come nothing near, than to keep too long a watch upon their approaches; for if a man watch too long, it is odds he will fall asleep. On the other side, to be deceived with too long shadows (as some have been when the moon was low and shone on their enemies' back), and so to shoot off before the time[9]; or to teach dangers to come on, by over early buckling[10] towards them; is another extreme. The ripeness or unripeness of the occasion (as we said) must ever be well weighed; and generally it is good to commit the beginnings of all great actions to Argus with his hundred eyes, and the ends to Briareus with his hundred hands,[11] first to watch, and then to speed. For the helmet of Pluto,[12] which maketh the politic man go invisible, is secrecy in the counsel and celerity in the execution. For when things are once come to the execution, there is no secrecy comparable to celerity; like the motion of a bullet in the air, which flieth so swift as it outruns the eye.

Of Suspicion.

Suspicions amongst thoughts are like bats amongst birds, they ever fly by twilight. Certainly they are to be repressed, or at the least well guarded[13]: for they cloud the mind; they lose friends; and they check with business, whereby business cannot go on currently and constantly. They dispose kings to tyranny, husbands to jealousy, wise men to irresolution and melancholy. They are defects, not in the heart, but in the brain; for they take place in the stoutest natures; as in the example of Henry the Seventh of England.[14] There was not a more suspicious man, nor a more stout. And in such composition they do small

---

[9]To mistake the actual nearness of a danger.

[10]Movement; literally, buckling up of armor.

[11]Mythical herdsman Argos had eyes all over his body (later they appeared on the tail of the peacock). Briareus was one of four giants, each of whom had a hundred hands.

[12]Roman god of the underworld.

[13]Loose.

[14]Henry VII defeated Richard III at Bosworth Field in 1485 to become king in 1486; he is reported by Edward Hall, in *The Union of the Two Noble Families of Lancaster and York* (1548), to have been suspicious of his father-in-law Lord Thomas Stanley, who might have sided with Richard III out of fear that the king would execute his son, Lord Strange.

hurt. For commonly they are not admitted, but with examination,[15] whether they be likely or no? But in fearful natures they gain ground too fast. There is nothing makes a man suspect much, more than to know little; and therefore men should remedy suspicion by procuring to know more, and not to keep their suspicions in smother. What would man have? Do they think those they employ and deal with are saints? Do they not think they will have their own ends, and be truer to themselves than to them? Therefore there is no better way to moderate suspicions, than to account upon such suspicions as true and yet to bridle them as false. For so far a man ought to make use of suspicions, as to provide, as if that should be true that he suspects, yet it may do him no hurt. Suspicions that the mind of itself gathers are but buzzes; but suspicions that are artificially nourished, and put into men's heads by the tales and whisperings of others, have stings. Certainly, the best mean to clear the way in this same wood of suspicions, is frankly to communicate them with the party that he suspects; for thereby he shall be sure to know more of the truth of them than he did before; and withal shall make that party more circumspect not to give further cause of suspicion. But this would not be done to men of base natures; for they, if they find themselves once suspected, will never be true. The Italian says, *Sospetto licentia fede*[16]; as if suspicion did give a passport to faith; but it ought rather to kindle it to discharge itself.

---

[15]A strong man examines the basis for his doubts and so remains free of their worst effects.

[16]"Suspicion drives out faith."

Suicide

When Hamlet considers death a "consummation devoutly to be wished" (3.1.63–64), his profound despair may keep him from respecting the Christian prohibition against "self-slaughter" (1.2.132). Shakespeare's audience would have known that suicide was also a crime in the eyes of the law: a person who committed suicide was termed *felo de se*, or a criminal against himself, and his property was forfeit to the crown. This did not stop writers and playwrights from representing suicide, especially if the cases they illustrated were drawn from the literature of the classical past (Dido, Queen of Carthage, and Lucrece, the wife of Tarquinius Collatinus of Rome, were favorite subjects). John Donne sees suicidal elements even in Christian martyrdom, arguing that suffering for others paradoxically entails a willingness both to destroy and to save the self, while John Sym and Michel de Montaigne sympathize with persons so driven by fear and shame that they see no other escape.

Michel de Montaigne (1533–1592)

The popular Essaies *of Michel de Montaigne, published in 1580, 1588, and 1592 in France and first translated into English by John Florio in 1603, are among the most daring expressions of sixteenth-century humanist thought. Relying on a rhetoric designed to explore rather than to define a topic, Montaigne made a practice of representing his subjects* in utremque partem, *from opposing points of view.*

"A custom of the Isle of Cea," while it establishes that Christian doctrine prohibits suicide, also shows why in certain circumstances it

212

was considered a plausible course of action in the pre-Christian world. Montaigne concludes by suggesting that he, at least, might find it possible to excuse a suicide in such situations as "a grieving-smart" and fear of "a worse death." Yet these categories are so vague that they could be imagined as covering many different situations. Their very vagueness in effect leaves conclusions to the reader.

from "A custom of the Isle of Cea"[1]

[The classical view of suicide]

Death is a remedy against all evils: It is a most assured haven, never to be feared and often to be sought. All comes to one period, whether man make an end of himself, or whether he endure it; whether he run before his day, or whether he expect it; whencesoever it come, it is ever his own; wherever the thread be broken, it is all there; it's the end of the web. The voluntariest death is the fairest. Life dependeth on the will of others, death on ours. In nothing should we so much accommodate ourselves to our humors as in that. Reputation doth nothing concern such an enterprise, it is folly to have any respect unto it. To live is to serve, if the liberty to die be wanting. The common course of curing any infirmity is ever directed at the charge of life; we have incisions made into us, we are cauterized, we have limbs cut and mangled, we are let blood, we are dieted. Go we but one step further, we need no more physic, we are perfectly whole. Why is not our jugular or throat-vein as much at our command as the mediane?[2] To extreme sicknesses, extreme remedies. [. . .]

The Stoics say, it is a convenient natural life for a wise man to forgo life although he abound in all happiness, if he do it opportunely; and for a fool to prolong his life, albeit he be most miserable, provided he be in most part of things which they say to be according unto nature.[3] As I offend not the laws made against thieves, when I cut mine own purse, and carry away mine own goods; nor of destroyers when I burn mine own wood, so am I

---

[1] Michel de Montaigne, *The Essays of Michael Lord of Montaigne*, trans. John Florio, 3 vols., London, 1910; vol. 2, pp. 27–29, 34–35, 41.

[2] One of the secondary veins of the body, i.e., the veins in the forearm.

[3] That he possess most of the things that are agreed to be essential to human nature.

nothing tied unto laws made against murderers, if I deprive myself of mine own life.

[Another view]

But this goeth not without some contradiction. For many are of the opinion that without the express commandment of him that hath placed us in this world, we may by no means forsake the garrison of it, and that it is in the hands of God only, who therein hath placed us, not for ourselves alone but for his glory and others' service, whenever it shall please him to discharge us hence and not for us to take leave; that we are not born for ourselves, but for our country. The laws for their own interest require an account at our hands for ourselves, and have a just action of murder against us; else as forsakers of our own charge, we are punished in the other world. [. . .] There is more constancy in using the chain that holds us, than in breaking the same; and more trial of steadfastness in Regulus than in Cato.[4]

[Extenuating circumstances, limiting cases]

Of all violences committed against conscience, the most in my opinion to be avoided is that which is offered against the chastity of women, forasmuch as there is naturally some corporal pleasure commixt[5] with it. And therefore the dissent cannot fully enough be joined thereunto: and it seemeth that force is in some sort intermixed with some will. [T]he ecclesiastical story hath in especial reverence sundry such examples of devout persons who called for death to warrant them from the outrages which some tyrants prepared against their religion and consciences. Pelagia and Sophronia [were] both canonized; the first, together with her mother and sisters, to escape the outrageous rapes of some soldiers, threw herself into a river; the other, to shun the force of Maxentius the Emperor,[6] slew herself.

---

[4]As consul, Regulus led the conquest of Africa; captured by the Carthaginians, he died under torture in 249 BCE. Cato supported Pompey against Julius Caesar. At Pompey's defeat in 47 BCE, Cato went to Utica near Carthage and, believing that his own cause was hopeless, committed suicide in 46 BCE.

[5]Desire; i.e., on the part of the rape victim.

[6]St. Augustine recounts the stories of Saints Pelagia and Sophronia in *The City of God*, written sometime after 413, Book I, Chapter 26. Maxentius, Emperor of Rome from 306 to 312, was defeated by Constantine, who succeeded him.

[An equivocal conclusion]

Grieving-smart, and a worse death seem to me the most excusable incitations.

John Sym (1581–1631)

John Sym, a Protestant clergyman sympathetic to Calvinism, wrote his treatise on "self-killing" in response to a growing number of reports of suicides in England during the first quarter of the seventeenth century. Although he could not excuse it on theological grounds, he described its psychological attractions: frustration or disappointment in love, hatred of a spouse, a sense of personal unworthiness, and particularly, shame at personal failure or loss of dignity. The example of the legendary Roman matron Lucretia (the heroine of Shakespeare's narrative poem "The Rape of Lucrece"), who stabbed herself after being raped, was often invoked as a limiting case. Dishonored in the terms her society professed, despairing of her reputation, traumatized by her victimization, her suicide appeared excusable. Few moralists condemned her, and some even thought that her action was highly moral.

from *Life's Preservative against Self-Killing*[1]

[The causes of suicide]

[An] extreme grief of mind and trouble of conscience [and] excessive discontentment for being crossed or disappointed. [. . .] This discontentment of mind arises from two causes. First, from want of that good, true or seeming, which we desire or expect. Secondly, from suffering of that evil which we would not. [. . .]

First, that which ariseth from the crossing or disappointment of the will of mens' affections and lusts: as those that immoderately affect and love to have and enjoy others of the other sex and are deeply overset in carnal or conjugal love, which is an unruly passion, and being disappointed, occasions people there-

---

[1]John Sym, *Life's Preservative against Self-Killing*, London, 1637; sigs. Gg verso–Gg3 verso.

fore to kill themselves. A wife kills herself because her husband crosses her will; either he will not do as she would have him or he will not let her have her will to go and do as she list.[2] Or [she] is displeased with her match, which proceeds from hatred to her husband, whom she envies the enjoying of her; and so I might instance in many like particulars.[3] But it is most unreasonable that because a body cannot have their love or will that therefore such an one should revenge the same upon himself by an act of the greatest hatred and hostility in the world; and that one should rather choose to kill himself than to live after a repulse in suit of love, or to see another brook what they impotently affected to enjoy.

The third kind of troubles of mind that sometimes occasions self-murder is shame and confusion, either for what a man hath ignominiously done or suffered or is certainly like to do or suffer, whereby he falls under contempt, scorn, and importable[4] disgrace with those whose respect he overvalues. And so, apprehending himself to be dejected and used more indignly[5] and unworthily than he thinks he hath deserved or can endure, he resolves to kill himself to free him from the same or at least from the sense of it. As did Lucretia, who, having been ravished by Tarquinius, stabbed herself to avoid the shame of it—of whom Augustine[6] says, that being sick and impatient of the villainy committed against her, she killed herself.

So intolerable a thing is shame to some, specially of the noblest natures, that they think the same worse than death, and that they had rather not to be than to live in shame; it confounds the judgment and drives [them] into desperate shifts and practices to be rid of it.

---

[2]Wants; wishes.

[3]There are many instances of suicide prompted by intolerable situations.

[4]Intolerable.

[5]Dishonorably.

[6]St. Augustine (354–430), Bishop of Hippo, gives an account of Lucretia in *The City of God*, Book I, Chapter 19.

John Donne (1572–1631)

Donne's career reveals his many talents. A brilliant poet and rising star in Queen Elizabeth's government, he sailed with Essex to sack Cadiz at the age of twenty-four and with Raleigh on a privateering expedition to the Azores the following year. He then became secretary to Sir Thomas Egerton, Lord Keeper of the Great Seal, but had to leave that office in 1601, after secretly marrying Ann More, Lady Egerton's neice. Surviving on patronage until 1615, Donne finally took orders and began his clerical career. Quite unlike the witty love lyrics of his youth or his passionate devotional verse and sober sermons of his mature years, Biothanatos *(probably written about 1611) boldly questions clerical and legal doctrine forbidding suicide. Donne's critique, although supported by passages from Scripture, was considered too radical for publication and appeared in print only after his death.*

From *Biathanatos*[1]

[Self-preservation and martyrdom]

Self-preservation, which we confess to be the foundation of general natural law, is no other thing than a natural affection and appetition[2] of good, whether true or seeming. For certainly the desire of martyrdom, though the body perish, is a self-preservation, because thereby, out of our election our best part is advanced. For heaven which we gain so, is certainly good; life, but probably and possibly. For here it holds well which Athenagoras says: Earthly things and heavenly differ so as *verisimile* and *verum*.[3] And this is the best description of felicity that I have found: That it is *reditus uniuscuiusque rei ad suum principium*.[4] Now since this law of self-preservation is accomplished in attaining that which conduces to our ends and is good to us (for our liberty, which is a faculty of doing that which I would, is as much of the law of nature as preser-

---

[1] John Donne, *Biathanatos: A Declaration of that Paradox or Thesis that Self-homicide is not so naturally sin, that it may never be otherwise,* London, 1647; pp. 49–50, 191–93.

[2] Desire.

[3] The verisimilar and the true." Athenagoras, second-century Greek philosopher, wrote the *Apology for Christians* to refute charges that Christianity promoted cannibalism, incest, and atheism.

[4] "The return of every individual entity to his [implied also to her] origin."

vation is) . . . for reasons seeming good to me, (as to preserve my life when I am justly taken prisoner, I will become a slave), I may do it without violating the law of nature. If I propose to myself in this self-homicide a greater good, though I mistake it, I perceive not wherein I transgress the general law of nature, which is an affection of good, true, or seeming; and if that which I affect by death, be truly a greater good, wherein is the other stricter law of nature, which is rectified reason,[5] violated?

And to my understanding there is a further degree of alacrity, and propenseness[6] to such a death, expressed in that phrase of John: He that hateth his life in this world, shall keep it unto life eternal.[7] And in that of Luke: Except he hate his own life, he cannot be my disciple.[8] Such a lothness[9] to live is that which is spoken of in the Hebrews: Some were racked and would not be delivered, that they might receive a better resurrection.[10] This place Calvin interprets of a readiness to die, and expresses it elegantly, To carry our life in our hands, offering it to God for a sacrifice. And this the Jesuits in their rule extend thus far, let every one think that this was said directly to him: Hate thy life. And they who in the other place, accept this phrase: No man hateth his own flesh, to yield an argument against self-homicide in any case, must also allow that the same hate being commanded here authorizes that act in some cases. . . . And therefore the holy ghost proceeds more directly in the first Epistle of Saint John,[11] and shows us a necessary duty: Because he laid down his life for us, therefore we ought to lay down our lives for our brethren. All these places work us to a true understanding of charity and to a contempt of this life in respect of it. And as these

[5]"Right reason," in accord with natural law.

[6]Propensity.

[7]John 12.25: "He that loveth his life shall lose it; and he that hateth his life in this world shall keep it unto life eternal."

[8]Luke 14.26: "If any man come to me, and hate not his father, and mother, and wife, and children, and brethren, and sisters, ye, and his own life also, he cannot be my disciple."

[9]Reluctance.

[10]Hebrews 11.35: "The women received their dead raised to life: others also were racked and would not be delivered, that they might receive a better resurrection."

[11]1 John 3.16: "Hereby have we perceived love, that he [Christ] laid down his life for us: therefore we ought also to lay down our lives for the brethren."

inform us how ready we must be, so all those places, which direct us by the example of Christ to do it as he did, show that in cases when our lives must be given, we need not ever attend extrinsic force of others.[12] But as he did in perfect charity, so we, in such degrees of it as this life and our nature are capable of, must die by our own will rather than his glory be neglected, whensoever, as Paul saith, Christ may be magnified in our bodies or the spiritual good of such another as we are bound to advance doth importune it.[13]

[12]Wait for outside forces.

[13]Philippians 1.20: "As I heartily look for and hope that in nothing I shall be ashamed, but that with all confidence, as always, so now Christ shall be magnified in my body, whether it be by life, or by death."

Sources

An important source for Shakespeare's *Hamlet* is the ancient story of Amleth, the heroic prince of Jutland, now modern Denmark, as told by the thirteenth-century historian Saxo Grammaticus in his *Historia Danica*. Also known as *Gesta Danorum* (that is, the deeds of the Danes), this history was first published in sixteen books in 1576 in Frankfurt. Saxo's contribution covers events through the early thirteenth century; later historians added a record of events to 1241. How this story came to Shakespeare's attention is not entirely clear: it was translated with embellishments from Saxo's Latin into Italian by Matteo Bandello (1485–1561), a writer of *novelle* or short stories, and then translated again into French with further embellishments by François de Belleforest (1530–1583), where it appears in the fifth volume of his *Histoires Tragiques* (1572). Shakespeare probably read Saxo's history as translated by Belleforest.

More recent versions of the Hamlet story existed in dramatic form and were likely to have been known to Shakespeare: one in particular, a play now lost but identified by recent critics as the Ur-Hamlet, may have been his principal source. This play is perhaps the one described by Thomas Nashe in his preface to Robert Greene's romance *Menaphon* (1589). Characterizing this play as a work by a "noverint" or public secretary, Nashe declares that it affords the audience "whole Hamlets." Nashe may be identifying a work by the playwright Thomas Kyd, whose *Spanish Tragedy* (1587) represents themes and characters somewhat similar to those in *Hamlet*, notably the character of the ghost of a murdered nobleman who converses with the figure of Revenge. The Ur-Hamlet, whether or not by Kyd, could also be implied in Thomas Lodge's reference to the character of a ghost—who cries "Hamlet, revenge"—in his *Wit's Misery and the World's Madness, Discovering the Devils Incarnate of This Age* (1596). Finally, Shakespeare may have profited from his connection with the theater. Hamlet's story is dramatized in an early version of a German play—based on the Ur-Hamlet—entitled *Der bestrafte Brudermord oder Prinz Hamlet aus Dannemark*, translated as *Fratricide Punished or Prince Hamlet in Denmark* (originally from a text dated 1710 but now lost) used by English players on tour in Europe in 1586 and afterward. In its present form, *Der bestrafte Brudermord* resembles Shakespeare's *Hamlet* in the details of its plot although not in their dramatic rendering. In the absence of any text of Ur-Hamlet, however, Saxo's account must serve as our point of comparison with Shakespeare's tragedy.

Saxo Grammaticus (fl. 1200, d. ca. 1204)

Even at its relatively far remove from Hamlet, *Saxo's heroic tale illustrates significant elements of Shakespeare's play: fratricide, incest, a contrived or feigned madness, and a duty to avenge the murder of a father. But unlike Amleth, whose superb cunning and roguish strategies allow him to achieve his revenge in an almost comic manner, Shakespeare's Hamlet is an eminently tragic figure. Amleth never betrays self-doubt, needs no ghost to tell him that his uncle Feng murdered his father (he knows this from the moment of the murder), and does not reflect on the propriety of the revenge to which he is committed. Hamlet, by contrast, made deeply melancholic by his father's death, has to struggle with myriad doubts and anxieties after he learns that his uncle Claudius has murdered his father. The fact that he is told of this crime by his father's ghost, who then demands revenge, further troubles his situation. Ghosts were notoriously hard to identify as good rather than evil spirits, and a ghost from purgatory challenged the Protestant claim that purgatory was itself merely a clerical invention. Saxo's Amleth succeeds his father after killing his uncle Feng and lives to reign in Jutland. Shakespeare's Hamlet dies of a lethal poison administered in the course of a sword fight in which he barely manages to kill*

Claudius, and the succession of the crown of Denmark goes to Fortinbras of Norway.

from *Historia Danica*[1]

[The revenge of Amleth of Jutland for the murder of his father Horwendil by his uncle Feng]

At this time Horwendil and Feng,[2] whose father Gerwendil had been governor of the Jutes, were appointed in his place by Rorik[3] to defend Jutland. But Horwendil held the monarchy for three years, and then, to win the height of glory, devoted himself to roving.[4] Then Koll,[5] King of Norway, in rivalry of his great deeds and renown, deemed it would be a handsome deed if by his greater strength in arms he could bedim the far-famed glory of the rover; and, cruising about the sea, he watched for Horwendil's fleet and came up with it. There was an island lying in the middle of the sea, which each of the rovers, bringing his ships up on either side, was holding. The captains were tempted by the pleasant look of the beach, and the comeliness of the shores led them to look through the interior of the spring-tide woods, to go through the glades, and roam over the sequestered forests. It was here that the advance of Koll and Horwendil brought them face to face without any witness. Then Horwendil endeavored to address the king first, asking him in what way it was his pleasure to fight, and declaring that one best which needed the courage of as few as possible. For, said he, the duel was the surest of all modes of combat for winning the meed[6] of bravery, because it relied only upon native courage, and excluded all help from the hand of another. Koll marvelled at so brave a judgment in a youth, and said: "Since thou hast granted me the choice of battle, I think it is best to employ that kind which needs only the

---

[1]Saxo Grammaticus, *Historia Danica*, trans. Oliver Elton, in *The First Nine Books of the Danish History of Saxo Grammaticus*, London, 1894; pp. 104–117.

[2]Horwendil is the basis for old king Hamlet. At this point in the "history," he appears to be merely a warrior appointed to defend Jutland (Denmark). He has actually been king of Jutland for three years, presumably in consequence of his successful defense of the kingdom. Feng is the basis for Hamlet's uncle Claudius.

[3]King of Denmark before Horwendil; he has no parallel in Shakespeare's play.

[4]Piracy.

[5]The basis for old king Fortinbras.

[6]Reward.

endeavors of two, and is free from all the tumult. Certainly it is more venturesome, and allows of a speedier award of the victory. This thought we share, in this opinion we agree of our own accord. But since the issue remains doubtful, we must pay some regard to gentle dealing, and must not give way so far to our inclinations as to leave the last offices undone. Hatred is in our hearts; yet let piety be there also, which in its due time may take the place of rigor. For the rights of nature reconcile us,[7] though we are parted by differences of purpose; they link us together, howsoever rancor estrange our spirits. Let us, therefore, have this pious stipulation, that the conqueror shall give funeral rites to the conquered. For all allow that these are the last duties of human kind, from which no righteous man shrinks. Let each army lay aside its sternness and perform this function in harmony. Let jealousy depart at death, let the feud be buried in the tomb. Let us not show such an example of cruelty as to persecute one another's dust, though hatred has come between us in our lives. It will be a boast for the victor if he has borne his beaten foe in a lordly funeral. For the man who pays the rightful dues over his dead enemy wins the goodwill of the survivor; and whoso devotes gentle dealing to him who is no more, conquers the living by his kindness. Also there is another disaster, not less lamentable, which sometimes befalls the living—the loss of some part of their body; and I think that succor is due to this just as much as to the worst hap[8] that may befall. For often those who fight keep their lives safe, but suffer maiming; and this lot is commonly thought more dismal than any death; for death cuts off memory of all things, while the living cannot forget the devastation of his own body. Therefore this mischief also must be helped somehow; so let it be agreed, that the injury of either of us by the other shall be made good with ten talents[9] of gold. For if it be righteous to have compassion on the calamities of another, how much more is it to pity one's own? No man but obeys nature's prompting; and he who slights it is a self-murderer."

After mutually pledging their faiths to these terms, they began the battle. Nor was their strangeness in meeting one another, nor

---

[7] Obsequies (formal ritual of prayer) owed to the dead.
[8] Event; chance occurrence. "Hap" is a medieval word for "fortune" or "chance."
[9] A talent was a unit of money.

the sweetness of that spring-green spot, so heeded as to prevent them from the fray. Horwendil, in his too great ardor, became keener to attack his enemy than to defend his own body; and, heedless of his shield, had grasped his sword with both hands; and his boldness did not fail. For by his rain of blows he destroyed Koll's shield and deprived him of it, and at last hewed off his foot and drove him lifeless to the ground. Then, not to fail of his compact, he buried him royally, gave him a howe[10] of lordly make and pompous obsequies. [. . .]

He had now passed three years in valiant deeds of war; and, in order to win higher rank in Rorik's favour, he assigned to him the best trophies and the pick of the plunder. His friendship with Rorik enabled him to woo and win in marriage his daughter Gerutha,[11] who bore him a son Amleth.

Such great good fortune stung Feng with jealousy, so that he resolved treacherously to waylay his brother, thus showing that goodness is not safe even from those of a man's own house. And behold, when a chance came to murder him, his bloody hand sated the deadly passion of his soul. Then he took the wife of the brother he had butchered, capping unnatural murder[12] with incest. For whoso yields to one iniquity, speedily falls an easier victim to the next, the first being an incentive to the second. Also the man veiled the monstrosity of his deed with such hardihood of cunning, that he made up a mock pretence of goodwill to excuse his crime, and glossed over fratricide with a show of righteousness. Gerutha, said he, though so gentle that she would do no man the slightest hurt, had been visited with her husband's extremest hate; and it was all to save her that he had slain his brother; for he thought it shameful that a lady so meek and unrancorous should suffer the heavy disdain of her husband. Nor did his smooth words fail in their intent; for at courts, where fools are sometimes favored and backbiters preferred, a lie lacks not credit. Nor did Feng keep from shameful embraces the hands that had slain a brother, pursuing with equal guilt both of his wicked and impious deeds.

---

[10]Grave.

[11]The basis for Gertrude.

[12]"Unnatural murder" translates *parricidium*, the murder of the father, in Saxo's original. These are also the words of the Ghost to Hamlet, 1.5.24.

Amleth beheld all this,[13] but feared lest too shrewd a behavior might make his uncle suspect him. So he chose to feign dulness, and pretend an utter lack of wits. This cunning course not only concealed his intelligence but ensured his safety. Every day he remained in his mother's house utterly listless and unclean, flinging himself on the ground, and bespattering his person with foul and filthy dirt. His discolored face and visage smutched with slime denoted foolish and grotesque madness. All he said was of a piece with these follies; all he did savored of utter lethargy. In a word, you would not have thought him a man at all, but some absurd abortion[14] due to a mad fit of destiny. He used at times to sit over the fire, and, raking up the embers with his hands, to fashion wooden crooks, and harden them in the fire, shaping at their tips certain barbs, to make them hold more tightly to their fastenings. When asked what he was about, he said that he was preparing sharp javelins to avenge his father. This answer was not a little scoffed at, all men deriding his idle and ridiculous pursuit; but the thing helped his purpose afterwards. Now it was his craft in this matter that first awakened in the deeper observers a suspicion of his cunning. For his skill in a trifling art betokened the hidden talent of the craftsman; nor could they believe the spirit dull where the hand had acquired so cunning a workmanship. Lastly, he always watched with the most punctual care over his pile of stakes that he had pointed in the fire. Some people, therefore, declared that his mind was quick enough, and fancied that he only played the simpleton in order to hide his understanding, and veiled some deep purpose under a cunning feint. His wiliness (said these) would be most readily detected, if a fair woman were put in his way in some secluded place, who should provoke his mind to the temptations of love; all men's natural temper being too blindly amorous to be artfully dissembled, and this passion being also too impetuous to be checked by cunning. Therefore, if his lethargy were feigned, he would seize the opportunity, and yield straightway to violent delights. So men were commissioned to draw the young man in his rides into a remote part of the forest, and there assail him with a temptation of this nature. Among these chanced to be a foster-

---

[13]Feng's crime. Amleth is not in doubt about his father's murderer.

[14]Monster; uninduced premature births and miscarriages were commonly called "abortions."

brother of Amleth, who had not ceased to have regard to their common nurture; and who esteemed his present orders less than the memory of their past fellowship. He attended Amleth among his appointed train, being anxious not to entrap, but to warn him; and was persuaded that he would suffer the worst if he showed the slightest glimpse of sound reason, and above all if he did the act of love openly. This was also plain enough to Amleth himself. For when he was bidden mount his horse, he deliberately set himself in such a fashion that he turned his back to the neck and faced about, fronting the tail; which he proceeded to encompass with the reins, just as if on that side he would check the horse in its furious pace. By this cunning thought he eluded the trick, and overcame the treachery of his uncle. The reinless steed galloping on, with the rider directing its tail, was ludicrous enough to behold.

Amleth went on, and a wolf crossed his path amid the thicket. When his companions told him that a young colt had met him, he retorted, that in Feng's stud there were too few of that kind fighting. This was a gentle but witty fashion of invoking a curse upon his uncle's riches. When they averred that he had given a cunning answer, he answered that he had spoken deliberately: for he was loth to be thought prone to lying about any mattter, and wished to be held a stranger to falsehood; and accordingly he mingled craft and candor in such wise that, though his words did lack truth, yet there was nothing to betoken the truth and betray how far his keenness went.

Again, as he passed along the beach, his companions found the rudder of a ship which had been wrecked, and said they had discovered a huge knife. "This," said he, "was the right thing to carve such a huge ham;" by which he really meant the sea, to whose infinitude, he thought, this enormous rudder matched. Also, as they passed the sandhills, and bade him look at the meal, meaning the sand, he replied that it had been ground small by the hoary tempests of the ocean. His companions praising his answer, he said that he had spoken it wittingly. Then they purposely left him, that he might pluck up more courage to practise wantonness. The woman whom his uncle had dispatched met him in a dark spot, as though she had crossed him by chance; and he took her and would have ravished[15] her, had not his foster-brother, by a secret device, given

[15]Raped.

him an inkling of the trap. For this man,[16] while pondering the
fittest way to play privily the prompter's part, and forestall the
young man's hazardous lewdness,[17] found a straw on the ground
and fastened it underneath the tail of a gadfly that was flying past;
which he then drove towards the particular quarter where he knew
Amleth to be: an act which served the unwary prince exceedingly
well. The token was interpreted as shrewdly as it had been sent. For
Amleth saw the gadfly, espied with curiosity the straw which it
wore embedded in its tail, and perceived that it was a secret warning to beware of treachery. Alarmed, scenting a trap, and fain to
possess his desire in greater safety, he caught up the woman in his
arms and dragged her off to a distant and impenetrable fen. Moreover, when they had lain together, he conjured her earnestly to dis-
close the matter to none, and the promise of silence was accorded as
heartily as it was asked. For both of them had been under the same
fostering in their childhood; and this early rearing in common had
brought Amleth and the girl into great intimacy.

So, when he had returned home, they all jeeringly asked him
whether he had given way to love, and he avowed that he had ravished the maid. When he was next asked where he did it, and what
had been his pillow, he said that he had rested upon the hoof of a
beast of burden, upon a cockscomb, and also upon a ceiling. For,
when he was starting into temptation, he had gathered fragments
of all these things, in order to avoid lying. And though his jest did
not take aught of the truth out of the story, the answer was greeted
with shouts of merriment from the bystanders. The maiden, too,
when questioned on the matter, declared that he had done no such
thing; and her denial was the more readily credited when it was
found that the escort had not witnessed the deed. Then he who had
marked the gadfly in order to give a hint, wishing to show Amleth
that to this trick he owed his salvation, observed that latterly he
had been singly devoted to Amleth. The young man's reply was
apt. Not to seem forgetful of his informant's service, he said that
he had seen a certain thing bearing a straw flit by suddenly, wearing a stalk of chaff fixed on its hinder parts. The cleverness of this

[16]Hamlet's foster-brother.
[17]Dangerous sexual aggression.

speech, which made the rest split with laughter, rejoiced the heart of Amleth's friend.

Thus all were worsted, and none could open the secret lock of the young man's wisdom. But a friend of Feng,[18] gifted more with assurance than judgment, declared that the unfathomable cunning of such a mind could not be detected by any vulgar plot, for the man's obstinacy was so great that it ought not to be assailed with any mild measures; there were many sides to his wiliness, and it ought not to be entrapped by any one method. Accordingly, said he, his own profounder acuteness had hit on a more delicate way, which was well fitted to be put in practice, and would effectually discover what they desired to know. Feng was purposely to absent himself, pretending affairs of great import. Amleth should be closeted alone with his mother in her chamber; but a man should first be commissioned to place himself in a concealed part of the room and listen heedfully to what they talked about. For if the son had any wits at all he would not hesitate to speak out in the hearing of his mother, or fear to trust himself to the fidelity of her who bore him. The speaker, loth to seem readier to devise than to carry out the plot, zealously proffered himself as the agent of the eavesdropping. Feng rejoiced at the scheme, and departed on pretence of a long journey. Now he who had given this counsel repaired privily to the room where Amleth was shut up with his mother, and lay down skulking in the straw. But Amleth had his antidote for the treachery. Afraid of being overheard by some eavesdropper, he at first resorted to his usual imbecile ways, and crowed like a noisy cock, beating his arms together to mimic the flapping of wings. Then he mounted the straw and began to swing his body and jump again and again, wishing to try if aught lurked there in hiding. Feeling a lump beneath his feet, he drove his sword into the spot, and impaled him who lay hid. Then he dragged him from his concealment and slew him. Then, cutting his body into morsels, he seethed it in boiling water, and flung it through the mouth of an open sewer for the swine to eat, bestrewing the stinking mire with his hapless limbs. Having in this wise eluded the snare, he went back to the room. Then his mother set up a great wailing, and began to lament her son's folly to his face; but he said: "Most infamous of women! dost

---

[18]The basis for Polonius.

thou seek with such lying lamentations to hide thy most heavy guilt? Wantoning like a harlot, thou hast entered a wicked and abominable state of wedlock, embracing with incestuous bosom thy husband's slayer, and wheedling with filthy lures of blandishment him who had slain the father of thy son. This, forsooth, is the way that the mares couple with the vanquishers of their mates; for brute beasts are naturally incited to pair indiscriminately; and it would seem that thou, like them, hast clean forgot thy first husband. As for me, not idly do I wear the mask of folly; for I doubt not that he who destroyed his brother will riot as ruthlessly in the blood of his kindred. Therefore it is better to choose the garb of dulness than that of sense, and to borrow some protection from a show of utter frenzy. Yet the passion to avenge my father still burns in my heart; but I am watching the chances, I await the fitting hour. There is a place for all things; against so merciless and dark a spirit must be used the deeper devices of the mind.[19] And thou, who hadst been better employed in lamenting thine own disgrace, know it is superfluity to bewail my witlessness; thou shouldst weep for the blemish in thine own mind, not for that in another's. On the rest see thou keep silence." With such reproaches he rent the heart of his mother and redeemed her to walk in the ways of virtue; teaching her to set the fires of the past above the seductions of the present.

When Feng returned, nowhere could he find the man who had suggested the treacherous espial; he searched for him long and carefully, but none said they had seen him anywhere. Amleth, among others, was asked in jest if he had come on any trace of him, and replied that the man had gone to the sewer, but had fallen through its bottom and been stifled by the floods of filth, and that he had then been devoured by the swine that came up all about that place. This speech was flouted by those who heard; for it seemed senseless, though really it expressly avowed the truth.

Feng now suspected that his stepson was certainly full of guile, and desired to make away with him, but durst not do the deed for fear of the displeasure, not only of Amleth's grandsire Rorik, but also of his own wife. So he thought that the King of Britain should be employed to slay him, so that another could do the deed, and he be able to feign innocence. Thus, desirous to hide his cruelty, he

---

[19]Compare Hamlet's resignation: "We defy augury" (5.2.204).

chose rather to besmirch his friend than to bring disgrace on his own head. Amleth, on departing, gave secret orders to his mother to hang the hall with knotted tapestry, and to perform pretended obsequies for him a year thence; promising that he would then return. Two retainers of Feng[20] then accompanied him, bearing a letter graven on wood—a kind of writing material frequent in old times; this letter enjoined the king of the Britons to put to death the youth who was sent over to him. While they were reposing, Amleth searched their coffers, found the letter, and read the instructions therein. Whereupon he erased all the writing on the surface, substituted fresh characters, and so, changing the purport of the instructions, shifted his own doom upon his companions. Nor was he satisfied with removing from himself the sentence of death and passing the peril on to others, but added an entreaty that the King of Britain would grant his daughter in marriage to a youth of great judgment whom he was sending to him. Under this was falsely marked the signature of Feng.

Now when they had reached Britain, the envoys went to the king, and proffered him the letter which they supposed was an implement of destruction to another, but which really betokened death to themselves. The king dissembled the truth, and entreated them hospitably and kindly. Then Amleth scouted all the splendor of the royal banquet like vulgar viands, and abstaining very strangely, rejected that plenteous feast, refraining from the drink even as from the banquet. All marvelled that a youth and a foreigner should disdain the carefully-cooked dainties of the royal board and the luxurious banquet provided, as if it were some peasant's relish. So, when the revel broke up, and the king was dismissing his friends to rest, he had a man sent into the sleeping-room to listen secretly, in order that he might hear the midnight conversation of his guests. Now, when Amleth's companions asked him why he had refrained from the feast of yestereve, as if it were poison, he answered that the bread was flecked with blood and tainted; that there was a tang of iron in the liquor; while the meats of the feast reeked of the stench of a human carcass, and were infected by a kind of smack of the odor of the charnel.[21] He further said that the king had the eyes of a slave, and that the queen had in three ways

---

[20]The basis for Rosencrantz and Guildenstern.
[21]Tomb.

shown the behavior of a bondmaid. Thus he reviled with insulting invective not so much the feast as its givers. And presently his companions, taunting him with his old defect of wits, began to flout him with many saucy jeers, because he blamed and cavilled at seemly and worthy things, and because he attacked thus ignobly an illustrious king and a lady of so refined a behavior, bespattering with the shamefullest abuse those who merited all praise.

All this the king heard from his retainer; and declared that he who could say such things had either more than mortal wisdom or more than mortal folly, in these few words fathoming the full depth of Amleth's penetration. Then he summoned his steward and asked him whence he had procured the bread. The steward declared that it had been made by the king's own baker. The king asked where the corn had grown of which it was made, and whether any sign was to be found there of human carnage? The other answered, that not far off was a field, covered with the ancient bones of slaughtered men, and still bearing plainly all the signs of ancient carnage; and that he had himself planted this field with grain in springtide, thinking it more fruitful than the rest, and hoping for plenteous abundance; and so, for aught he knew, the bread had caught some evil savor from this bloodshed. The king, on hearing this, surmised that Amleth had spoken truly, and took the pains to learn also what had been the source of the lard. The other declared that his hogs had, through negligence, strayed from keeping, and battened on the rotten carcass of a robber, and that perchance their pork had thus come to have something of a corrupt smack. The king, finding that Amleth's judgment was right in this thing also, asked of what liquor the steward had mixed the drink? Hearing that it had been brewed of water and meal, he had the spot of the spring pointed out to him, and set to digging deep down; and there he found, rusted away, several swords, the tang whereof it was thought had tainted the waters. Others relate that Amleth blamed the drink because, while quaffing it, he had detected some bees that had fed in the paunch of a dead man; and that the taint, which had formerly been imparted to the combs,[22] had reappeared in the taste. The king, seeing that Amleth had rightly given the causes of the taste he had found so faulty, and learning that the ignoble eyes wherewith Amleth had

[22]Catacombs, a subterranean receptacle for dead bodies.

reproached him concerned some stain upon his birth, had a secret interview with his mother, and asked her who his father had really been. She said she had submitted to no man but the king. But when he threatened that he would have the truth out of her by a trial, he was told that he was the offspring of a slave. By the evidence of the avowal thus extorted he understood the whole mystery of the reproach upon his origin. Abashed as he was with shame for his low estate, he was so ravished with the young man's cleverness, that he asked him why he had aspersed the queen with the reproach that she had demeaned herself like a slave? But while resenting that the courtliness of his wife had been accused in the midnight gossip of a guest, he found that her mother had been a bondmaid. For Amleth said he had noted in her three blemishes showing the demeanor of a slave; first, she had muffled her head in her mantle as bondmaids do; next, that she had gathered up her gown for walking; and thirdly, that she had first picked out with a splinter, and then chewed up, the remnant of food that stuck in the crevices between her teeth. Further, he mentioned that the king's mother had been brought into slavery from captivity, lest she should seem servile only in her habits, yet not in her birth.

Then the king adored the wisdom of Amleth as though it were inspired, and gave him his daughter to wife; accepting his bare word as though it were a witness from the skies. Moreover, in order to fulfil the bidding of his friend, he hanged Amleth's companions on the morrow. Amleth, feigning offence, treated this piece of kindness as a grievance, and received from the king, as compensation, some gold, which he afterwards melted in the fire and secretly caused to be poured into some hollowed sticks.

When he had passed a whole year with the king he obtained leave to make a journey, and returned to his own land, carrying away of all his princely wealth and state only the sticks which held the gold. On reaching Jutland, he exchanged his present attire for his ancient demeanor, which he had adopted for righteous ends, purposely assuming an aspect of absurdity. Covered with filth, he entered the banquet-room where his own obsequies were being held, and struck all the men utterly aghast, rumor having falsely noised abroad his death. At last terror melted into mirth, and the guests jeered and taunted one another, that he whose last rites they were celebrating as though he were dead, should appear in the flesh.

When he was asked concerning his comrades, he pointed to the sticks he was carrying, and said, "Here is both the one and the other." This he observed with equal truth and pleasantry; for his speech, though most thought it idle, yet departed not from the truth; for it pointed at the weregild[23] of the slain as though it were themselves. Thereon, wishing to bring the company into a gayer mood, he joined the cupbearers, and diligently did the office of plying the drink. Then, to prevent his loose dress hampering his walk, he girded his sword upon his side, and purposely drawing it several times, pricked his fingers with its point. The bystanders accordingly had both sword and scabbard riveted across with an iron nail.[24] Then, to smooth the way more safely to his plot, he went to the lords and plied them heavily with draught upon draught, and drenched them all so deep in wine, that their feet were made feeble with drunkenness, and they turned to rest within the palace, making their bed where they had revelled. Then he saw they were in a fit state for his plots, and thought that here was a chance offered to do his purpose. So he took out of his bosom the stakes he had long ago prepared, and went into the building, where the ground lay covered with the bodies of the nobles wheezing off their sleep and their debauch. Then, cutting away its supports, he brought down the hanging his mother had knitted, which covered the inner as well as the outer walls of the hall. This he flung upon the snorers, and then applying the crooked stakes, he knotted and bound them up in such insoluble intricacy, that not one of the men beneath, however hard he might struggle, could contrive to rise. After this he set fire to the palace. The flames spread, scattering the conflagration far and wide. It enveloped the whole dwelling, destroyed the palace, and burnt them all while they were either buried in deep sleep or vainly striving to arise. Then he went to the chamber of Feng, who had before this been conducted by his train into his pavilion; plucked up a sword that chanced to be hanging to the bed, and planted his own in its place.[25] Then, awakening his uncle, he told him that his nobles were perishing in the flames, and that Amleth was here, armed with

---

[23]Compensatory payment by one responsible for a person's death to his or her family.

[24]Fearful bystanders nailed his sword in its holder.

[25]Amleth arranges his meeting with Feng so that he fights with Feng's sword while Feng has the sword the bystanders have rendered useless. The exchange of weapons is repeated in Hamlet's sword fight with Laertes. See 5.2.288.1–2 s.d.

his old crooks to help him, and thirsting to exact the vengeance, now long overdue, for his father's murder. Feng, on hearing this, leapt from his couch, but was cut down while, deprived of his own sword, he strove in vain to draw the strange one.[26] O valiant Amleth, and worthy of immortal fame, who being shrewdly armed with a feint of folly, covered a wisdom too high for human wit under a marvellous disguise of silliness! and not only found in his subtlety means to protect his own safety, but also by its guidance found opportunity to avenge his father. By this skilful defence of himself, and strenuous revenge for his parent, he has left it doubtful whether we are to think more of his wit[27] or his bravery.

[26] Amleth's sword.
[27] Quick intelligence.

Performance and Interpretation

A play is realized only in performance, animated by actors, their actions on stage, and the responses of the audience. Because a play is a living work of art, no single performance can define it. In the history of theater, there are only performances, shaped by the cultures in which they are staged. Thus past performances, even when they are described by historians of the stage, are by definition elusive. By contrast, performances created as part of a literary fiction endure even as they illustrate some of the conditions of theatricality. Henry Fielding's account of a fictional performance of *Hamlet* focuses on the playgoer, Charles Dickens' on the role of the actor. Samuel Clemens, by his satirical recreation of a ludicrous performance of Hamlet's speech "To be or not to be," tells us that, in effect, a playgoer experiences two performances: one on stage (however inept) and another in his mind, an idealized re-vision of what he is actually seeing. The critics Samuel Taylor Coleridge and William Hazlitt study the character of Hamlet to better understand the play as a whole. They see Hamlet as if he were one of them, a real man and not one playing a part on stage. A. C. Bradley follows Coleridge and Hazlitt as an analyst of character, although with an appreciation for the play as a literary work.

Henry Fielding (1707-1754)

In his comic novel Tom Jones *(1749), Henry Fielding chose an inexperienced and naive spectator, the schoolmaster Partridge, to reveal the conditions in which many audiences find themselves even after years of going to plays. On the one hand, Fielding shows us that Partridge knows that Hamlet on stage is not continuous with daily reality; on the other hand, Fielding shows us how often Partridge cannot help but believe that Hamlet is, somehow, answerable to that reality. As a result, Partridge wavers between a studied detachment from and an instinctive identification with the play's characters. Not surprisingly, it is the actor who plays the King, whose performance is the most affected and therefore the least realistic, that Partridge chooses as the "best" actor—the King, at least, has not frightened him by seeming to be real.*

from *The History of Tom Jones: A Foundling*[1]

[Partridge attends a performance of Hamlet]

As soon as the play, which was *Hamlet, Prince of Denmark*, began, Partridge was all attention, nor did he break silence till the entrance of the Ghost; upon which he asked Jones, "what man that was in the strange dress; something," said he, "like what I have seen in a picture. Sure it is not armor, it is?"

Jones answered, "That is the Ghost."

To which Partridge replied with a smile, "Persuade me to that, sir, if you can. Though I can't say I ever actually saw a ghost in my life, yet I am certain I should know one, if I saw him, better than that comes to. No, no, sir, ghosts don't appear in such dresses as that neither." In this mistake, which caused much laughter in the neighborhood of Partridge, he was suffered to continue, until the scene between the Ghost and Hamlet, when Partridge gave that credit to Mr. Garrick[2] which he had denied to Jones, and fell into so violent a trembling, that his knees knocked against each other. Jones asked him what was the matter, and whether he was afraid of the warrior upon the stage?

"Oh, la! sir," said he, "I perceive now it is what you told me. I am not afraid of anything, for I know it is but a play; and if it was really a ghost, it could do one no harm at such a distance, and in so much company: and yet if I was frightened, I am not the only person."

"Why, who," cries Jones, "dost thou take to be such a coward here besides thyself?"

[1]Henry Fielding, *The History of Tom Jones: A Foundling*, 2 vols., London, 1882; vol. 2, pp. 125–27.
[2]David Garrick, 1717–1779, leading actor and playwright, who produced many of Shakespeare's plays at The Theater Royal, Drury Lane.

"Nay, you may call me coward if you will: but if that little man there upon the stage is not frightened, I never saw any man frightened in my life. Ah, ah: go along with you! Lord have mercy upon such foolhardiness! Whatever happens it is good enough for you. Follow you?— I'd follow the devil as soon. Nay, perhaps it is the devil, for they say he can put on what likeness he pleases. Oh! here he is again. No farther! No, you have gone far enough already; farther than I'd have gone for all the king's dominions." Jones offered to speak, but Partridge cried, "Hush, hush, dear sir, don't you hear him?!" And during the whole speech of the Ghost, he sat with his eyes fixed partly on the Ghost and partly on Hamlet, and with his mouth open; the same passions which succeeded each other in Hamlet succeeding likewise in him.

When the scene was over, Jones said, "Why Partridge, you exceed my expectations. You enjoy the play more than I conceived possible."

"Nay, sir," answered Partridge, "if you are not afraid of the devil, I can't help it; but to be sure it is natural to be surprised at such things, though I know there is nothing in them; not that it was the Ghost that surprised me neither, for I should have known that to have been only a man in a strange dress; but when I saw the little man so frightened himself, it was that which took hold of me."

"And dost thou imagine then, Partridge," cries Jones, "that he was really frightened?"

"Nay, sir," said Partridge, "did not you yourself observe afterwards, when he found out it was his own father's spirit, and how he was murdered in the garden, how his fear forsook him by degrees, and he was struck dumb with sorrow, as it were, just as I should have been had it been my own case. But hush! oh, la! What noise is that? There he is again. Well, to be certain though I know there is nothing at all in it, I am glad I am not down yonder where those men are." Then turning his eyes again upon Hamlet, "Ay you may draw your sword; what signifies a sword against the power of the devil?"

During the second act, Partridge made very few remarks. He greatly admired the fineness of the dresses; nor could he help observing upon the King's countenance. "Well," said he, "how people may be deceived by faces? *Nulla fides fronti*[3] is, I find, a true saying. Who would think, by looking in the King's face, that he had ever committed a murder?" He then inquired after the Ghost; but

---

[3]There is no proof in appearance.

Jones, who intended he should be surprised, gave him no other satisfaction than that he might possibly see him again soon, and in a flash of fire.

Partridge sat in fearful expectation of this; and now, when the ghost made his next appearance, Partridge cried out: "There, sir, now; what say you now? Is he frightened now or no? As much frightened as you think me; and to be sure, nobody can help some fears. I would not be in so bad a condition as what's-his-name, Squire Hamlet, is there, for all the world. Bless me! What's become of the spirit? As I am a living soul, I thought I saw him sink into the earth."

"Indeed, you saw right," answered Jones.

"Well, well," cries Partridge, "I know it is only a play; and besides, if there was anything in all this, Madame Miller[4] would not laugh so, for as to you, sir, you would not be afraid, I believe, if the devil was here in person. There, there—ay, no wonder you are in such a passion; shake the vile wicked wretch to pieces. If she was my own mother I should serve her so. To be sure, all duty to a mother is forfeited by such wicked doings. Ay, go about your business; I hate the sight of you."

Our critic was now pretty silent till the play, which Hamlet introduces before the King. This he did not at first understand, till Jones explained it to him; but he no sooner entered into the spirit of it, than he began to bless himself that he had never committed murder. Then turning to Mrs. Miller, he asked her if she did not imagine the King looked as if he was touched; "though he is," said he, "a good actor, and doth all he can to hide it. Well, I would not have so much to answer for as that wicked man there hath, to sit upon a much higher chair than he sits upon. No wonder he ran away: for your sake I'll never trust an innocent face again."

The grave digging scene next engaged the attention of Partridge, who expressed much surprise at the number of skulls thrown upon the stage. To which Jones answered, "That it was one of the most famous burial-places about town."

"No wonder then," cries Partridge, "that the place is haunted. But I never saw in my life a worse grave-digger. I had a

[4]Another playgoer in Tom Jones's party.

sexton, when I was clerk, that should have dug three graves while he is digging one. The fellow handles a spade as if it was the first time he had ever had one in his hand. Ay, ay, you may sing. You had rather sing than work, I believe." Upon Hamlet's taking up the skull, he cried out, "Well it is strange to see how fearless some men are: I never could bring myself to touch anything belonging to a dead man on any account. He seemed frightened enough too at the Ghost I thought. *Nemo omnibus horis sapit.*[5]"

Little more worth remembering occurred during the play; at the end of which Jones asked him, which of the players he had liked best?

To this he answered, with some appearance of indignation at the question, "The King, without doubt."

"Indeed, Mr. Partridge," says Mrs. Miller, "you are not of the same opinion with the town; for they are all agreed that Hamlet is acted by the best player who was ever on the stage."

"He the best player!" cries Partridge, with a contemptuous sneer, "why I could act as well as he myself. I am sure if I had seen a ghost, I should have looked in the very same manner, and done just as he did. And then, to be sure, in that scene, as you called it, between him and his mother, where you told me he acted so fine, why, Lord help me, any man, that is any good man, that had had such a mother, would have done exactly the same. I know you are only joking with me; but, indeed, madam, though I was never at a play in London, yet I have seen acting before in the country; and the King for my money; he speaks all his words distinctly, half as loud again as the other. Anybody may see he is an actor."

. . . . Thus ended the adventure at the playhouse; where Partridge had afforded great mirth, not only to Jones and Mrs. Miller, but to all who sat within hearing, who were more attentive to what he said than to anything that passed on the stage.

He durst not go to bed all that night for fear of the Ghost; and for many nights after, sweat two or three hours before he went to sleep, with the same apprehensions; and waked several times in great horrors, crying out, "Lord have mercy upon us! there it is."

[5]No one is wise all the time.

Samuel Taylor Coleridge (1772–1834)

A poet and critic of English Romanticism, Samuel Taylor Coleridge interpreted Hamlet *almost as if it were a novel. In his* Notes on Some Other Plays of Shakespeare *(1806–1808) and his* Lectures on Shakespeare and Milton *(1813), he does not tell his reader how the play is to be performed or how it was performed on a particular occasion. His interest is chiefly in what makes the play's hero so disinclined to take action, to be so deeply committed to a life of contemplation. He sees in Shakespeare's hero the image of a thinker whose connection to the everyday is tenuous, who lives almost entirely in a mental world of his own construction. Coleridge sees this aspect of Hamlet's character sympathetically: To be immersed in reflection, to crave "that which is not," is, Coleridge declares, the fate of "men of genius."*

from Notes on Some Other Plays of Shakespeare[1]

[The character of Hamlet]

The seeming inconsistencies in the conduct and character of Hamlet have long exercised the conjectural ingenuity of critics; and, as we are always loth to suppose that the cause of defective apprehension is in ourselves, the mystery has been too commonly explained by the very easy process of setting it down as in fact inexplicable, and by resolving the phenomenon into a misgrowth or *lusus*[2] of the capricious and irregular genius of Shakespeare. The shallow and stupid arrogance of these vulgar and indolent decisions I would fain do my best to expose. I believe the character of Hamlet may be traced to Shakespeare's deep and accurate science in mental philosophy. Indeed, that this character must have some connection with the common fundamental laws of our nature may be assumed from the fact, that Hamlet has been the darling of every country in which the literature of England has been fostered. In order to understand him, it is essential that we should reflect on the constitution of our own minds. Man is distinguished from the brute animals in proportion as thought prevails over sense; but in the healthy processes of the mind, a balance is constantly maintained between the impressions from

---

[1]Samuel Taylor Coleridge, *Notes on Some Other Plays of Shakespeare* and *Lectures on Shakespeare and Milton* in *Lectures and Notes on Shakespeare and Other English Poets,* London, 1885; pp. 343–345 and 473–474, respectively.

[2]Trick.

outward objects and the inward operations of the intellect; for if there be an overbalance in the contemplative faculty, man thereby becomes the creature of mere meditation, and loses his natural power of action. Now one of Shakespeare's modes of creating characters is, to conceive any one intellectual or moral faculty in morbid excess, and then to place himself, Shakespeare, thus mutilated or diseased, under given circumstances. In Hamlet he seems to have wished to exemplify the moral necessity of a due balance between our attention to the objects of our senses, and our meditation on the workings of our minds,—an equilibrium between the real and the imaginary worlds. In Hamlet this balance is disturbed: his thoughts, and the images of his fancy are far more vivid than his actual perceptions, and his very perceptions, instantly passing through the medium of his contemplations, acquire, as they pass, a form and a color not naturally their own. Hence we see a great, an almost enormous, intellectual activity, and a proportionate aversion to real action consequent upon it, with all its symptoms and accompanying qualities. This character Shakespeare places in circumstances, under which it is obliged to act on the spur of the moment: Hamlet is brave and careless of death; but he vacillates from sensibility, and procrastinates from thought, and loses the power of action in the energy of resolve. Thus it is that this tragedy presents a direct contrast to that of *Macbeth*; the one proceeds with the utmost slowness, the other with a crowded and breathless rapidity.

The effect of this overbalance of the imaginative power is beautifully illustrated in the everlasting broodings and superfluous activities of Hamlet's mind, which, unseated from its healthy relation, is constantly occupied with the world within, and abstracted from the world without, giving substance to shadows, and throwing a mist over all common-place actualities. It is the nature of thought to be indefinite; definiteness belongs to external images alone. Hence it is that the sense of sublimity arises, not from the sight of an outward object, but from the beholder's reflection upon it; not from the sensuous impression, but from the imaginative reflex. Few have seen a celebrated waterfall without feeling something akin to disappointment: it is only subsequently that the image comes back full into the mind, and brings with it a train of grand or beautiful associations. Hamlet feels this; his senses are in a state of trance, and he looks upon external things as hieroglyphics. His soliloquy—

O! that this too too solid flesh would melt, &c.

springs from that craving after the indefinite—for that which is not—which most easily besets men of genius; and the self-delusion common to this temper of mind is finely exemplified in the character which Hamlet gives of himself:

> it cannot be
> But I am pigeon-liver'd and lack gall
> To make oppression bitter.

He mistakes the seeing his chains for the breaking of them, delays action till action is of no use, and dies the victim of mere circumstance and accident.

from *Lectures on Shakespeare and Milton,*[3] *at Bristol*

The lecturer, in descending to particulars, took occasion to defend from the common charge of improbable eccentricity, the scene which follows Hamlet's interview with the Ghost. He showed that after the mind has been stretched beyond its usual pitch and tone, it must either sink into exhaustion and inanity, or seek relief by change. Persons conversant with deeds of cruelty contrive to escape from their conscience by connecting something of the ludicrous with them; and by inventing grotesque terms, and a certain technical phraseology, to disguise the horror of their practices.

The terrible, however paradoxical it may appear, will be found to touch on the verge of the ludicrous. Both arise from the perception of something out of the common nature of things, something out of place; if from this we can abstract danger, the uncommonness alone remains, and the sense of the ridiculous is excited. The close alliance of these opposites appears from the circumstance that laughter is equally the expression of extreme anguish and horror as of joy: in the same manner that there are tears of joy as well as tears of sorrow, so there is a laugh of terror as well as a laugh of merriment. These complex causes will naturally have produced in Hamlet the disposition to escape from his own feelings of the overwhelming

---

[3]These lectures were transcribed from notes by John Payne Collier, 1789–1883, Shakespearean critic, editor, and journalist.

and supernatural by a wild transition to the ludicrous, a sort of cunning bravado, bordering on the flights of delirium.

Mr. Coleridge instanced, as a proof of Shakespeare's minute knowledge of human nature, the unimportant conversation which takes place during the expectation of the Ghost's appearance; and he recalled to our notice what all must have observed in common life, that on the brink of some serious enterprise, or event of moment, men naturally elude the pressure of their own thoughts by turning aside to trivial objects and familiar circumstances. So in *Hamlet*, the dialogue on the platform begins with remarks on the coldness of the air, and inquiries, obliquely connected indeed with the expected hour of the visitation, but thrown out in a seeming vacuity of topics, as to the striking of the clock. The same desire to escape from the inward thoughts is admirably carried on in Hamlet's moralizing on the Danish custom of wassailing; and a double purpose is here answered, which demonstrates the exquisite judgment of Shakespeare. By thus entangling the attention of the audience in the nice distinctions and parenthetical sentences of Hamlet, he takes them completely by surprise on the appearance of the Ghost, which comes upon them in all the suddenness of its visionary character. No modern writer would have dared, like Shakespeare, to have preceded this last visitation by two distinct appearances, or could have contrived that the third should rise upon the two former in impressiveness and solemnity of interest.

William Hazlitt (1778–1830)

Like Coleridge's Hamlet, William Hazlitt's character is preeminently an intellectual. He is not a hero in the usual sense of that word; he lives unto himself and ignores "the practical consequence of things." Hazlitt reads but does not see the play; for him, it might well be a study in human psychology, one that represents the mentality of its hero, not the situations in which he finds himself. In his Characters of Shakespeare's Plays *(1818), he observes: "We do not like to see our author's plays acted and least of all* Hamlet*"—a statement that reveals in a rather backhanded way how brilliantly Shakespeare dramatized the inner life of thought, conscience, and will in the most popular of his plays.*

from *Characters of Shakespeare's Plays*[1]

This is that Hamlet the Dane whom we read of in our youth, and whom we may be said almost to remember in our after-years; he who made that famous soliloquy on life, who gave the advice to the players, who thought "this goodly frame, the earth," a sterile promontory, and "this brave o'er-hanging firmament, the air, this majestical roof fretted with golden fire," "a foul and pestilent congregation of vapors;" whom "man delighted not, nor woman neither"; he who talked with the grave-diggers, and moralized on Yorick's skull; the school-fellow of Rosencrantz and Guildenstern at Wittenberg; the friend of Horatio; the lover of Ophelia; he that was mad and sent to England; the slow avenger of his father's death; who lived at the court of Horwendillus[2] five hundred years before we were born, but all whose thoughts we seem to know as well as we do our own, because we have read them in Shakespeare.

Hamlet is a name; his speeches and sayings but the idle coinage of the poet's brain. What then, are they not real? They are as real as our own thoughts. Their reality is in the reader's mind. It is *we* who are Hamlet.[3] This play has a prophetic truth, which is above that of history. Whoever has become thoughtful and melancholy through his own mishaps or those of others; whoever has borne about with him the clouded brow of reflection, and thought himself "too much i' th' sun"; whoever has seen the golden lamp of day dimmed by envious mists rising in his own breast, and could find in the world before him only a dull blank with nothing left remarkable in it; whoever has known "the pangs of despised love, the insolence of office, or the spurns which patient merit of the unworthy takes"; he who has felt his mind sink within him, and sadness cling to his heart like a malady, who has had his hopes blighted and his youth staggered by the apparitions of strange things; who cannot be well at ease, while he sees evil hovering near him like a specter; whose powers of action have been eaten up by thought, he to whom the universe seems infinite, and himself nothing; whose bitterness of soul makes him careless of consequences, and who goes to a play as his best resource to shove off, to a second remove, the evils of life by a mock representation of them—this is the true Hamlet.

[1]William Hazlitt, *Characters of Shakespeare's Plays*, London, 1901; pp. 73–81.
[2]Horwendil, a king of Jutland; see Saxo Grammaticus, pp. 221–34.
[3]A. C. Bradley calls this mode of engagement "sentimental" reading.

We have been so used to this tragedy that we hardly know how to criticize it any more than we should know how to describe our own faces. But we must make such observations as we can. It is the one of Shakespeare's plays that we think of the oftenest, because it abounds most in striking reflections on human life, and because the distresses of Hamlet are transferred, by the turn of his mind, to the general account of humanity. Whatever happens to him we apply to ourselves, because he applies it so himself as a means of general reasoning. He is a great moralizer; and what makes him worth attending to is, that he moralizes on his own feelings and experience. He is not a common-place pedant. If 'Lear' is distinguished by the greatest depth of passion, 'Hamlet' is the most remarkable for the ingenuity, originality, and unstudied development of character. Shakespeare had more magnanimity than any other poet, and he has shown more of it in this play than in any other. There is no attempt to force an interest: everything is left for time and circumstances to unfold. The attention is excited without effort, the incidents succeed each other as matters of course, the characters think and speak and act just as they might do if left entirely to themselves. There is no set purpose, no straining at a point. The observations are suggested by the passing scene—the gusts of passion come and go like sounds of music borne on the wind. The whole play is an exact transcript of what might be supposed to have taken place at the court of Denmark, at the remote period of time fixed upon, before the modern refinements in morals and manners were heard of. It would have been interesting enough to have been admitted as a bystander in such a scene, at such a time, to have heard and witnessed something of what was going on. But here we are more than spectators. We have not only "the outward pageants and the signs of grief;" but "we have that within which passes show." We read the thoughts of the heart, we catch the passions living as they rise. Other dramatic writers give us very fine versions and paraphrases of nature; but Shakespeare, together with his own comments, gives us the original text, that we may judge for ourselves. This is a very great advantage.

The character of Hamlet stands quite by itself. It is not a character marked by strength of will or even of passion, but by refinement of thought and sentiment.[4] Hamlet is as little of the hero as a man can

[4]See also Coleridge, pp. 240–42.

well be: but he is a young and princely novice, full of high enthusiasm and quick sensibility—the sport of circumstances, questioning with fortune and refining on his own feelings, and forced from the natural bias of his disposition by the strangeness of his situation. He seems incapable of deliberate action, and is only hurried into extremities on the spur of the occasion, when he has no time to reflect, as in the scene where he kills Polonius, and again, where he alters the letters which Rosencrantz and Guildenstern are taking with them to England, purporting his death. At other times, when he is most bound to act, he remains puzzled, undecided, and sceptical, dallies with his purposes, till the occasion is lost, and finds out some pretence to relapse into indolence and thoughtfulness again. For this reason he refuses to kill the King when he is at his prayers, and by a refinement in malice, which is in truth only an excuse for his own want of resolution, defers his revenge to a more fatal opportunity, when he shall be engaged in some act "that has no relish of salvation in it."

He is the prince of philosophical speculators; and because he cannot have his revenge perfect, according to the most refined idea his wish can form, he declines it altogether. So he scruples to trust the suggestions of the Ghost, contrives the scene of the play to have surer proof of his uncle's guilt, and then rests satisfied with this confirmation of his suspicions, and the success of his experiment, instead of acting upon it. Yet he is sensible of his own weakness, taxes himself with it, and tries to reason himself out of it [3.8].

Still he does nothing; and this very speculation on his own infirmity only affords him another occasion for indulging it. It is not from any want of attachment to his father or of abhorrence of his murder that Hamlet is thus dilatory; but it is more to his taste to indulge his imagination in reflecting upon the enormity of the crime and refining on his schemes of vengeance, than to put them into immediate practice. His ruling passion is to think, not to act: and any vague pretext that flatters this propensity instantly diverts him from his previous purposes.

The moral perfection of this character has been called in question, we think, by those who did not understand it. It is more interesting than according to rules; amiable, though not faultless. The ethical delineations of "that noble and liberal casuist" (as Shakespeare has been well called) do not exhibit the drab-colored quakerism of morality. His plays are not copied either from the 'Whole

Duty of Man,' or from 'The Academy of Compliments!'⁵ We confess we are a little shocked at the want of refinement in those who
are shocked at the want of refinement in Hamlet. The neglect of
punctilious exactness in his behavior either partakes of the "licence
of the time," or else belongs to the every excess of intellectual
refinement in the character, which makes the common rules of life,
as well as his own purposes, sit loose upon him. He may be said to
be amenable only to the tribunal of his own thoughts, and is too
much taken up with the airy world of contemplation to lay as much
stress as he ought on the practical consequences of things. His
habitual principles of action are unhinged and out of joint with the
time. His conduct to Ophelia is quite natural in his circumstances.
It is that of assumed severity only. It is the effect of disappointed
hope, of bitter regrets, of affection suspended, not obliterated, by
the distractions of the scene around him! Amidst the natural and
preternatural horrors of his situation, he might be excused in delicacy from carrying on a regular courtship. When "his father's spirit
was in arms," it was not a time for the son to make love in. He
could neither marry Ophelia, nor wound her mind by explaining
the cause of his alienation, which he durst hardly trust himself to
think of. It would have taken him years to have come to a direct
explanation on the point. In the harassed state of his mind, he could
not have done much otherwise than he did. His conduct does not
contradict what he says when he sees her funeral,

> "I loved Ophelia. Forty thousand brothers
> Could not with all their quantity of love
> Make up my sum."— [5.1.257–59]

Nothing can be more affecting or beautiful than the Queen's
apostrophe to Ophelia on throwing the flowers into the grave.

> "Sweets to the sweet! Farewell.   [*Scattering flowers.*]
> I hoped thou shouldst have been my Hamlet's wife.
> I thought thy bride-bed to have decked, sweet maid,
> And not t' have strewed thy grave."[5.1.228–31]

Shakespeare was thoroughly a master of the mixed motives of
human character, and he here shows us the Queen, who was so crimi-

⁵Generic titles for late Renaissance tracts on conduct and manners.

nal in some respects, not without sensibility and affection in other relations of life. Ophelia is a character almost too exquisitely touching to be dwelt upon. Oh rose of May, oh flower too soon faded! Her love, her madness, her death, are described with the truest touches of tenderness and pathos. It is a character which nobody but Shakespeare could have drawn in the way that he has done, and to the conception of which there is not even the smallest approach, except in some of the old romantic ballads. Her brother, Laertes, is a character we do not like so well: he is too hot and choleric, and somewhat rhodomontade.[6] Polonius is a perfect character in its kind; nor is there any foundation for the objections which have been made to the consistency of this part. It is said that he acts very foolishly and talks very sensibly. There is no inconsistency in that. Again, that he talks wisely at one time and foolishly at another; that his advice to Laertes is very excellent, and his advice to the King and Queen on the subject of Hamlet's madness very ridiculous. But he gives the one as a father, and is sincere in it; he gives the other as a mere courtier, a busy-body, and is accordingly officious, garrulous, and impertinent. In short, Shakespeare has been accused of inconsistency in this and other characters, only because he has kept up the distinction which there is in nature, between the understandings and the moral habits of men, between the absurdity of their ideas and the absurdity of their motives. Polonius is not a fool, but he makes himself so. His folly, whether in his actions or speeches, comes under the head of impropriety of intention.

We do not like to see our author's plays acted, and least of all, *Hamlet*. There is no play that suffers so much in being transferred to the stage. Hamlet himself seems hardly capable of being acted. Mr. Kemble[7] unavoidably fails in this character from a want of ease and variety. The character of Hamlet is made up of undulating lines; it has the yielding flexibility of "a wave o' th' sea." Mr. Kemble plays it like a man in armor, with a determined inveteracy of purpose, in one undeviating straight line, which is as remote from the natural grace and refined susceptibility of the character, as the sharp angles and abrupt starts which Mr. Kean[8] introduces into the part. Mr. Kean's Hamlet is

---

[6]Boastful.

[7]Charles Kemble, 1775–1854, a leading actor who played on the London stage for twenty years, mostly in comic roles.

[8]Edmund Kean, 1787–1833, a great charismatic tragic actor, featured in many of Shakespeare's plays.

as much too splenetic[9] and rash as Mr. Kemble's is too deliberate and formal. His manner is too strong and pointed. He throws a severity, approaching to virulence, into the common observations and answers. There is nothing of this in Hamlet. He is, as it were, wrapped up in his reflections, and only *thinks aloud*. There should therefore be no attempt to impress what he says upon others by a studied exaggeration of emphasis or manner; no *talking at* his hearers. There should be as much of the gentleman and scholar as possible infused into the part, and as little of the actor. A pensive air of sadness should sit reluctantly upon his brow, but no appearance of fixed and sullen gloom. He is full of weakness and melancholy, but there is no harshness in his nature. He is the most amiable of misanthropes.

Charles Dickens (1812–1870)

Actors, like audiences, can be inexperienced and naive. In the actor Mr. Wopsle, Charles Dickens creates the counterpart to Fielding's Mr. Partridge. Great Expectations *(1860–1861) illustrates how a great play can survive inept acting. Pip and his fellow spectators can have their mocking fun of Wopsle's performance because they know well and love the play that they are not, in fact, seeing. They do not walk out of the theater, not because they are loyal to Wopsle (whom presumably many do not know), but because his touching though inadequate efforts have the power to conjure up in their minds the* Hamlet *of their dreams. Implied, perhaps, in the hopelessness of Wopsle's performance is the absolute elusiveness of the perfect performance, one that can only be imagined.*

from *Great Expectations*[1]

[Pip goes to see his friend Mr. Wopsle act the part of Hamlet]

On our arrival in Denmark,[2] we found the king and queen of that country elevated in two arm-chairs on a kitchen-table, holding a Court. The whole of the Danish nobility were in attendance, con-

[9]Ill-tempered, bitter.

---

[1]Charles Dickens, *Great Expectations*, Boston, 1861; pp. 228–230.
[2]The theater at which *Hamlet* was to be performed.

sisting of a noble boy in the wash-leather boots of a gigantic ancestor,[3] a venerable Peer with a dirty face who seemed to have risen
from the people late in life,[4] and the Danish chivalry with a comb in
its hair and a pair of white silk legs, and presenting on the whole a
feminine appearance.[5] My gifted townsman stood gloomily apart,
with folded arms, and I could have wished that his curls and forehead had been more probable.[6]

Several curious little circumstances transpired as the action proceeded. The late king of the country[7] not only appeared to have been
troubled with a cough at the time of his decease, but to have taken it
with him to the tomb, and to have brought it back. The royal phan-
tom also carried a ghostly manuscript round its truncheon, to which it
had the appearance of occasionally referring, and that too, with air of
anxiety and a tendency to lose the place of reference which were sug-
gestive of a state of mortality. It was this, I conceive, which led to the
Shade's being advised by the gallery to "turn over!"—a recommendation which it took extremely ill. It was likewise to be noted of this
majestic spirit that whereas it always appeared with an air of having
been out a long time and walked an immense distance, it perceptibly
came from a closely continuous wall. This occasioned its terrors to be
received derisively. The Queen of Denmark, a very buxom lady,
though no doubt historically brazen, was considered by the public to
have too much brass about her; her chin being attached to her diadem
by a broad band of that metal (as if she had a gorgeous toothache), her
waist being encircled by another, and each of her arms by another, so
that she was openly mentioned as "the kettledrum." The noble boy in
the ancestral boots, was inconsistent; representing himself, as it were
in one breath, as an able seaman, a strolling actor, a grave-digger, a
clergyman, and a person of the utmost importance at a Court fencing-
match, on the authority of whose practiced eye and nice discrimina-
tion the finest strokes were judged. This gradually led to a want of
toleration for him, and even—on his being detected in holy orders,
and declining to perform the funeral service—to the general indigna-

[3]Osric.
[4]Polonius.
[5]Laertes.
[6]Hamlet, played by Mr. Wopsle.
[7]The old king Hamlet.

tion taking the form of nuts. Lastly, Ophelia was a prey to such slow musical madness, that when, in course of time, she had taken off her white muslin scarf, folded it up, and buried it, a sulky man who had been long cooling his impatient nose against an iron bar in the front row of the gallery, growled, "Now the baby's put to bed let's have supper!" which, to say the least of it, was out of keeping.

Upon my unfortunate townsman all these incidents accumulated with playful effect.[8] Whenever that undecided Prince had to ask a question or state a doubt, the public helped him out with it. As for example: on the question whether 'twas nobler in the mind to suffer, some roared yes, and some no, and some inclining to both opinions said "toss up for it;" and quite a Debating Society arose. When he asked what should such fellows as he do crawling between earth and heaven, he was encouraged with loud cries of "Hear, hear!" When he appeared with his stocking disordered (its disorder expressed, according to usage, by one very neat fold at the top, which I suppose to be always got up with a flat iron), a conversation took place in the gallery respecting the paleness of his leg, and whether it was occasioned by the turn the Ghost had given him. On his taking the recorders—very like a little black flute that had just been played in the orchestra and handed out at the door—he was called on unanimously for Rule Britannia. When he recommended the player not to saw the air thus, the sulky man said, "And don't you do it neither: you're a deal worse than him!" And I grieve to add that peals of laughter greeted Mr. Wopsle on every one of these occasions.

But his greatest trials were in the churchyard; which had the appearance of a primeval forest, with a kind of small ecclesiastical wash-house on one side, and a turnpike gate on the other. Mr. Wopsle in a comprehensive black cloak, being descried entering at the turnpike, the grave-digger was admonished in a friendly way, "Look out! Here's the undertaker a coming to see how you're a getting on with your work!" I believe it is well known in a constitutional country that Mr. Wopsle could not possibly have returned the skull, after moralizing over it, without dusting his fingers on a white napkin taken from his breast; but even that innocent and indispensable action did not pass without the comment "Wai-ter!" The arrival of the body for interment (in an empty black box with

---

[8]Hamlet.

the lid tumbling open), was the signal for a general joy which was much enhanced by the discovery, among the bearers, of an individual obnoxious to identification. The joy attended Mr. Wopsle through his struggle with Laertes on the brink of the orchestra and the grave, and slackened no more until he had tumbled the king off the kitchen-table, and died by inches from the ankles upward.

We had made some pale efforts in the beginning to applaud Mr. Wopsle; but they were too hopeless to be persisted in. Therefore we had sat, feeling keenly for him, but laughing, nevertheless, from ear to ear.

Samuel Clemens (1835–1910)

In his Adventures of Huckleberry Finn *(1885), Samuel Clemens, known to his readers as Mark Twain, creates a* Hamlet *designed especially for Americans. The duke's ludicrous parody of the best-known and most-quoted of Hamlet's lines—"To be or not to be"—paradoxically preserves this soliloquy: it expects that readers can and will recall its true form. In so doing, Clemens shows how deeply* Hamlet *has penetrated the culture of the American continent; he implies that Shakespeare's drama can and will survive its representations, however comic, even in settings quite alien to any its author could have imagined. Like Wopsle's* Hamlet, *the duke's* Hamlet *functions as a comic aide-memoire; it shadows the character Shakespeare actually created.*

from *The Adventures of Huckleberry Finn*[1]

[Huck hears the king rehearse Hamlet's soliloquy[2]]

After dinner, the duke says:

"Well, Capet,[3] we'll want to make this a first-class show, you know, so I guess we'll add a little more to it. We want a little something to answer encores with, anyway."

---

[1]Samuel Clemens, *The Adventures of Huckleberry Finn*, New York, 1889; pp. 178–179.

[2]Huckleberry Finn, Clemens's youthful hero, is in the company of two con men, nicknamed the duke and the king. They are on their way down the Mississippi River.

[3]Probably a reference to Hugh Capet, who acceded to the French throne in 987; Capetian monarchs ruled France to 1328.

"What's onkores, Bilgewater?⁴"

The duke told him, and then says:

"I'll answer by doing the Highland fling or the sailor's horn-pipe; and you—well, let me see—Oh, I've got it—you can do Hamlet's soliloquy."

"Hamlet's which?"

"Hamlet's soliloquy, you know; the most celebrated thing in Shakespeare. Ah, it's sublime, sublime! Always fetches the house. I haven't got it in the book—I've only got one volume—but I reckon I can piece it out from memory. I'll just walk up and down a minute, and see if I can call it back from recollection's vaults."

So he want to marching up and down, thinking, and frowning horrible every now and then; then he would hoist up his eyebrows; next he would squeeze his hand on his forehead and stagger back and kind of moan; next he would sigh, and next he'd let on to drop a tear. It was beautiful to see him. By-and-by he got it. He told us to give attention. Then he strikes a most noble attitude, with one leg shoved forwards, and his arms stretched away up and his head tilted back, looking up at the sky; and then he begins to rip and rave and grit his teeth; and after that, all through his speech he howled, and spread around, and swelled up his chest, and just knocked the spots out of any acting ever I see before. This is the speech—I learned it, easy enough, while he was learning it to the king:

> To be, or not to be; that is the bare bodkin
> That makes calamity of so long life;
> For who would fardels bear, till Birnam Wood do come to
>   Dunsinane,⁵
> But that the fear of something after death
> Murders the innocent sleep,
> Great nature's second course,
> And makes us rather sling the arrows of outrageous fortune
> Than fly to others that we know not of.

⁴Probably a reference to Francis Egerton, the last Duke of Bridgewater, 1736–1803, who built canals throughout England and was celebrated as the founder of British inland navigation.

⁵The duke interpolates phrases from *Macbeth* as well as other parts of *Hamlet* throughout this parody of Hamlet's soliloquy.

There's the respect must give us pause:
Wake Duncan with thy knocking! I would thou couldst;
For who would bear the whips and scorns of time,
The oppressor's wrong, the proud man's contumely,
The law's delay, and the quietus which his pangs might take,
In the dead waste and middle of the night, when churchyards yawn
In customary suits of solemn black,
But that the undiscovered country from whose bourn no traveler
    returns,
Breathes forth contagion on the world,
And thus the native hue of resolution, like the poor cat i' the adage,
Is sicklied o'er with care,
And all the clouds that lowered o'er our housetops,
With this regard their currents turn awry,
And lose the name of action.
'Tis a consummation devoutly to be wished. But soft you, the fair
    Ophelia:
Ope not thy ponderous and marble jaws,
But get thee to a nunnery—go!

Well, the old man he liked that speech, and he mighty soon got it so he could do it first rate. It seemed like he was just born for it; and when he had his hand in and was excited, it was perfectly lovely the way he would rip and tear and rair up behind when he was getting it off.

A. C. Bradley (1851–1935)

Shakespearean Tragedy (1905) dismisses two popular representations of Hamlet's character: the epitome of oversensitivity (as Goethe saw him) and the inward, brooding man of thought (as Coleridge read him). Rather, A. C. Bradley sees that Hamlet is beset with melancholy, a maladjustment of the psyche. Like Coleridge and Hazlitt, Bradley does not take account of Hamlet's situation, the constraints it puts on him as a prince called to avenge his father's murder. What focuses Bradley's attention is Hamlet's particular cast of mind and his unusual behavior, both symptomatic of disease.

from *Shakespearean Tragedy*[1]

We come next to what may be called the sentimental view of Hamlet, a view common both among his worshippers and among his defamers. Its germ may perhaps be found in an unfortunate phrase of Goethe's (who of course is not responsible for the whole view): "a lovely, pure and most moral nature, *without the strength of nerve which forms a hero*, sinks beneath a burden which it cannot bear and must not cast away." When this idea is isolated, developed and popularised, we get the picture of a graceful youth, sweet and sensitive, full of delicate sympathies and yearning aspirations, shrinking from the touch of everything gross and earthly; but frail and weak, a kind of Werther,[2] with a face like Shelley's[3] and a voice like Mr. Tree's.[4] And then we ask in tender pity, how could such a man perform the terrible duty laid on him?

How, indeed! And what a foolish Ghost even to suggest such a duty! But this conception, though not without its basis in certain beautiful traits of Hamlet's nature, is utterly untrue. It is too kind to Hamlet on one side, and it is quite unjust to him on another. The "conscience" theory at any rate leaves Hamlet a great nature which you can admire and even revere. But for the "sentimental" Hamlet you can feel only pity not unmingled with contempt. Whatever else he is, he is no *hero*.

But consider the text. This shrinking, flower-like youth—how could he possibly have done what we *see* Hamlet do? What likeness to him is there in the Hamlet who, summoned by the Ghost, bursts from his terrified friends with the cry:

> Unhand me, gentlemen!
> By heaven, I'll make a ghost of him that lets me;

the Hamlet who scarcely once speaks to the King without an insult, or to Polonius without a gibe; the Hamlet who storms at Ophelia

---

[1]A. C. Bradley, *Shakespearean Tragedy: Lectures on Hamlet, Othello, King Lear, and Macbeth*, London, 1905; pp. 101–108, 120–128.

[2]The sensitive and unfortunate artist is the hero of Goethe's novel *The Sorrows of Young Werther*, 1774.

[3]Percy Bysshe Shelley, 1792–1822, English poet of the romantic period, noted for his "feminine" beauty.

[4]Sir Herbert Beerbohm Tree, 1853–1917, actor and manager of the Haymarket Theater and later Her Majesty's Theater, produced and acted in many of Shakespeare's plays.

and speaks daggers to his mother; the Hamlet who, hearing a cry behind the arras, whips out his sword in an instant and runs the eavesdropper through; the Hamlet who sends his 'school-fellows' to their death and never troubles his head about them more; the Hamlet who is the first man to board a pirate ship, and who fights with Laertes in the grave; the Hamlet of the catastrophe, an omnipotent fate, before whom all the court stands helpless, who, as the truth breaks upon him, rushes on the King, drives his foil right through his body, then seizes the poisoned cup and forces it violently between the wretched man's lips, and in the throes of death has force and fire enough to wrest the cup from Horatio's hand ("By heaven, I'll have it!") lest he should drink and die? This man, the Hamlet of the play, is a heroic, terrible figure. He would have been formidable to Othello or Macbeth. If the sentimental Hamlet had crossed him, he would have hurled him from his path with one sweep of his arm.

This view, then, or any view that approaches it, is grossly unjust to Hamlet, and turns tragedy into mere pathos. But, on the other side, it is too kind to him. It ignores the hardness and cynicism which were indeed no part of his nature, but yet, in this crisis of his life, are indubitably present and painfully marked. His sternness, itself left out of sight by this theory, is no defect; but he is much more than stern. Polonius possibly deserved nothing better than the words addressed to his corpse:

> Thou wretched, rash, intruding fool, farewell!
> I took thee for thy better: take thy fortune:
> Thou find'st to be too busy is some danger;

yet this was Ophelia's father, and, whatever he deserved, it pains us, for Hamlet's sake, to hear the words:

> This man shall set me packing:
> I'll lug the guts into the neighbor room.

There is the same insensibility in Hamlet's language about the fate of Rosencrantz and Guildenstern; and, observe, their deaths were not in the least required by his purpose. Grant, again, that his cruelty to Ophelia was partly due to misunderstanding, partly forced on him, partly feigned; still one surely cannot altogether so account for it, and still less can one so account for the disgusting and insulting grossness of his language to her in the play-scene. I know this is said to be merely an example of the custom of Shakespeare's time. But it is not so. It is such language as you will find addressed to a woman by no other hero of Shakespeare's, not even in that dreadful scene where Othello accuses Desdemona.[5] It is a great mistake to ignore these things, or to try to soften the impression which they naturally make on one. That this embitterment, callousness, grossness, brutality, should be induced on a soul so pure and noble is profoundly tragic; and Shakespeare's business was to show this tragedy, not to paint an ideally beautiful soul unstained and undisturbed by the evil of the world and the anguish of conscious failure.

There remains, finally, that class of view which may be named after Schlegel[6] and Coleridge. According to this, *Hamlet* is the tragedy of reflection. The cause of the hero's delay is irresolution; and the cause of this irresolution is excess of the reflective or speculative habit of mind. He has a general intention to obey the ghost, but "the native hue of resolution is sicklied o'er with the pale cast of thought." He is "thought-sick." "The whole," says Schlegel, "is intended to show how a calculating consideration which aims at exhausting, so far as human foresight can, all the relations and possible consequences of a deed, cripples the power of acting. . . . Hamlet is a hypocrite towards himself; his far-fetched scruples are often mere pretexts to cover his want of determination. . . . He has no firm belief in himself or in anything else. . . . He loses himself in labyrinths of thought." So Coleridge finds in Hamlet "an almost enormous intellectual activity and a proportionate aversion to real action consequent upon it" (the aversion, that is to say, is consequent on the activity). Professor Dowden[7] objects to this view, very justly, that it neglects the emotional side of Hamlet's character, "which is quite as important as the intellectual"; but, with this supplement, he appears on the whole to adopt it. Hamlet, he says, "loses a sense of fact because with him each object and event transforms and expands itself into an idea. . . . He cannot steadily keep alive within himself a sense of the importance of any positive, lim-

---

[5]See *Othello* 5.2.23–103.

[6]August Wilhelm von Schlegel, 1767–1845, critic and exponent of the movement of German Romanticism who wrote on theater and Shakespeare and visibly influenced Coleridge's Shakespeare criticism.

[7]Edward Dowden, 1843–1913, Professor of English at Trinity College, Dublin, a scholar who wrote on Shakespeare and the romantic poets.

ited thing,—a deed, for example." And Professor Dowden explains this condition by reference to Hamlet's life. "When the play opens he has reached the age of thirty years . . . and he has received culture of every kind except the culture of active life. During the reign of the strong-willed elder Hamlet there was no call to action for his meditative son. He has slipped on into years of full manhood still a haunter of the university, a student of philosophies, an amateur in art, a ponderer on the things of life and death, who has never formed a resolution or executed a deed."

On the whole, the Schlegel-Coleridge theory (with or without Professor Dowden's modification and amplification) is the most widely received view of Hamlet's character. And with it we come at last into close contact with the text of the play. It not only answers, in some fundamental respects, to the general impression produced by the drama, but it can be supported by Hamlet's own words in his soliloquies—such words, for example, as those about the native hue of resolution, or those about the craven scruple of thinking too precisely on the event. It is confirmed, also, by the contrast between Hamlet on the one side and Laertes and Fortinbras on the other; and, further, by the occurrence of those words of the King to Laertes (IV. vii. 119 f.), which, if they are not in character, are all the more important as showing what was in Shakespeare's mind at the time:

> that we would do
> We should do when we would; for this "would" changes,
> And hath abatements and delays as many
> As there are tongues, are hands, are accidents;
> And then this "should" is like a spendthrift sigh
> That hurts by easing.

And, lastly, even if the view itself does not suffice, the *description* given by its adherents of Hamlet's state of mind, as we see him in the last four Acts, is, on the whole and so far as it goes, a true description. The energy of resolve is dissipated in an endless brooding on the deed required. When he acts, his action does not proceed from this deliberation and analysis, but is sudden and impulsive, evoked by an emergency in which he has no time to think. And most of the reasons he assigns for his procrastination are evidently not the true reasons, but unconscious excuses.

Nevertheless this theory fails to satisfy. And it fails not merely in this or that detail, but as a whole. We feel that its Hamlet does not fully answer to our imaginative impression. He is not nearly so inadequate to this impression as the sentimental Hamlet, but still we feel he is inferior to Shakespeare's man and does him wrong. And when we come to examine the theory we find that it is partial and leaves much unexplained. I pass that by for the present, for we shall see, I believe, that the theory is also positively misleading, and that in a most important way. And of this I proceed to speak.

Hamlet's irresolution, or his aversion to real action, is, according to the theory, the *direct* result of "an almost enormous intellectual activity" in the way of "a calculating consideration which attempts to exhaust all the relations and possible consequences of a deed." And this again proceeds from an original one-sidedness of nature, strengthened by habit, and, perhaps, by years of speculative inaction. The theory describes, therefore, a man in certain respects like Coleridge himself, on one side a man of genius, on the other side, the side of will, deplorably weak, always procrastinating and avoiding unpleasant duties, and often reproaching himself in vain; a man, observe, who at *any* time and in *any* circumstances would be unequal to the task assigned to Hamlet. And thus, I must maintain, it degrades Hamlet and travesties the play. For Hamlet, according to all the indications in the text, was not naturally or normally such a man, but rather, I venture to affirm, a man who at any *other* time and in any *other* circumstances than those presented would have been perfectly equal to his task; and it is, in fact, the very cruelty of his fate that the crisis of his life comes on him at the one moment when he cannot meet it, and when his highest gifts, instead of helping him, conspire to paralyze him. This aspect of the tragedy the theory quite misses; and it does so because it misconceives the cause of that irresolution, which, on the whole, it truly describes. For the cause was not directly or mainly an habitual excess of reflectiveness. The direct cause was a state of mind quite abnormal and induced by special circumstances,—a state of profound melancholy. Now, Hamlet's reflectiveness doubtless played a certain part in the *production* of that melancholy, and was thus one indirect contributory cause of his irresolution.[8] And, again, the melancholy, once

---

[8] On melancholy, see pp. 172–80.

established, displayed, as one of its *symptoms,* an excessive reflection on the required deed. But excess of reflection was not, as the theory makes it, the *direct* cause of the irresolution at all; nor was it the *only* indirect cause; and in the Hamlet of the last four Acts it is to be considered rather a symptom of his state than a cause of it. [. . .]

"Melancholy," I said, not dejection, nor yet insanity. That Hamlet was not far from insanity is very probable. His adoption of the pretence of madness may well have been due in part to fear of the reality; to an instinct of self-preservation, a fore-feeling that the pretence would enable him to give some utterance to the load that pressed on his heart and brain, and a fear that he would be unable altogether to repress such utterance. And if the pathologist calls his state melancholia, and even proceeds to determine its species, I see nothing to object to in that; I am grateful to him for emphasizing the fact that Hamlet's melancholy was no mere common depression of spirits; and I have no doubt that many readers of the play would understand it better if they read an account of melancholia in a work on mental diseases. If we like to use the word "disease" loosely, Hamlet's condition may truly be called diseased. No exertion of will could have dispelled it. Even if he had been able at once to do the bidding of the Ghost he would doubtless have still remained for some time under the cloud. It would be absurdly unjust to call *Hamlet* a study of melancholy, but it contains such a study.

But this melancholy is something very different from insanity, in anything like the usual meaning of that word. No doubt it might develop into insanity. The longing for death might become an irresistible impulse to self-destruction; the disorder of feeling and will might extend to sense and intellect; delusions might arise; and the man might become, as we say, incapable and irresponsible. But Hamlet's melancholy is some way from this condition. It is a totally different thing from the madness which he feigns; and he never, when alone or in company with Horatio alone, exhibits the signs of that madness. Nor is the dramatic use of this melancholy, again, open to the objections which would justly be made to the portrayal of an insanity which brought the hero to a tragic end. The man who suffers as Hamlet suffers—and thousands go about their business suffering thus in greater or less degree—is considered irresponsible neither by other people nor by himself: he is only too keenly conscious of his responsibility. He is therefore, so far, quite capable of being a tragic agent, which an insane person, at any rate according to Shakespeare's practice, is not. And, finally, Hamlet's state is not one which a healthy mind is unable sufficiently to imagine. It is probably not further from average experience, nor more difficult to realize, than the great tragic passions of Othello, Antony or Macbeth.

Let me try to show now, briefly, how much this melancholy accounts for.

It accounts for the main fact, Hamlet's inaction. For the *immediate* cause of that is simply that his habitual feeling is one of disgust at life and everything in it, himself included,—a disgust which varies in intensity, rising at times into a longing for death, sinking often into weary apathy, but is never dispelled for more than brief intervals. Such a state of feeling is inevitably adverse to *any* kind of decided action; the body is inert, the mind indifferent or worse; its response is, "it does not matter," "it is not worth while," "it is no good." And the action required of Hamlet is very exceptional. It is violent, dangerous, difficult to accomplish perfectly, on one side repulsive to a man of honor and sensitive feeling, on another side involved in a certain mystery (here come in thus, in their subordinate place, various causes of inaction assigned by various theories). These obstacles would not suffice to prevent Hamlet from acting, if his state were normal; and against them there operate, even in his morbid state, healthy and positive feelings, love of his father, loathing of his uncle, desire of revenge, desire to do duty. But the retarding motives acquire an unnatural strength because they have an ally in something far stronger than themselves, the melancholic disgust and apathy; while the healthy motives, emerging with difficulty from the central mass of diseased feeling, rapidly sink back into it and "lose the name of action." We *see* them doing so; and sometimes the process is quite simple, no analytical reflection on the deed intervening between the outburst of passion and the relapse into melancholy. But this melancholy is perfectly consistent also with that incessant dissection of the task assigned, of which the Schlegel-Coleridge theory makes so much. For those endless questions (as we may imagine them), "Was I deceived by the Ghost? How am I to do the deed? When? Where? What will be the consequence of attempting it—success, my death, utter misunderstanding, mere mischief to the State? Can it be right to do it, or noble to kill a defenseless man? What is the good of doing it in such a world as this?"—all this, and whatever else passed in a sickening round through Hamlet's mind, was not the healthy and right deliberation of a man with such a task, but otiose thinking hardly deserving the name of thought, an unconscious weaving of pretexts for inaction, aimless tossings on a sick bed, symptoms of melancholy which only increased it by deepening self-contempt.

Again, this state accounts for Hamlet's energy as well as for his lassitude, those quick decided actions of his being the outcome of a nature normally far from passive, now suddenly stimulated, and producing healthy impulses which work themselves out before they have time to subside. It accounts for the evidently keen satisfaction which some of these actions give to him. He arranges the play-scene with lively interest, and exults in its success, not really because it brings him nearer to his goal, but partly because it has hurt his enemy and partly because it has demonstrated his own skill (2.2.513–23). He looks forward almost with glee to countermining the King's designs in sending him away (3.4.204–11), and looks back with obvious satisfaction, even with pride, to the address and vigor he displayed on the voyage (5.2.1–55). These were not *the* action on which his morbid self-feeling had centered; he feels in them his old force, and escapes in them from his disgust. It accounts for the pleasure with which he meets old acquaintants, like his "school-fellows" or the actors. The former observed (and we can observe) in him a "kind of joy" at first, though it is followed by "much forcing of his disposition" as he attempts to keep this joy and his courtesy alive in spite of the misery which so soon returns upon him and the suspicion he is forced to feel. It accounts no less for the painful features of his character as seen in the play, his almost savage irritability on the one hand, and on the other his self-absorption, his callousness, his insensibility to the fates of those whom he despises, and to the feelings even of those whom he loves. These are frequent symptoms of such melancholy, and they sometimes alternate, as they do in Hamlet, with bursts of transitory, almost hysterical, and quite fruitless emotion. It is to these last (of which a part of the soliloquy, "O what a rogue," gives a good example) that Hamlet alludes when, to the Ghost, he speaks of himself as "lapsed in *passion,*" and it is doubtless partly his conscious weakness in regard to them that inspires his praise of Horatio as a man who is not "passion's slave."

Finally, Hamlet's melancholy accounts for two things which seem to be explained by nothing else. The first of these is his apathy or "lethargy." We are bound to consider the evidence which the text supplies of this, though it is usual to ignore it. When Hamlet mentions, as one possible cause of his inaction, his "thinking too precisely on the event," he mentions another, "bestial oblivion"; and the thing against which he inveighs in the greater part of that soliloquy (4.4) is not the excess or the misuse of reason (which for him here and always is god-like), but this *bestial* oblivion or "*dullness,*" this "letting all *sleep,*" this allowing of heaven-sent reason to "fust unused":

> What is a man,
> If his chief good and market of his time
> Be but to *sleep* and feed? a *beast*, no more.

So, in the soliloquy in 2.2. he accuses himself of being "a *dull* and muddy-mettled rascal," who "peaks [mopes] like John-a-dreams, unpregnant of his cause," dully indifferent to his cause. So, when the Ghost appears to him the second time, he accuses himself of being tardy and lapsed in *time;* and the Ghost speaks of his purpose being almost *blunted*, and bids him not to *forget* (cf. "oblivion"). And so, what is emphasized in those undramatic but significant speeches of the player-king and of Claudius is the mere dying away of purpose or of love. Surely what all this points to is not a condition of excessive but useless mental activity (indeed there is, in reality, curiously little about that in the text), but rather one of dull, apathetic, brooding gloom, in which Hamlet, so far from analyzing his duty, is not thinking of it at all, but for the time literally *forgets* it. It seems to me we are driven to think of Hamlet *chiefly* thus during the long time which elapsed between the appearance of the Ghost and the events presented in the Second Act. The Ghost, in fact, had more reason than we suppose at first for leaving with Hamlet as his parting injunction the command, "Remember me," and for greeting him, on re-appearing, with the command, "Do not forget." These little things in Shakespeare are not accidents.

The second trait which is fully explained only by Hamlet's melancholy is his own inability to understand why he delays. This emerges in a marked degree when an occasion like the player's emotion or the sight of Fortinbras's army stings Hamlet into shame at his inaction. "*Why,*" he asks himself in genuine bewilderment, "do I linger? Can the cause be cowardice? Can it be sloth? Can it be thinking too precisely of the event? And does *that* again mean cowardice? What is it that makes me sit idle when I feel it is shameful to do so, and when I have *cause, and will, and strength, and means,* to act?" A man irresolute merely because he was considering a proposed action too minutely would not feel this bewilderment. A man might feel it whose conscience secretly condemned the act which his explicit consciousness approved; but we have seen that there is no sufficient evidence to justify us in conceiving Hamlet thus. These are the questions of a man stimulated for the moment to shake off the weight of his melancholy, and, because for the moment he is free from it, unable to understand the paralyzing pressure which it exerts at other times.

I have dwelt thus at length on Hamlet's melancholy because, from the psychological point of view, it is the center of the tragedy, and to omit it from consideration or to underrate its intensity is to make Shakespeare's story unintelligible. But the psychological point of view is not equivalent to the tragic; and, having once given its due weight to the fact of Hamlet's melancholy, we may freely admit, or rather may be anxious to insist, that this pathological condition would excite but little, if any, tragic interest if it were not the condition of a nature distinguished by that speculative genius on which the Schlegel-Coleridge type of theory lays stress. Such theories misinterpret the connection between that genius and Hamlet's failure, but still it is this connection which gives to his story its peculiar fascination and makes it appear (if the phrase may be allowed) as the symbol of a tragic mystery inherent in human nature. Wherever this mystery touches us, wherever we are forced to feel the wonder and awe of man's godlike "apprehension" and his "thoughts that wander through eternity," and at the same time are forced to see him powerless in his petty sphere of action, and powerless (it would appear) from the very divinity of his thought, we remember Hamlet. And this is the reason why, in the great ideal movement which began towards the close of the eighteenth century, this tragedy acquired a position unique among Shakespeare's dramas, and shared only by Goethe's *Faust*.[9] It was not that *Hamlet* is Shakespeare's greatest tragedy or most perfect work of art; it was that *Hamlet* most brings home to us at once the sense of the soul's infinity, and the sense of the doom which not only circumscribes that infinity but appears to be its offspring.

---

[9]*Faust*: a play by Goethe, published in two parts, 1808 and 1832. Unlike the hero of Christopher Marlowe's early 17th-century play *Dr. Faustus*, Goethe's Faust is not damned but is carried off to heaven by angels after a period of purification and service to mankind.

Further Reading

On Shakespeare and *Hamlet*:

Adelman, Janet. *Suffocating Mothers: Fantasies of Maternal Origin in Shakespeare's Plays,* Hamlet *to* The Tempest. London: Routledge, 1992.

Ayer, P. K. "Reading, Writing and *Hamlet*." *Shakespeare Quarterly* 44 (1993): 423–439.

Bate, Jonathan. *The Genius of Shakespeare.* Oxford: Oxford University Press, 1998.

Belsey, Catherine. *The Subject of Tragedy: Identity and Difference in Renaissance Drama.* London: Methuen, 1985.

Bevington, David, ed. "Hamlet." In *The Complete Works of Shakespeare.* 5th ed. New York: Longman, 2004, 1097–1149.

Booth, Stephen. "On the Value of Hamlet." In *Reinterpretations of Elizabethan Drama.* Ed. Norman Rabkin. New York: Columbia University Press, 1969, 137–176.

Bowers, Fredson Thayer. *Hamlet as Scourge and Minister.* Charlottesville: University of Virginia Press, 1989.

Cary, Louise D. "Hamlet Recycled, or the Tragical History of the Prince's Prints." *ELH* 61 (1994): 783–805.

Cohen, Walter. *The Drama of a Nation: Public Theater in Renaissance England and Spain.* Ithaca: Cornell University Press, 1985.

Colie, Rosalie. *Shakespeare's Living Art.* Princeton: Princeton University Press, 1974.

Dawson, Anthony B. "The Impasse over the Stage." *ELR* 21 (1991): 309–327.

Dollimore, Jonathan, and Alan Sinfield, eds. *Political Shakespeare: New Essays in Cultural Materialism.* Ithaca: Cornell University Press and Manchester University Press, 1985.

Eagleton, Terry. *William Shakespeare.* Oxford: Basil Blackwell, 1986.

Erickson, Peter. *Patriarchal Structures in Shakespeare's Drama.* Berkeley: University of California Press, 1985.

Foakes, R. A. Hamlet *versus* Lear: *Cultural Politics and Shakespeare's Art.* Cambridge: Cambridge University Press, 1993.

Goldman, Michael. *Shakespeare and the Energies of Drama.* Princeton: Princeton University Press, 1993, 74–93.

Grady, Hugh. *Shakespeare, Machiavelli, and Montaigne: Power and Subjectivity from* Richard II *to* Hamlet. Oxford: Oxford University Press, 2002.

Grazia, Margreta de. "*Hamlet* Before its Time." *MLQ* 62 (2001): 355–375.

Greenblatt, Stephen. *Hamlet in Purgatory*. Princeton: Princeton University Press, 2001.

———. "The Mousetrap." *Shakespeare Studies* 35 (1997): 1–32.

———. "Introduction to *Hamlet*." In *The Norton Shakespeare*. Eds. Stephen Greenblatt, Walter Cohen, Jean E. Howard, and Katharine Eisaman Maus. New York: W.W. Norton, 1997, 1659–1666.

Gross, Kenneth. "The Rumor of *Hamlet*." *Raritan* 14 (1994): 43–76.

Holland, Norman. *Psychoanalysis and Shakespeare*. New York: Octagon, 1989.

Howard, Jean, and Marion O'Connor, eds. *Shakespeare Reproduced: The Text in History and Ideology*. New York: Methuen, 1987.

Jardine, Lisa. *Still Harping on Daughters: Women and Drama in the Age of Shakespeare*. Brighton: Harvester, 1983.

Jones, Ernest. Hamlet *and* Oedipus. New York: Norton, 1976.

Kahn, Coppelia. *Man's Estate: Masculine Identity in Shakespeare*. Berkeley: University of California Press, 1981.

Kastan, David Scott. *Shakespeare and the Book*. Cambridge: Cambridge University Press, 2001.

———. "'His Semblable in His Mirror': *Hamlet* and the Imitation of Revenge." *Shakespeare Studies* 19 (1991): 111–124.

Kerrigan, William. *Hamlet's Perfection*. Baltimore: Johns Hopkins University Press, 1996.

Kliman, Bernice, ed. *Approaches to Teaching Shakespeare's* Hamlet. New York: The Modern Language Association of America, 2001.

Knight, G. Wilson. *Wheel of Fire: Interpretations of Shakespearian Tragedy*. London: Methuen, 1949.

Knights, L. C. *An Approach to* Hamlet. London: Chatto and Windus, 1960.

Kurland, Stuart. "Hamlet and the Scottish Succession?" *Studies in English Literature* 34 (1994): 279–300.

Lenz, Carolyn Ruth Swift, Gayle Greene, and Carol Thomas Neely, eds. *Woman's Part: Feminist Criticism of Shakespeare*. Urbana: University of Illinois Press, 1980.

Levao, Ronald. "King of Infinite Space: Hamlet and His Fictions." *Renaissance Minds and Their Fictions*. Berkeley: University of California Press, 1986, 334–364.

Leverenz, David. "The Woman in *Hamlet*: An Interpersonal View." *Journal of Women in Culture and Society* 4:2 (1978): 291–308.

Levin, Harry. *The Question of Hamlet*. New York: Oxford University Press, 1959.

Low, Anthony. "*Hamlet* and the Ghost of Purgatory: Intimations of Killing the Father." *ELR* 29 (1999): 443–467.

Lupton, Julia Reinhard, and Kenneth Reinhard. *After Oedipus: Shakespeare in Psychoanalysis*. Ithaca: Cornell University Press, 1993.

Mack, Maynard. "The World of *Hamlet*." *The Yale Review* 41 (1852): 502–523. Rpt. in *Twentieth-Century Interpretations of Hamlet*. Ed. David Bevington. Englewood Cliffs, New Jersey: Prentice Hall, 1968.

Mallette, Richard. "From Gyves to Graces: *Hamlet* and Free Will." *Journal of English and Germanic Philology* 93 (1994): 336–355.

Marcus, Leah. *Unediting the Renaissance: Shakespeare, Marlowe, Milton*. London: Routledge, 1996.

Neely, Carol Thomas. *Broken Nuptials in Shakespeare's Plays*. New Haven: Yale University Press, 1985.

Newman, Karen. *Fashioning Femininity and English Renaissance Drama*. Chicago: University of Chicago Press, 1991.

Novy, Marianne. *Love's Argument: Gender Relations in Shakespeare*. Chapel Hill: University of North Carolina Press, 1984.

Parker, Patricia. *Shakespeare from the Margins: Language, Culture, Context*. Chicago: Chicago University Press, 1996.

Parker, Patricia, and Geoffrey Hartman, eds. *Shakespeare and the Question of Theory*. New York: Methuen, 1985.

Paster, Gail Kern. "The Body and Its Passions." *Shakespeare Studies* 29 (2001): 44–50.

Patterson, Annabel. *Shakespeare and the Popular Voice*. Oxford: Basil Blackwell, 1989.

Rabkin, Norman. *Shakespeare and the Common Understanding*. New York: The Free Press, 1967.

Rosenberg, Marvin. *The Masks of Hamlet*. Newark: University of Delaware Press, 1992.

Sanders, Eve Rachele. *Gender and Literacy on Stage in Early Modern England*. Cambridge: Cambridge University Press, 1998.

Stoppard, Tom. *Rosencrantz and Guildenstern Are Dead*. New York: Grove Press, 1967.

Targoff, Ramie. "The Performance of Prayer: Sincerity and Theatricality in Early Modern England." *Representations* 60 (1997): 49–64.

Watson, Robert N. "Giving up the Ghost in a World of Decay: Hamlet's Revenge and Denial." *Renaissance Drama* 21 (1990): 199–223.

Wilson, J. Dover. *What Happens in* Hamlet. Cambridge: Cambridge University Press, 1951.

Wilson, Luke. *Theaters of Intention: Drama and the Law in Early Modern England*. Stanford: Stanford University Press, 2000.

Wright, George T. "Hendiadys and *Hamlet*." *PMLA* 96 (1981): 168–193.

On Shakespeare and the London Theater:

Agnew, Jean-Christophe. *Worlds Apart: The Market and the Theater in Anglo-American Thought, 1550–1750*. Cambridge: Cambridge University Press, 1986.

Bristol, Michael. *Big-Time Shakespeare*. London: Routledge, 1996.

Gurr, Andrew. *The Shakespearean Playing Companies*. Oxford: Oxford University Press, 1996.

———. *The Shakespearean Stage, 1574–1642*. Cambridge: Cambridge University Press, 1992.

———. *Playgoing in Shakespeare's London*. Cambridge: Cambridge University Press, 1988.

Howard, Jean E. *Shakespeare's Art of Orchestration: Stage Technique and Audience Response.* Urbana: University of Illinois Press, 1984.

Hunter, G. K. *English Drama 1586–1642: The Age of Shakespeare.* Oxford: Clarendon Press, 1997.

Kernan, Alvin. *Shakespeare, The King's Playwright, 1603–1613.* New Haven and London: Yale University Press, 1995.

Mullaney, Steven. *The Place of the Stage: License, Play and Power in Renaissance England.* Chicago: University of Chicago Press, 1988.

Thomson, Peter. *Shakespeare's Professional Career.* Cambridge: Cambridge University Press, 1994.

Wells, Stanley. *Shakespeare: A Life in Drama.* New York, London: W.W. Norton, 1995.

Yachnin, Paul Edward. *Stage-Wrights: Shakespeare, Johnson, Middleton, and the Making of Theatrical Value.* Philadelphia: University of Pennsylvania Press, 1997.

On Shakespeare and Contemporary Culture:

Bradshaw, Graham. *Shakespeare's Scepticism.* New York: St. Martin's Press, 1987.

Berry, Ralph. *Shakespeare and Social Class.* Atlantic Highlands, NJ: Humanities Press, 1988.

Engle, Lars. *Shakespearean Pragmatism: Market of His Time.* Chicago: University of Chicago Press, 1993.

Knapp, Jeffrey. *Shakespeare's Tribe: Church, Nation, and Theater in Renaissance England.* Chicago: Chicago University Press, 2002.

Manley, Lawrence. *Literature and Culture in Early Modern London.* Cambridge: Cambridge University Press, 1995.

Marx, Steven. *Shakespeare and the Bible.* Oxford: Oxford University Press, 2000.

Orgel, Stephen. *Impersonations: The Performance of Gender in Shakespeare's England.* Cambridge: Cambridge University Press, 1996.

Shuger, Debora Kuller. *The Renaissance Bible: Scholarship, Sacrifice and Subjectivity.* Berkeley, University of California Press, 1994.

Smith, Bruce R. *Homosexual Desire in Shakespeare's England.* Chicago: University of Chicago Press, 1991.

Traub, Valerie. *Desire and Anxiety: Circulations of Sexuality in Renaissance Drama.* London: Routledge, 1992.

Woodbridge, Linda. *The Scythe of Saturn: Shakespeare and Magical Thinking.* Urbana: University of Illinois Press, 1994.

———. *Women and the English Renaissance, 1540–1620.* Urbana: University of Illinois Press, 1984.

On the Text of *Hamlet:*

Bertram, Paul, and Bernice W. Kliman, eds. *The Three-Text Hamlet: Parallel Texts of the First and Second Quartos and First Folio.* New York: AMS Press, 1991.

Furness, Horace Howard, ed. *New Variorum Edition of Shakespeare.* 1877. 2 vols. n.p., 1963.

Irace, Kathleen O., ed. *The First Quarto of* Hamlet. Cambridge: Cambridge University Press, 1998.

Wells, Stanley, and Gary Taylor. "*Hamlet.*" *William Shakespeare: A Textual Companion.* Oxford: Oxford University Press, 1987, 396–420.

Movies of *Hamlet*, with Actors in the Title Role and Directors:

1996 Kenneth Branagh, directed by Kenneth Branagh
1990 Mel Gibson, directed by Franco Zefferelli
1980 Derek Jacobi, directed by Rodney Bennett
1969 Nicoll Williamson, directed by Tony Richardson
1964 Richard Burton, directed by John Gielgud
1948 Lawrence Olivier, directed by Lawrence Olivier